BETTY JO: A LIFE REMEMBERED

Betty Jo

A LIFE REMEMBERED

* *

A PROFILE

VOLUME I

by

William R. Simon

Pictorial research and design by

James A. Ledbetter

Edited by Mia Squilla Pavelle

Publication of this book was made possible in part by a generous grant from Robert H. Bohannon, given in memory of Betty Jo Hay.

Jess Thomas Hay
P.O. Box 239
Dallas, Texas 75221-0239

ISBN: 978-0-615-23650-6

Library of Congress Control Number: 2008935362

© 2008 by Jess Thomas Hay

Written by William R. Simon
Designed and produced by James A. Ledbetter
Edited by Mia Squilla Pavelle
Indexed by Kay Banning

Printed and bound in China

Cover:
Betty Jo Hay at the time of her installation as president of the
Mental Health Association of Texas. Circa 1981.
Photograph by Gittings.

Frontispiece:
Betty Jo and Jess Hay by the lake behind their home on
Lupton Circle, Dallas. Published in *The Houston Post*,
Sunday, November 9, 1986.

This book, like most, was a collective effort. But primacy has its place, and Jess Hay, Betty Jo's husband, towered above all. It was his vision, inspiration, and guidance that directed the project from beginning to end. Ramona Taylor, Jess Hay's strong right-hand for 46 years, did all the logistical heavy lifting. Her coordination, organization, and attention to detail kept the project on course and moving forward. Jim Ledbetter's artistic eye shaped the book's outstanding design and photographic layout, including the impressive pictorial essays presented after each chapter. WordScribe owner Barbara Springfield's superb interview transcriptions greatly facilitated my research. Her professionalism and friendship were, as always, indispensable assets for project success. Mia Squilla Pavelle deserves special kudos for navigating the manuscript around all the dangerous shoals this writer placed in her path. The clear-eyed perspective and editing skill she brought to the task were invaluable.

My greatest thanks belong to the Hay extended family and their many friends who openly shared insightful stories about Betty Jo. Without their interview contributions, this remarkable woman's story would have been impossible to tell.

And finally, I owe a debt of gratitude to my wife, Elaine. Her sharp-eyed proofreading eliminated numerous errors, and her wise counsel provided a constant source of support that kept me moored to both the task at hand and to our family.

William R. Simon

Betty Jo Hay was an incredible woman who enriched the lives of the people she touched.

She was warm and funny, and possessed a razor sharp wit and amazing insight into people and their circumstances. Her intelligent mind often was focused on helping people to overcome their personal challenges so they could reach for the stars.

While Betty Jo's passion encompassed many topics and fields of interest, I got to know her in connection with our shared interest in and concern for issues related to mental health, including those designed to prevent mental illness and those aimed at enhancing the quality of care available to the mentally ill. In the late 1980s, I responded affirmatively to her invitation to join the National Mental Health Board. We both felt strongly about trying to end the stigma and discrimination that millions of ordinary Americans endure when they or their families are confronted with mental health needs. On this front, Betty Jo led the way for many years.

She was a spirited fighter for what she believed in, and inspired in me a confidence that no matter what the endeavor, if she was involved, the cause of justice always would be served.

Above all, Betty Jo loved her husband, Jess, and her family. But, because her life was rooted in her faith, her intellect, and her compassion for others, the larger common good was served wherever she walked.

I was honored to call her my friend, and to have walked some of the way with her.

Tipper Gore

Christmas 2004

My dearest Betty Jo,

By my reckoning, this is our 55th Christmas together as a couple and our 54th as partners for life. Every single day of our relationship has brought joy and meaning and purpose to my life, and I fervently hope to yours as well.

At the risk of excessive redundancy, please know that I love you to the depths of my being, and that I am profoundly grateful to you for all you have added to my life and for all we have shared together.

Love, Jess

Two months after I wrote this letter—on February 16, 2005—Betty Jo died of the cancer she courageously had battled for twenty-seven months. In the wake of her death, I was consumed by a mystical blend of despair and disbelief, gnawing grief, yet overwhelming gratitude. Gratitude for all she had given to me as my wife and constant companion, despair at the realization that our life together had come to an end.

No matter how much I tried to deny it, and hoped it wasn't true, the awful reality was that Betty Jo was gone. Betty Jo. The woman I had spent my entire adult life with, and who had shared all of my dreams, aspirations, accomplishments, and failures. Gone.

In the year-and-a-half following her death, I struggled to find my way without her, unsure of how to respond to the blow, but certain that I had to. Slowly, as I was able to reflect on the joyful and productive life I was lucky enough to have shared with Betty Jo, I found what I was looking for. This story is my response, my way of thanking a truly wonderful woman, and of sharing with family, friends, and generations of our descendants yet to be, all that Betty Jo Hay was. In this way, Betty Jo's impact on her family and friends and on her society will be remembered, and I will have satisfied a deep personal need to contribute my modest bit to that desirable end.

As for her impact on my life, personally, Betty Jo was the core from which all the rest derived. She was the force that inspired me to aim higher, to pursue broader and more commendable goals, and to believe those goals actually could be achieved. By her example, she showed me that life—thoughtfully and enthusiastically embraced—is good, meaningful, and filled with purpose and potential significance. How grateful I am for these gifts, and for the fifty-five years of sustained joy and limitless expectation that defined my life with Betty Jo.

During those many years, I tried always to respond to her constant support of my interests by doing the same for hers. In this way we were able to move through life together, as equal partners, in pursuit of common goals. While each of us functioned independently, it was with the assurance that the other would be supportive of any particular undertaking as and to the extent needed. Thus, ours became a partnership of the rarest kind—a relationship driven by trust, mutual respect, and an abiding confidence in one another. It resulted in a fulfilling and shared life.

From the beginning, I knew that in Betty Jo I had been touched by a remarkable and very special woman, and after she died, as I searched for the appropriate words to convey my deep gratitude, I discovered that those words of thanks could be found in some of my earlier letters to her.

December 25, 1967
My darling,

'Tis sad to say, but time's sole commitment seemingly is to passing, change its only certain result.

Yet time reminds and change confirms that meaning, elusive as it is, does prevail, perhaps only in a love profound and deep

- *but certainly there.*

Such is my love for you.

And so, with gratitude for a glimpse of purpose, meaning, direction, hope, and sustaining grace within this transitory life

- *I abide in your debt and trust in your love.*

Jess

December 24, 1968

My Darling,

> *Another year has come and now is nearly gone. As life is wont to be, 1968 has been a year of highs and lows; of uncertainty blended almost imperceptibly with renewed hope and a keener sense of direction; of thwarted expectation and unanticipated progress; of anxiety and freedom; of despondency and determination; of hang-up and, hopefully, some enhanced clarity.*

> *And yet, I would describe 1968 as a year of great joy*
>> • *for I believe it to have been a year of deepening love between us*
>>> ○ *a year of sharing*
>>> ○ *a year of being one in two.*

For my own part, I know (although I would not have believed it possible) that I love you more today than on Christmas Eve one year ago; and I abide in the faith that our love will grow richer and deeper with each passing day. And this faith makes life worthwhile and a joy to embrace.

> *Thus, in gratitude, may I borrow words from the great Bard to say to you, my wife and my love:*
>> *"For thy sweet love remembered, such wealth brings that then I scorn*
>> *To change my state with kings."*
>>> *All my love, all my life,*
>>>> *Jess*

The following Valentine message, two months later on February 14, 1969, captures as nearly as possible the essence of marriage as Betty Jo and I experienced it.

February 14, 1969

Seeing	*Dancing*	*Learning*	*Teaching*	*Waking*
Hearing	*Courting*	*Knowing*	*Working*	*Sleeping*
Speaking	*Kissing*	*Believing*	*Thinking*	*Laughing*
Feeling	*Conceiving*	*Doubting*	*Playing*	*Crying*

Done Together   Equal   Sharing

Assume qualities mutually attracting and add to sharing

- *a bit of caring*
- *a sense of belonging*
- *a commitment uniting*
- *and a trust sustaining.*

The sum is loving,

In life the heart of being.

Sharing the last 19 years, eight months, and eight days with you has been a great joy. Thanks for being my Valentine!

Love,

Jess

August 3, 1999

My dear Betty Jo,

Nearly 50 years ago I fell head over heels in love with you and, fortunately for me, some seven months later you reciprocated. Then, about one year thereafter on this very day in 1951, we were married. The resulting relationship has been the central blessing of my life, and I am grateful for it, for all of our shared experiences (past, present, and future), and for the depth of our love and companionship.

Thanks for all the fond memories and for all you have contributed and continue to contribute to my life.

I love you very much.

Jess

Betty Jo and I frequently acknowledged that together we had been blessed with a life grander in its dimension and joy than either of us ever dreamed possible. The finest fruits of that life, of course, are our two daughters and three grandchildren, our extended family, and our hundreds of friends. The foundation provided by these vital relationships and by our faith enriched our lives beyond measure, and inspired, enabled, and drove every endeavor we undertook, both individually and as a couple. For that faith, and for those relationships, Betty Jo and I were—and I remain—deeply indebted and very grateful.

Yes, we shared a wonderful and fulfilling life together, and as I reflect more and more on that life, I am struck by a deepened sense of wonder. How could such joy have come our way? Why were we the beneficiaries of so much, while many others did without? I have no answers to these mysteries, but I have found peace in the knowledge that ours truly was a good life. I thank God for the gift of that life, and I thank Betty Jo Peacock Hay, who was, without question, my grandest gift of all.

But, lest I leave you with the impression that Betty Jo was a saint, let me be clear. She was no saint, no Miss Goodie Two Shoes, nor did she aspire to be so. More appropriately, she might be described as one who responded joyfully to the clarion call of "Lord of the Dance," one of her favorite hymns.

Dance, then, wherever you may be;
I am the Lord of the Dance, said he.
And I'll lead you all wherever you may be,
And I'll lead you all in the dance, said he.

She was good—clean-down-to-the-bone good—but neither pretense nor phoniness constituted any part of her make-up. Although she engaged in diligent work, thoughtful reflection, and productive outreach, she loved life, enjoyed dancing, fun and games, and frolicsome play fully as much. Throughout her life, she was who she was, no more and no less.

She was a woman of independent thought and intense personal integrity who provided a moral compass and an inspiring example to me, to her daughters and grandchildren, and to her extended family of relatives and friends. She also cared for and found ways and means to respond lovingly to people along her path who were in need or who sought her guidance, counsel or help. She was a focused woman, whose priorities always were apparent and, with few exceptions, clearly defined. I was extremely fortunate to have been among those priorities, still marvel at this fact, and will remain eternally grateful that it was so.

And, thus it is, that gratitude appears finally to be achieving the upper hand in my internal struggle, though admittedly I remain given to moments of melancholy and recurring tears. My hope is that over time, these debilitating counterweights will abate still further, thereby enabling unequivocal application of my thousands of happy memories in pursuit of full and enthusiastic embrace of the future. Perhaps *Betty Jo: A Life Remembered* will be another significant step in that direction.

August 3, 2006

CHAPTER
1

HERITAGE
through
AUGUST 1948

Betty Jo was born in McAlester, Oklahoma during hard times. She arrived on June 6, 1931, in the midst of widespread economic devastation. For nearly two years the Great Depression had taken its toll, causing people to lose hope as the economy spiraled downward toward rock bottom. The crisis challenged the American spirit and created hardship and suffering the likes of which hadn't been seen by this nation since the Civil War.

It was against the backdrop of these dire economic conditions that Betty Jo's young mother faced her own serious—and very personal—challenge. Seventeen-year-old Kathryn Albert had just completed an outstanding high school career when she made a decision that would alter the course of her life. Rather than go on to college as she had planned, Kathryn chose, instead, to get married shortly after her graduation from McAlester High School in 1930. Within months of marrying Lige Cantrell, Kathryn was pregnant and their relationship was in jeopardy. "Young love" is how Kathryn's brother, Earl Albert, would explain his otherwise level-headed sister's lapse of judgment in looking back on what would be her brief and unfortunate marriage to the young man known around town as "Dude." Earl was a little boy of nine at the time, the youngest of Kathryn's four brothers.

"He was 'Dude' to me," Earl, 85, recalled from his home in McAlester. "Everybody called him Dude—Dude Cantrell. Nobody knew him by anything else. He wasn't very good material for a husband, but sometimes you go through those things."

By the time Betty Jo was born, Cantrell was gone, leaving Kathryn no choice but to move back home, where her father, Ernest—a coal miner and farmer—welcomed her and the baby. Soon, in the sanctuary of her family's warm, loving embrace, Kathryn resumed the role she previously had played, a role thrust upon her five years earlier following her mother's tragic death from tuberculosis in 1926. Though only thirteen at the time, it fell on Kathryn—the only remaining female in a household with a father and four brothers—to do what she could to restore stability to her grief-stricken family. And so, driven by a strong personality and the rigid gender roles of the times, Kathryn Albert willingly accepted the burden and would continue to bear it throughout her high school years.

By 1931, when she returned home with Betty Jo, Kathryn's two older brothers were grown and gone. Carl, the oldest, had just graduated from the University of Oklahoma with a stellar record that included a Phi Beta Kappa key and a Rhodes scholarship to attend Oxford University in England. Noal—nicknamed, Budge—was twenty-one-years-old and on his own. The youngest brothers, Homer, 13, and Earl, 9, no longer required close care, and were the perfect age for bonding with and babysitting their small niece. Earl remembered the day Betty Jo was born, and how he helped care for her over the next few years:

> She was a beautiful child, and, of course, I loved her the minute I saw her. Homer and I took care of entertaining Betty Jo. She didn't need any babysitter. Sis didn't need any outside help. We answered any needs Betty Jo had. I don't remember ever hearing her cry. . . . If you woke her up at two o'clock in the morning, she'd wake up with a smile. She was a beautiful and pleasant child to be around. We took care of her, and we loved her, and we'd kill for her. . . . I enjoyed every day she was at home with us.

Theirs was a family where love and ties to kin ran deep. "We were always a close family," said Earl. "We loved one another. We took up for one another." Indeed, family loyalty and mutual support were traits that had connected generations of Alberts. Such qualities reflected the importance of kinship networks not uncommon in Southeastern Oklahoma, an island of southern culture known as "Little Dixie," whose population bore the imprint of settlers from southern Missouri, Arkansas, and northern Louisiana. It was a section of the state noted for its adherence to southern cultural characteristics that stressed, among other things, family solidarity.

The earliest Albert ancestors reached America by the 1700s. Described as "common pioneer stock," they joined the westward migration that settled the continent. In a family history written by Carl Albert in 1976, he recalled his grandfathers often spoke about "territorial fever," a condition which stirred the family for several generations and was driven by their quest for rich farmland. In the 1800s, their restless pursuit took the Alberts to Illinois and then back and forth between Kansas and Missouri. By the close of the nineteenth century, with most of the continental United States settled, there remained one large patchwork of Indian domains west of Arkansas, and it was towards this final frontier that Kathryn's grandfather—Granville Albert—was drawn. His search for better land, better crops, and new opportunity took him to Choctaw Nation land, which occupied eight million acres in the southeast corner of what eventually would become Oklahoma. It was there, near the town of McAlester, that they settled in 1889.

McAlester enjoyed the advantages of a dual economy. On one hand, it became an important market for agricultural products, with cotton as its main cash crop. Within the city limits there were three cotton gins and a cotton compress that, in 1900 alone, processed 40,000 bales. In addition, the discovery of rich coal deposits led to a substantial mining industry when the Missouri, Kansas, and Texas (MK&T or Katy) railroad reached the coalfields in 1872. Before the turn of the century, some 50 mining companies had opened more than 100 mines in the area, which annually produced three million tons of what some called the "best steam coal west of Pennsylvania." At the center of this activity was the town of McAlester. Founded by storekeeper and Indian trader J. J. McAlester, the sleepy little village of 646 people became Oklahoma's first industrial city boasting a population of 12,000 residents by the first decade of the twentieth century.

Granville Albert's son, Ernest, profited from both economies. Ernest began coal mining at age sixteen, and later, became state certified as a gas man, while also developing expertise as a shot fireman—two particularly dangerous mining jobs. But, farming was the Albert family's principal occupation, and although it didn't pay as much as mining, Ernest was equally skilled at growing corn and cotton.

In 1907, the year Oklahoma joined the union as the nation's forty-sixth state, Ernest married Leona Ann Scott. Her family had come from Gainesville, Texas, and like the Alberts, found the prospect of good farm land sufficient lure to leave Texas for Indian Territory and settle near McAlester. "Mother was a dynamic woman," said oldest son Carl Albert, of his mother, Leona. "She was a sparkling brunette who measured five feet and two inches and weighed one hundred and ten pounds. Many people told me that when she was a teenager she was the prettiest girl in the whole area."

A few years after they married, and with two children in the family, Leona convinced Ernest to quit mining following an accident which nearly took his life. As it happened, he'd been struck by a falling rock one day while working underground, and many people believe he would have died had there not been another miner to pull him out.

So, with the support of Leona's father—Robert Carlton Scott—Ernest turned to farming, the only other occupation he knew. Scott helped Ernest find a farm to rent near the community of Bug Tussle, about ten miles northeast of McAlester. In time, the Albert family found itself drawing strength not only from its personal relationships, but also from the economic opportunities that came its way. Such was the case when Ernest Albert found a piece of rich bottom land too large to work by himself, and, as would be expected, he called on his father and brother, who agreed to share the rental cost and the acreage.

Yet it was family-centered activities that dominated most aspects of their lives, and which provided a much-needed respite from farm work. One of Carl Albert's earliest memories was a family trip by covered wagon to visit grandfather Granville Albert and an uncle and aunt who lived on farms between Wayne and Rosedale, Oklahoma:

> It was great fun to camp by the side of the road and watch my mother cook our meals over an open campfire. It took us three days to reach our relatives' farms. One can now make the trip by automobile in an hour and a half.

On another occasion, Carl remembered visiting his mother's sister, Aunt Myrtle Williams, for the Christmas holiday. "We had a big Christmas," Carl said, "but the most important event of the season was the birth of my cousin, Merle Williams." Merle and her brother Earl formed close ties to the Albert family. Later, when the Williams family moved closer to Bug Tussle, the cousins frequently exchanged visits. "They were almost as close to me as my own brothers and sister," Carl said. So close, in fact, that the Alberts named Kathryn's youngest brother after Aunt Myrtle's husband and son. Liberty Earl Albert was so christened in honor of Uncle *Liberty* Centennial Williams and cousin *Earl* Williams in a show of their deep family bond.

During those years, Ernest and Leona may not have had much money, but there was no shortage of family, many of whom lived in close proximity, as Carl recalled:

> All of my living grandparents lived nearby. Grandpa and Grandma Albert lived on our place, and my father's only brother lived two hundred yards away with his two children. Grandpa Scott and my mother's stepmother lived a quarter mile up the road. My mother's sister, Myrtle, lived just a few miles away. Dozens of other relatives lived nearby. Our family ties were strong and deep.

Those family ties, and the support that went along with them, helped smooth the rough edges of pioneer life experienced by those who resided in the Bug Tussle community.

To be sure, they lived a hardscrabble, frontier existence in the early years of Oklahoma statehood. Tenant farming offered the Alberts little more than bare subsistence, and even that required the hardest kind of physical effort. But they came from tough pioneer stock and were up to the task. "A vigorous breed, all of them endowed with a huge capacity for work," as one writer put it.

Take Granville and Mary Jane Albert's home, for example. It was nothing more than a "two-room log shack," remembered grandson Carl, yet his grandmother labored to transform her family's meager circumstances into a comfortable environment:

> She was tiny, quick, intelligent, and extremely industrious. She could do more for an old run down log house and weed-ridden yard than anyone I ever saw. . . . There were flowers all over the yard. There was never a stick or tin can out of place. She had little money to buy nice things, but she could make them. She crocheted floor rugs out of old rags. She could knit and sew and had the prettiest lace curtains I ever saw. She dusted her furniture every day and scrubbed her floors at least twice a week.

And all the while—though she may not have realized it—Mary Jane was leaving an indelible mark on her son, Ernest Albert, who inherited his mother's devotion to hard work, as son, Carl, relates in the family history:

> My father had gray eyes and black hair. He was a short, stocky built man and very muscular. At the prime of his life he was five feet, five and one-half inches tall and weighed 165 pounds. He was one of the most powerful men for his size I have ever known. He loved physical labor of any kind and would work on the farm constantly from sun up until sun down with only a short time off for lunch.

Ernest's passion for work brought the family farming success. By the time Kathryn Albert was born in 1913, Ernest and Leona not only were growing cotton, corn, oats, wheat, peanuts, and vegetables, but they also raised a variety of livestock, including pigs and cattle. Oral history accounts made by Kathryn's older brother, Carl, provide a glimpse into Albert family farm life at the time of her birth:

> The old double log house . . . consisted of two log rooms separated by a wide breezeway running north and south. Behind the east log room there was a small

lean-to which we used as a kitchen. A frame smoke house sat [nearby]. . . . Our drinking water came from an old well near the house. In our back yard there was a big, black iron boiling pot which stood on three short legs. It was a multipurpose instrument found in about every rural community yard in Pittsburg County, Oklahoma. It converted ashes and hog fat into lye soap. It was used to boil clothes after they had been washed by my mother using lye soap and a scrub board set inside a No. 3 galvanized washtub. It was also used to render lard and to heat water for bathing. The children had their baths on Saturday. We went barefoot in the summertime and had to wash our feet every night.

The barn was about thirty yards west of the house. It was surrounded by cattle and horse lots, pig pens, and chicken coops. My father usually raised ten or twelve hogs. We had milk cows and raised a few calves to butcher. Next to the barn lots we had a large vegetable garden. Our corn crib was full of corn, our shed with hay, and the smoke house with smoked hams and bacon.

Inside the house, there was no sign of luxury. A wood cook stove and family dining table occupied the lean-to. The children slept in the west log room. My parents slept in the east room, which was also our living room, where we gathered around the pot-bellied wood stove that was our sole source of winter heat. Other than the Bible, there were never many books. Newspapers covered the walls. They were all we could afford for wallpaper.

Few Bug Tussle people had more worldly goods than we. Several had much less. Most people were poor. Only a few owned their farms or even had any idea of ever owning them. They usually had large families. The kids had no Sunday clothes. Most of them went barefoot until the frost came. Some of the grown people did, too.

Kathryn's birth on April 26, 1913, remained a vivid and lasting memory for Carl:

The most important event in our lives as a family while . . . living in the old log house was the birth of my sister. . . . I well remember the day of her birth. She was delivered by old Doc Tennant, a confederate Civil War veteran and the neighborhood doctor. . . . I walked out of my bedroom across the breezeway into my parents' bedroom. . . . My mother was lying in a bed and Grandma Albert was washing a baby in a galvanized dish pan a few feet away. Grandma said, "You have a little sister.". . . I will never forget the thrill it was for me and the whole family to have a baby sister in the house.

Besides inheriting Leona's brunette appearance, Kathryn possessed her mother's vivacious personality and quick intelligence. "Kathryn matured rapidly as a baby," said Carl. "Her hair was black and before she was two months old her eyes were black and sparkling. Before she was old enough to walk she had learned to talk as plainly as an adult. As she lay on her pallet I used to ask her to repeat all kinds of words, and she always shot them right back at me." Young Kathryn, he said, also was comfortable with leadership:

Kathryn started to the Bug Tussle school when she was six-years-old. . . . Kathryn was by far the best student in her class. [The teacher] Mrs. Ross would line her first graders up to read, and Kathryn would walk back and forth in front of the line to help the children read.

Then during World War I, while Kathryn was still a toddler, good fortune smiled on the Alberts as the price of farm products rose. Prosperity for American farms and factories, however, meant enormous debt for the European countries caught in the conflict. The human toll was even more costly. Trench warfare brought unprecedented slaughter to combatants on all sides, as evidenced in 1916, when—on the first day of the Battle of the Somme—20,000 British soldiers were killed, and 38,000 were wounded.

As the stalemate in Europe dragged on, farm prices soared. America entered the war in 1917 and prices climbed higher, providing the Alberts with their first taste of financial good fortune, according to Carl:

Cotton went to as high as forty cents a pound. We had customarily been getting ten to 15 cents a pound. . . . While we were not able to own a car . . . our standard of living went up. Mama was able to paper the house with store-bought wallpaper and to get her Aunt Minnie to come out from town and help put it up. Aunt Minnie was a very good poor-woman's interior decorator. My father's bank account reached four figures for the first time since he had moved to the farm. Everybody wore better clothes. We were able to buy a hack which . . . was thought of as a poor man's surrey. We had curtains to keep the rain out. . . . We loved this new luxury. Before this, we had never been able to afford more than a second hand buggy or Springfield wagon.

In 1917, Ernest Albert rented a farm from Guy McCullough about a mile east of where Kathryn was born, but still within the Bug Tussle community. Two years later, in 1919, thanks to their newly acquired prosperity, the Alberts at long last became landowners when Ernest bought the 120-acre farm from McCullough. This purchase ended their restless search for new land, and proclaimed Pittsburg County and McAlester—the county seat and principal town—as their home, and the place they put down permanent roots.

Ernest never left the county. Most of his children, despite eventual careers in other parts of the country, returned to Pittsburg County and the family farm during retirement. When the creation of Lake Eufaula in the 1960s submerged a portion of their property, Kathryn and her husband Duncan Peacock took advantage of the family's lakefront property and built a retirement house. They were later joined by Carl and Mary Albert. Earl Albert, his wife Doris and children Kathy, Nancy, and Polly, lived several years in Mangum, Oklahoma before moving permanently to McAlester. And, Budge and Betty relocated there after many years in Wichita, Kansas.

But retirement was nothing more than a distant dream for Ernest and his family in 1922. That was the year farm prices collapsed, leaving him no choice but to return to coal mining. In what would be a wise decision—especially where his children were concerned— he accepted a job at the Number Four Samples Mine located on the grounds of the state penitentiary in McAlester. Besides enabling Ernest to earn good wages as a gas man and shot firer, relocating to town also made it possible for his children to attend the county's only high school. While neither Ernest nor Leona had more than a fifth grade education, Leona, in particular, encouraged her children's scholastic ambitions. Their academically-gifted oldest son, Carl, set the highest possible standard. He not only excelled as a championship debater, but he also earned the highest grade point average ever attained by a McAlester High School student and graduated valedictorian in 1927. Eventually, Carl would go on to become a U.S. Congressman and Speaker of the House of Representatives.

Carl's high school achievements, however, were overshadowed by family tragedy. Leona had contracted tuberculosis the previous year, and although Ernest had the financial resources to send her to Albuquerque where the drier climate was considered beneficial, she failed to recover. Leona Scott Albert died in December 1926, at the age of forty, dealing the family a severe blow.

Forced to shoulder the twin burdens of grief and new family responsibilities, thirteen-year-old Kathryn did her best to meet the challenge. "This was an ordeal for all of us," said Carl Albert, "and especially for the youngest three (Kathryn, Homer, and Earl). Kathryn literally had to be the mother to her two younger brothers—Earl was only five years old." Earl vividly remembers his sister's household contributions:

> Kathryn was our keeper. She cooked and kept house and did those things. . . . We helped her. We'd do dishes and things that needed to be done, but she was the head one. . . . From time to time Papa would get a housekeeper, somebody to come in and help cook and clean. But between those, Kathryn did it.

Sara Lane, former congressional staff member for Carl Albert during his years in the U.S. House of Representatives, recalled Kathryn's accounts of those difficult days:

> Kathryn was thirteen-years-old when her mother died, and she had to fix Ernie's lunch every day. She baked a pie every day. . . . That's what he took in his lunch bucket, along with whatever meat she fixed. But I'm telling you, she ran a home and she took care of Earl and Homer.

Lane and others agreed Kathryn continued this role later in life, becoming the family matriarch, and as such, assuming much of the responsibility for preserving family ties and initiating occasions of celebration. Older brother Carl called her "the hub around which the whole family turns." It was a trait she passed on to her daughter, Betty Jo, who would embrace it with joy and enthusiasm.

Meanwhile, and quite remarkably, neither the loss of her mother nor the resulting duties at home distracted Kathryn from her avid interest in high school. She demonstrated her desire to excel by building an outstanding scholastic record and participating in numerous school activities. The roster of achievement in Kathryn's 1930 senior yearbook included membership in the Honor Society, as well as the following clubs: mathematics, poetry, glee, dramatics, government, Spanish, Latin, and debate. The girl's negative debate team, of which Kathryn was a member, earned yearbook kudos for defeating rival Oklahoma teams from Sapulpa and Muskogee. And, by her side all the while was fellow senior and best friend Lorene Craighead, who participated in many of the same clubs as Kathryn, and

28

whose loyal friendship would prove invaluable during another crucial turning point in Kathryn's life.

At the end of her senior year, despite a superior academic performance, Kathryn failed to receive the ultimate honor—class valedictorian—because of a school policy. Younger brother Earl explained that while Kathryn had earned the highest grade point average of all the students in her senior class, she was ineligible for valedictory honors because of the semester she had spent in Albuquerque while her mother was ill. "Kathryn was a sharp girl, and she tried hard," said Earl. "She wanted to be tops in her class. Whatever she did, she wanted to be the best."

While Kathryn aspired to a college education, she chose instead to get married after she graduated, and became pregnant soon after. However, as it turned out, her marriage was brief, and her pregnancy and daughter's birth proved only a temporary setback. Four years after Betty Jo was born—with help from Lorene Craighead's family—Kathryn was able to pursue her educational goal. It so happened that the Craigheads had moved to Durant, Oklahoma, and, once aware of Kathryn's desire to attend college, they invited her and Betty Jo to live with them so Kathryn could enroll at Southeastern Oklahoma State University in Durant. It was a gesture of kindness that went to the heart of the deep friendship the Craigheads and Alberts formed during their years together in Bug Tussle where Robert Craighead had taught school.

Eventually, after settling into her new town and college, Kathryn developed a serious friendship with a Texan—Duncan Peacock—who lived across the state line in Denison, about twenty miles south of Durant. Kathryn had known Duncan before she moved to Durant, having dated him on the occasional weekend when he made the two-hour drive from Denison to McAlester to see her. And while it isn't clear exactly how they met, letters from

Kathryn Myrtle Albert, mother of Betty Jo Peacock Hay, circa 1933.

Duncan to Kathryn beginning in early 1935, reveal he had fallen in love with the attractive young mother. In late February 1935, Duncan's letters spoke about the couple's growing attachment:

> makes life seem more worthwhile to have somebody you really like all the way and have reason to think that perhaps they value your friendship a little bit too. . . .

> It's good news to hear that you still plan to come down to school and that your dad also favors the plan. . . .

> So little old Betty told them all about me did she. Bless her little heart. Tell her I said howdy.

Duncan's fondness for Betty Jo made a favorable impression on Kathryn. This was apparent from letters he wrote to Kathryn while she was home briefly in McAlester helping to look after some of the family's younger children.

In one letter, Duncan asked: "What are you doing in your spare time since you got back? Spanking kids? I don't care how many others you let have it, but leave Betty alone because she doesn't need it."

Then there was the occasional loving bribe: "Kathryn, I am enclosing a dime for Betty," he wrote. "Tell her I am giving it to her, and want her to be a good girl and not tell you that she is not going to do things you ask her to do."

Duncan's relationship with Kathryn often included Betty Jo: "Wonder if Betty still wants to go home with me tonight?" he inquired in another letter. "Tell her that I am coming over after her and take her fishing sometime soon and for her to have an old pair of overalls handy. Talk our picnic for Friday up, and we will go early enough to catch a fish."

Thoughtful consideration for her child wasn't the only thing Kathryn liked about Duncan. He offered reliability. At age thirty-one, he was what people referred to as "a solid citizen," steady, sensible, and sober-minded. He also was financially stable, earning a good living at a Denison cotton compress, which, during the Depression, was no small achievement. In addition, Duncan had an entrepreneurial spirit that he would turn to financial advantage on more than one occasion in the coming years.

It was this kind of dependability, coupled with adoration from a man deeply in love with her, that twenty-two-year-old Kathryn found hard to pass up. So on September 22, 1935—following the successful completion of her first semester of college—Kathryn Albert

30

and Duncan Peacock were married. It was a good decision. From that moment on, Kathryn's unfortunate first marriage would be remembered as a learning experience, lending truth to the sage observation of Oklahoma humorist Will Rogers that: "Good judgment comes from experience, and a lot of that comes from bad judgment."

■

It appears unlikely Kathryn continued her college education in Durant after 1935. By 1936, she and Betty Jo—an active five-year-old—were living in Denison with Duncan, who continued to work at the cotton compress.

The marriage of Kathryn and Duncan and the move to Texas enhanced Betty Jo's childhood in a number of ways. The most significant enrichment, of course, was Duncan himself, a father whom Betty Jo adored and from whom she acquired many of her core and lasting values. The marriage also provided warm relationships with her new paternal grand-parents—Nina and Sam Peacock—and with additional aunts and uncles, including Myrtle Peacock, Harry Peacock, Rowe and Samye Peacock Newman, Charles and Sara Peacock Terry, Max and Grace Peacock Arterberry, and Ruth and Edgar Peacock. The Albert-Peacock union also brought cousins into Betty Jo's life for the first time. Betty Jean Newman and Max Edgar "Sonny" Arterberry were a year or so older than Betty Jo, and the three of them became lifelong friends and childhood playmates. Lance and Elaine Terry, the son and daughter of Sara and Charles, arrived later, as did Ruth Ellen Peacock, the daughter of Ruth and Edgar. Ruth Ellen, who was born in 1946, would play a special role in 1951 as the flower girl in Jess and Betty Jo's wedding.

Duncan had grown up about ten minutes away from Denison, in the larger town of Sherman, Texas. His father and mother, Sam and Nina Peacock, were well-established Sherman residents who owned a 200-acre farm five miles south of town, as well as fifteen acres on the outskirts. Situated on the fifteen acres was a sprawling two-story home, large enough to accommodate the Peacocks and their seven children: Duncan, his two brothers, Edgar and Harry, and four sisters, Myrtle, Sara, Grace, and Samye.

Duncan's father, Sam Peacock, spent most of his professional life working as a freight agent for a railroad company, but at one point he managed a cotton compress and even had a small income tax preparation business. Grandson Max Edgar Arterberry, Grace Peacock Arterberry's son, remembers his grandfather, Sam, as "a very civic-minded person," adding that, ". . . some of his close friends were . . . the movers and shakers in Sherman."

Meanwhile, Nina Peacock, a former teacher, guided her children toward higher education, a reality and privilege made possible for each of them by the steady financial resources Sam provided.   As a result, Duncan and several of his sisters attended Austin College in Sherman, while brothers Edgar and Harry went to Baylor University in Waco. Duncan's oldest sister, Myrtle, who never married, earned a master's degree and taught history at Sherman High School.

To be sure, the Peacocks were a close-knit family, as close as any, Duncan had thought. That is, until he fell in with Kathryn and the Albert family. Then, it became clear that if Duncan hoped to find his place among the tightly-woven Albert clan, he'd better learn to navigate carefully, so as not to step on any toes. This was evident from at least one letter Duncan wrote to Kathryn during their courtship:

> This week end is Easter. You have already told me that you are going home to McAlester. Wonder if you mind if I came up Saturday night or Sunday morning? I know you will want to go to church. . . . Perhaps Carl will be there too, and I would be in the way.

While Duncan's apprehension certainly was reasonable for a young man in a new and growing relationship, his worries weren't so great that they overshadowed the loving bond he and Kathryn were forging together. Yet the pull of family remained a powerful force in Kathryn's married life, and when it called, Duncan often had no choice but to be patient. Such was the case when Kathryn was considering a trip to visit her older brother, Budge, who lived in Wichita, Kansas at the time:

> It will more than likely be two weeks before I see you again because I'd bet my pants that you go to Wichita for about two weeks to visit Budge.

A strong-willed Kathryn did make the trip to Wichita and another to McAlester—one month later—for a family gathering. On that occasion, Duncan accompanied Kathryn. However, in a letter upon his return, the still-uncertain young suitor couldn't help wondering whether he'd measured up. "Hope I did not leave an unfavorable impression upon the minds of your kin," he wrote.

More often than not though, during their first year of marriage, Duncan stayed home in Denison, while Kathryn—in an effort to surround her little girl with family, as she herself had been—traveled to Oklahoma with Betty Jo. One of those trips prompted a letter to Kathryn from a lonely Duncan who missed his family:

Seems funny for you and Betty Jo not to be here tonight. I have a touch of the blues or heebie jeebies. . . . If I were you, I do not think I would let Betty go home with Budge and Betty [Budge's wife]. No telling when you could go after her, and I know you wouldn't want to be away from her for any considerable length of time.

The letters also reveal that something of a rivalry had developed between Duncan, and Budge and Betty, at the center of which was Betty Jo, and at its core, the deep love and affection they felt for her. And though Duncan understood Budge and Betty's enthusiasm for Betty Jo—since they, as yet, had no children of their own—he had no desire to be too generous with her, and not even the semi-humorous tone in his letters could hide that message:

Tell Budge and Betty that *I said* if they wanted one to watch and enjoy that they had better get one because we are going to quit sharing ours. Looks like Budge would want one to call him papa or pap or something similar instead of just Uncle Budge.

This not-so-subtle tension and mild competition for Betty Jo's attention resulted in part from the fact that she was the first and for nine years the only grandchild of Ernest Albert. As a result, throughout her early years she was a central focus of the Albert family's devotion, which gave her every reason to emerge as a spoiled child. But Betty Jo never yielded to such temptation, and instead was as thrilled as her aunts and uncles when the first of her Albert cousins, Judy Albert, arrived in 1940. Ultimately, Betty Jo enjoyed sharing the Albert limelight with seven cousins, including:

- Judy and Anne, the two daughters of Budge and Betty Albert,
- Mary Frances and David Albert, the daughter and son of Mary and Carl, and
- Doris and Earl Albert's three daughters, Kathy, Nancy, and Polly.

Over time—as the prior generation had done—these seven cousins and Betty Jo established a remarkably close bond, thereby continuing the rich family tradition of the Albert clan.

Meanwhile, regardless of his mild aggravation at having to share Betty Jo with her aunts and uncles, Duncan endured, and at every opportunity rolled out the welcome mat for the Alberts. Once, as Kathryn prepared to return home to Denison after a trip to

McAlester, Duncan told her to, "Bring everyone with you that will come." Another time, he offered to open their home to Kathryn's younger brother, Homer, who recently had graduated from high school. "Ask Homer if he would like to stay with us and go to school in Durant," Duncan wrote.

Time and again, Duncan proved himself to be the solid, steady man described by people who knew him, and, eventually, those very qualities helped him achieve the sense of belonging within the Albert family which he sought. As his love for Kathryn and Betty Jo continued to grow, he was inspired to look toward the future, certain that with sound economics and hard work he could build a successful life for them. "I practically worship you," Duncan told Kathryn in a letter during their courtship, "and with the money that I will have saved and what I will make, looks to me we should command somewhat of a margin on life to start with." He elaborated on that theme in the fall of 1936, shortly after their first anniversary:

> I hope our turn of fortune enables us to do the things for Betty Jo that we want to do as she gets older. . . . I do a lot of dreaming, I know, but I am convinced that if we drive hard enough, we can and will realize the dreams most important to our happiness and satisfaction. Probably you and Betty are the stimulants that prompt the pipe dreams anyway; so let's not be content, let's use our heads, use good judgment, and get somewhere.

As it happened, Duncan's desire to "get somewhere" coincided with the arrival of the Works Progress Administration (WPA), one of President Franklin D. Roosevelt's New Deal relief programs aimed at providing construction and other jobs for out-of-work Americans during the Depression. Sensing there was money to be made—and hoping to supplement his income from the cotton compress—Duncan's entrepreneurial instincts led him to purchase two dump trucks which he felt certain could be put to good use by the WPA. Kathryn's brother, Earl, who was a teenager at the time, witnessed Duncan's small business operation firsthand:

> The WPA was going big about this time. Duncan had two dump trucks that he worked on the WPA; got about eight bucks a day for each one of them. He drove one of them himself and had a guy on the other one. I'd ride with him when I'd go down there to visit. They [the WPA] were building bridges and roads and stuff all the time. Duncan would haul gravel, or whatever, dump it, and go get another

load. . . . I went with him one time. He was always into something.

The extra income permitted Kathryn and Duncan to add dimension to Betty Jo's life. Now there was money enough to indulge their little girl in such luxuries as tap dancing class and tumbling lessons, which new skills she enjoyed performing for her family, according to first cousin, Betty Jean Martino, the daughter of Duncan's sister, Samye Peacock Newman and her husband, Rowe. Betty Jean also remembered the personalities of her Aunt Kathryn and specifically her Uncle Duncan—whom she recalled possessed a dry wit, and was the quieter of the two: "But, Kathryn made up for it," Betty Jean added, "because she was always so bubbly and busy all the time. . . . She always made the best pies, wonderful fruit pies. Anything Kathryn did, she did well."

By 1940 or 1941, improved financial circumstances enabled Duncan to buy a new car—a Chevrolet. The car carried the Peacocks across the Southwest United States on a memorable family vacation to Carlsbad Caverns, in New Mexico, which included a stop at the Pecos River for a refreshing swim. Cousin Max Edgar Arterberry kept Betty Jo company on the trip, and, even at age seventy-six, remembered the thrill of riding in the back seat of the brand new Chevrolet.

The relaxed routine that came from a happy marriage and a better bank account ended on December 7, 1941, when Japan attacked Pearl Harbor. America was at war. Laissez faire isolationism gave way to danger, tension, and uncertainty. In Dallas, seventy miles south of Denison, fear of attack prompted city officials to tighten security, according to Southern Methodist University historian Darwin Payne:

The city immediately stationed armed guards at properties feared vulnerable to sabotage, including Love Field, radio station WRR, and Bachman Lake. At the latter site, Texas Defense Guardsmen bearing rifles with fixed bayonets patrolled to prevent contamination of the water supply by foreign agents. . . . Citizens were advised that in case of an air raid a siren atop the Adolphus Hotel would signal a city-wide blackout in which all lights would be extinguished. At the end of the first week, a school . . . to train 5,000 air raid wardens was announced. "We don't believe an air raid on Dallas or its defense industries is imminent, but nobody can be sure," Mayor Woodall Rodgers said. In stores throughout Dallas, clerks began removing Japanese-made goods from display shelves.

Neither the Peacocks nor the Alberts were spared the consequences of America's entry into World War II. Three of the Albert brothers—Carl, Homer, and Earl—enlisted in the Army, as did Duncan's brothers, Edgar and Harry. For his part, Duncan, now in his late thirties, supported the war effort by working for the national defense industry. In 1943, he, Kathryn, and Betty Jo packed up and moved to Dallas, the industrial hub for military contractors in North Texas. Duncan found work at North American Aviation, an aircraft manufacturing company, and one of the largest defense contractors in the area, which, by Payne's account, "employed as many as 30,000 workers who built 24,000 B-24 Bombers, P-51 Mustangs, and AT Texan Trainers." Kathryn did her part as well, finding employment within the cotton industry. Helped, perhaps, by Duncan's many years in the cotton compress business, she went to work at the Dallas Cotton Exchange for the R. M. Noblitt Cotton Company.

Once in Dallas, Duncan and Kathryn settled in Oak Cliff, a thriving blue-collar community west of the Trinity River. They rented a small duplex apartment on South Brighton Street in a lower middle-class neighborhood of modest single-family frame homes. Blue collar occupations predominated what one of Betty Jo's former classmates, Chuck Stahl, described as a "family neighborhood." Much of its vitality came from the sheer number of children living in the neighborhood—fifteen on the South Brighton block alone. Up and down South Brighton Street, boys and girls passed the hot summer days playing kick the can, capture the flag, and hopscotch. "The boys played football in the yards, and baseball in the street, because there weren't many cars in those days," Stahl remembered. "We made rubber band guns, slingshots, and built tree houses."

And on warm summer nights it wasn't unusual to find Betty Jo and her friends lounging on and around her front porch swing, hoping for whatever stray breezes might wander by. As she got older, she and her friends often would hop a streetcar and head to the nearby Teen-Canteen for an evening of socializing, always under the watchful eye of vigilant parents, according to former classmate and friend Gene Austin. "They had a teen club down on Jefferson Boulevard. We went there and danced. . . . It was a good, clean, Christian environment."

Concern about the war, however, was never far away. Daily life revolved around scrap rubber, tin foil and paper drives, gasoline coupons, and sugar and meat rationing. And for the Peacocks, there was the added anxiety of knowing close relatives were serving as combat soldiers. In a show of support and love, Kathryn dedicated herself to regular letter-writing—the only form of communication with members of the military—and she enlisted Betty Jo's help in the cause. The letters helped boost morale, as Betty Jo learned when she received the following response from her Uncle Carl Albert, who, at the time, was serving in the judge advocate general's office under General Douglas MacArthur:

> I've been working all day and half the night lately. I am feeling fine, though. The main thing in my life these days is letters from home. So, "keep them flying."
>
> Love, Uncle Carl

It was particularly difficult for Kathryn to see Homer and Earl—the two brothers she had helped raise after their mother's death—serving in combat units under threat of violent injury or death. The depth of her concern prompted this response from Earl, who was serving in the Pacific with the 11th Airborne Division's 457th Parachute Field Artillery Battalion:

> Sis, there isn't any need for you to choke up when you are eating something that you know we like. Keep right on cooking and eating it so you will be in practice to cook us the things we want when we get home. . . . Sis, there isn't any need for you to worry about us. You are just making yourself grow old, and besides why worry until you are sure you have something to worry about.

Kathryn would continue to worry, not only about her own brothers, but Duncan's, as well, including Harry Peacock, who also served in the Pacific Theater. On the chance that Harry might be stationed near Earl, and hopeful the two could somehow connect, Kathryn made sure her brother had Harry's contact information. In a return letter dated October 2, 1944, Earl told Kathryn: "I'm keeping Harry's address. I may meet him where you said. I hope to be there for Christmas." But there would be no meeting. Harry Peacock had been killed six days earlier. He and 207 other men from the 81st Wildcat Infantry Division died during the battle of Peleliu, a small island of steep coral ridges, honey-combed with caves, tunnels, and 10,500 veteran Japanese soldiers honor-bound to die for their emperor.

Max Edgar Arterberry—Grace Peacock Arterberry's son—remembers first learning about the attack while he and his family visited the farm of his grandparents, Sam and Nina Peacock, in late September 1944. "This was when we heard the news over the radio that they were fighting on Peleliu," said Max Edgar. "I remember my grandmother said, 'Well, I guess he's fighting now.' Then, we found out two or three weeks later that he had been killed."

Kathryn's deep concern for her family proved justified. Not only had the war claimed the life of Duncan's younger brother, Harry Peacock, but tragedy also struck the Albert family, when Kathryn's twenty-six-year-old brother, Homer, was wounded in action. Three months before Harry's death, the Alberts learned that Homer, stationed in England with the 90th Division, had taken part in the Normandy invasion on June 6, 1944. When Duncan forwarded a letter from Homer to Kathryn—who was visiting Budge in Wichita— he added the following note:

> You had a letter from Homer, and I am enclosing it to you. I hope he wasn't in the first wave of those invasion forces. . . . I am really thinking and pulling for Homer. I hope the kid gets out of it alright and I feel that he will. It will certainly be a great day to see all those boys coming home.

Homer did come home, but he wasn't "alright." Though spared from participating in the first wave of the attack, he was wounded by a grenade within days of the landing and sent to a military hospital in England. On June 17, 1944, in a letter to his father, Ernest Albert, Homer wrote:

> Dear Papa and family: I have been away from the war sometime now. I had my leg worked on twice. I can tell the world you get plenty scared when your ears start ringing. . . . I will be well soon. The whole thing just goes to show you war is close, and I did not realize it until I had shot a German.

> Love to all, Homer.

As it turned out, his physical injuries proved less debilitating than the emotional trauma he suffered. In an October letter to his father, Homer wondered whether he could:

> make a start in life. Things are different than they were back in the states. I have cried for home but I didn't know I was so low down. . . . As you know I felt like a boy when I left home and now I am really a boy. . . . Even if the world tries to help me out I can not be helped by the world.

According to his brother, Earl Albert, Homer failed to make a satisfactory start in life. "He never was mentally right after the war," said Earl. "He was in bad shape."

But he wasn't so troubled that he couldn't appreciate Kathryn's attention and unflagging support, which he expressed in a January 1945 letter to his niece, Betty Jo: "Always help your mother because she has helped you a lot, and she has been better to me than all the others, and I really want her to rest plenty and not worry about me."

Following his release from the hospital in England, and in need of psychiatric care, Homer was admitted to the Veteran's Administration hospital in San Antonio, Texas. While there, he received periodic visits from concerned family members, and a year later, returned to the Bug Tussle family farm in Oklahoma where he would be cared for by his father and stepmother, Irene.

Betty Jo, meanwhile, continued making frequent trips to the farm as she had throughout her childhood, which enabled her to develop a close bond with her grandfather, Ernest Albert, and with the Albert family's rural heritage. One memorable part of that heritage was Ernest's enthusiasm for large country breakfasts. His well-stocked farm-fresh larder supplied the basics, and Irene prepared the meals, leaving Betty Jo with lasting memories of bountiful breakfast spreads anchored by fresh eggs, thick-slab smokehouse bacon, sausage, and that indispensable "Little Dixie" staple, biscuits and gravy.

Ernest Homer Albert would die in 1947 when Betty Jo was sixteen, and though deeply saddened by the loss of her grandfather, poignant memories of him would surface in years to come. On those occasions, Betty Jo, now married and with a family of her own, would announce peremptorily, "We're going to have my grandfather's breakfast," and then proceed to serve up that delicious piece of Albert family history.

Unfortunately, pleasant family moments failed to improve Homer's condition. Mental impairment and the loss of his father forced him to return to the VA hospital in 1947, this time in North Little Rock, Arkansas. Homer's adjustment to institutional life proved difficult, and his psychological condition deteriorated. He responded to patients who disturbed him or his belongings by fighting. In 1950, doctors at the VA hospital concluded that, "further medical or psychiatric treatment will not bring about improvement," and recommended a prefrontal lobotomy, which Kathryn authorized. While the operation successfully curtailed Homer's aggressive behavior, it also damaged his personality, leaving him impassive and apathetic. "All the life went out of him after that operation," said Earl. "When they did that surgery, they finished him off." Homer remained in the VA hospital until his death in 1962.

In her last act of love on his behalf, Kathryn planned Homer's funeral. At one point during family discussions about the arrangements, Aunt Myrtle Williams suggested covering Homer's war-injured hand. Kathryn refused. Sara Lane, close friend and former congressional staff member for Carl Albert, recalled Kathryn's opposition to Myrtle's proposal. "Carl, I'm not covering that hand," she told her older brother. "I've looked at it for twenty years and the public can look at it today." Kathryn never flinched from looking at reality straight on, and she had no patience with those who wished to sugarcoat life and disguise its truth. It was a trait adopted by her daughter. While diplomacy certainly had its place, more often than not an honest appraisal is what people could expect from Betty Jo.

Many of Betty Jo's distinctive characteristics and values gathered definition during high school. Most notable among these were self-confidence and the desire to excel— qualities she applied successfully to a wide range of endeavors at Sunset High School in Dallas, a public school with plenty to offer in the 1940s.

"Sunset in that day was one of the premier high schools," said Mary (Gilmore) Bevins, a former classmate. With its first-class academic program, strong athletic and debate teams, and experienced, dedicated teachers, Spencer Relyea, another classmate, said he considered Sunset the best high school in the city:

> Sunset had very good faculty. I remember taking four years of Spanish from Mr. Johns, who later became the director of foreign languages for all the Dallas public schools, and we spoke nothing but Spanish in the classroom my last two years. One of the boys who graduated in the highest honor group went to Yale and won some prize up there his first year for proficiency in Latin. . . .Typically, that was only won by students who had gone to Eastern prep schools.

Betty Jo responded to the excellent teaching by consistently achieving at an honors level. She finished her high school academic career with a flourish—as one of a select group of thirteen students to graduate with high honors. Furthermore, by placing a priority on academic achievement and becoming involved in school activities, Betty Jo and several of her close friends—including Patsy (McDonough) Smith—distinguished themselves from the other girls in their class:

> Both of us were achievers. We were both very independent, we both strived for A's,

40

and we both tried very hard to win. Winning was very important to both of us. . . . We were both blondes, but we didn't want to fit the stereotype of the ditsy blonde. . . . Boys were not the most important thing in our lives. We wanted good grades to get into college.

Lofty goals, no doubt, but certainly within reach of the tenacious, hard-working Betty Jo, who fellow classmate Jan (Clancy) Amos characterized as stable and serious:

She had goals, and her goals were intellectual. . . . There was no question that Betty was going to graduate and go to college and excel. . . . Anyone that was close to her knew that she wasn't going to let anything stand in her way.

In fact, Betty Jo's chosen priorities in high school and her sense of determination, according to Amos, ran counter to the prevailing teenage girl culture in Dallas in the 1940s:

Marriage and children were the goals most of the girls had when we graduated. Cinderella was going to get kissed by the prince . . . and going to marry and be happy the rest of her life, which was a bunch of crap, but that was the way we felt and thought. . . . I can tell you most of them married out of high school, and that was their big goal.

Betty Jo's most avid interest outside of school was the Methodist youth group at Brooklyn Avenue Methodist Church in Oak Cliff. It provided fellowship and fun, and a chance for Betty Jo to demonstrate her ability as a leader. Gene Austin, former classmate and youth group president, recalls her leadership skills and their friendship:

The youth group was active and Betty was an important part of it. She was a good leader. She helped us plan worship services and summer work projects. She was a happy, upbeat person, and people liked her. In my case, she made me feel worthwhile. . . . I felt like she was a friend that I could go to with anything. She was open and approachable.

Austin remembers Betty Jo had a particular fondness for the hymn, "I Would Be True," perhaps because of its inspirational message, which, for an idealistic adolescent, might have struck a responsive chord:

I would be true, for there are those who trust me;
I would be pure, for there are those who care;
I would be strong, for there is much to suffer;
I would be brave, for there is much to dare;
I would be brave, for there is much to dare.

With her religious values securely grounded in the Methodist church, Betty Jo, early on, accepted the challenge presented to all members of her faith: to seek a purposeful life. And in keeping with one of the major tenets of that faith, she embarked on what would become a lifelong commitment to the service of others. Her church youth group focused on what Austin described as making "the world a better place because you live here. . . . It was our job to love your neighbor and try to improve society." Dr. Richard Gelwick, a close friend who first met Betty Jo during a high school debate tournament, believes many of the most important values she held had been firmly fixed since childhood:

> She got her compass right when she was a child. At the time I met her in high school, she had pretty much gotten her course clear. . . . She knew where her true north was and could always find her way.

One line of direction pointed toward debate, which quickly became a passion. Following in the footsteps of her mother and her Uncle Carl, Betty Jo joined the school debate club. This extracurricular activity, more than any other, blended interests and abilities that would play a significant role in her later life.

Blessed with an outgoing, extroverted personality, Betty Jo enjoyed the limelight and relished opportunities to perform, just as she had when she was a little girl. "She loved anything to do with speaking," said former debate partner and friend, Patsy (McDonough) Smith. "She was a good speaker. . . . She loved to be out front—definitely not a shy violet." Several former classmates recalled Betty Jo's confidence and eagerness to speak up, characteristics not common among typically shy, and often insecure, adolescents. Smith remembered her friend as "self-confident, smart, pretty."

Former high school boyfriend Chuck Stahl had no trouble responding to Betty Jo's physical appeal. Their acquaintance, first as neighbors and friends, later evolved into a romance and steady dating relationship. "Poise," Stahl said, contributed to his attraction. "She held herself properly and didn't slouch around. Obviously, she had good upbringing."

Meanwhile, the debate program proved a perfect match for Betty Jo. Her graceful

Five Cliff Girls Throw Big Dance

A Spring dance was given in honor of six Sunset High School girls at Arlington Hall, Lee Park, last weekend.

The hostesses were Misses Joan Brimberry, daughter of Mr. and Mrs. S. O. Brimberry, 411 S. Mont Clair; Marjorie Jaffa, daughter of Mr. and Mrs. W. H. Farner, 2118 Barberry; Ida Nelle Tunnell, daughter of Mr. and Mrs. S. B. Tunnell, 1007 S. Windomere; Betty Peacock, daughter of Mr. and Mrs. Duncan Peacock, 600 S. Erigh on; Patsy Johnson, daughter of Mr. and Mrs. Pat Johnson, 1203 N. Clinton, and Jan Clancy, daughter of Mr. and Mrs. D. M. Clancy, N Hampton..

More than fifty couples attended the dance which was semi-formal Refreshments were served by the girls' mothers.

Joan Brimberry   Betty Peacock

Marjorie Jaffa   Patsy Johnson

Ida Nelle Tunnell   Jan Clancy

Invite You To

a

SPRING DANCE

at

LEE HALL

Eight to Twelve

Friday, April Eleventh

Semi-Formal

Date Of Your Choice

While a student at Sunset High School, finishing her junior year, Betty Jo and five of her friends were honored with a Spring Dance at Arlington Hall in Lee Park on Friday, April 11, 1947.

manner lent itself to the program's presentation aspect and caught the eye of Miss Rebecca Thayer, the school's debate coach and speech teacher. According to former classmate and debate team member Eldred Barrick, Miss Thayer understood the vital role presentation played in debate and effectively conveyed that to her students:

> She would coach you on speaking, on pronouncing words properly, and your floor presence and delivery—your posture at the podium, the way you used your hands to express yourself. You learned to look people in the eye. . . . Betty Jo had a lot of floor presence.

She also had something to say. Betty Jo found the debate topics absorbing and intellectually challenging. "You had to know something about a subject of some importance nationally," said Barrick. "Debate team members developed an interest in government, economics, and world affairs." And, it was no wonder. Arguing the affirmative and negative sides of such issues as the Taft-Hartley Act, universal health care, and compulsory military service required the gathering of many facts, and Miss Thayer demanded highly-organized presentations. Patsy Smith remembered their debate coach as an encourager and a great role model:

> She encouraged us to do research . . . to be original in our thinking and bring up statements that the opposing team could not refute in any way. We had the facts. . . . If you have the facts, then you cannot easily be refuted.

Betty Jo earned a reputation for presenting precise, well-researched arguments, the product of hard work and long hours at the downtown Dallas public library. Her competitive spirit drove her to research the coming year's debate topic during summer vacation. "Even in the summer," said Patsy Smith, "we were preparing cases. We knew what the topic was, and we wanted to get a jump ahead of everybody."

Debate teammate Eldred Barrick recalled Betty Jo's mental agility during tournaments:

> She knew her subject well, and she was able to take the argument from the other team and turn it to her advantage without using memorized material—what we called "canned material." Betty Jo was really good at rebuttal. . . . She was very good at thinking on her feet and presenting it in an organized manner. It doesn't matter what you know if you're not organized, and the judges are unable to

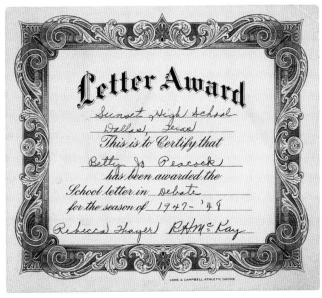

During Betty Jo's high school years she developed an inquiring interest in debate and government and became an effective member of the Sunset debate team. At the end of her senior year at Sunset she was awarded her third "letter" in debate.

44

follow your argument and understand the point you're trying to make.

Self-confidence, excellent research, and flawless delivery came together masterfully during an Oklahoma City tournament in 1947 when Betty Jo was a high school junior. Her performance left opponent Richard Gelwick, who would become her good friend, stunned and amazed. At the time, Gelwick and his debate partner were representing Bristow High School of Oklahoma, a school with a reputation for debating success. In an unexpected turn of events just before the competition, illness prevented Betty Jo's debate partner from participating. Fully expecting Betty Jo to withdraw from the tournament, Gelwick watched, as she approached the lectern alone. Instead of withdrawing, she calmly and confidently announced she would present all the arguments for her team. Gelwick vividly remembered the moment:

> The first thing I noticed was she was beautiful and blonde and very well-dressed. Her appearance was outstanding. And then when she said, "My colleague is ill, but I am prepared to do both speeches," I thought, well, it's all over, and it was. We lost the debate. . . . She was a spectacularly effective debater.

Betty Jo's interest in politics and government affairs spiked sharply in 1946 when her uncle, Carl Albert, was elected to the U.S. House of Representatives. On January 3, 1947, as he took the oath of office to represent Oklahoma's third congressional district, fifteen-year-old Betty Jo Peacock witnessed the event from the V.I.P. gallery of the House chamber.

One year later, she returned to Washington, D.C. for yet another visit with her aunt and uncle, and this trip was even more significant. Betty Jo's future husband, Jess Hay, recounted her remembrance of the exciting experience:

> On this trip she attended her first White House dinner, at which she was seated at a table with her aunt and uncle, Mary and Carl Albert, Speaker of the House Sam Rayburn, and other dignitaries. To her great delight, the occasion included dancing to the music of one of the military bands of the day, and her dance card was filled primarily by attending cadets from West Point and midshipmen from the Naval Academy. For a sixteen-year-old girl, it indeed was an exciting time. This experience was to be the first of many White House visits, and it clearly whetted her interest in the political process.

During dinner at the White House, freshman Congressman Carl Albert introduced his niece to the nation's thirty-third president, Harry Truman, a thrilling occasion that earned a certain amount of celebrity for Betty Jo upon her return to Sunset High School. The school paper—*The Sunset Stampede*—carried a brief, front-page story about the event in its March 4, 1948 issue under the headline, "Sunset Senior Meets President in White House." The article read in part:

> "Good evening, Miss Peacock," said Harry S. Truman, as he smiled and shook hands with Betty. "I had to swallow my heart two or three times to get out 'Good evening, Mr. President,' explained Betty.
>
> "Mr. Truman is just like any average man," said Betty, "and he looks just like all his pictures. Mrs. Truman was nice-looking and well dressed."
>
> At the President's Ball, Betty danced with many of the military aides from Annapolis and West Point, and many "old bachelor senators."

"She was very proud," said classmate Gene Austin. "She talked to us about the trip and how many congressmen she met and danced with. As soon as she saw me she shook my hand and said, 'Shake hands with the hand that shook the hand of the president.'"

Coming face to face with elected congressmen and senators not only gave a decidedly human touch to the business of politics, but it also provided Betty Jo with her first personal connection to national legislative issues. These experiences solidified her interest in the political arena. Fellow debater Eldred Barrick was convinced that Betty Jo's uncle, Carl Albert, had a profound impact on the direction of her life. "I think that had a lot to do with shaping her ambition," Barrick said. "She knew more about politics . . . than the rest of us did. . . . She was more intimately acquainted with politics."

Although the Debate Club claimed Betty Jo's keen interest and commitment, she pursued numerous other high school activities. Among them—National Honor Society, Student Council, National Thespian Club, Drama Club, Speaker Club, National Forensic League, Good Scholarship Club, Sodalitas Latina, Senior Play, Senior Day Skit, Junior Red Cross, Linz Pin Recipient, and Office Helper. Her wide-ranging interests reflected the desire to fully embrace high school life and actively participate on many levels. Like her mother, Betty Jo possessed energy and initiative.

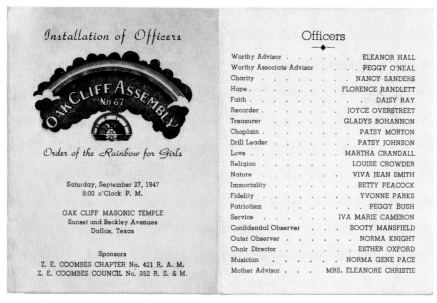

As a part of an active social life in high school, Betty Jo Peacock served as an officer in the Order of the Rainbow for Girls in the capacity of "Immortality." Just what she would do in this position remains a mystery.

At home, Betty Jo had the love of her parents to help support her busy school life. When close friend Patsy (McDonough) Smith looked back, she remembered Kathryn as a "protective" mother, an enviable quality from her perspective:

> Betty Jo's mother was there for her, which mine wasn't. When we had assemblies, she was there. . . . When school was out, all Betty Jo had to do was walk down the steps and get inside her mother's car. . . . They lived in a very small house, but neat as a pin, always lovely. Her mother was the perfect role model for a mother.

Friend and youth group president, Gene Austin, shared similar memories of Kathryn and the influence she had on Betty Jo. "I remember Mrs. Peacock as a kind, loving mother type," he said. "She was encouraging, like Betty was encouraging. She had that openness trait."

In their daily lives, Kathryn and Duncan continued to model hard work, and soon would enjoy its benefits. With the war over, and America in the midst of an economic boom, Dallas experienced unprecedented growth and prosperity, according to SMU historian Darwin Payne:

> Dallas' future never seemed brighter. . . . Businesses flourished, incomes rose, and schools became crowded. . . . Voters approved in late 1945 a $40 million bond issue to implement a new master plan for municipal buildings, streets and boulevards, parks, and schools. . . . In 1948, the year when the *Wall Street Journal* recognized Dallas as a financial center by establishing there a southwest edition . . . what was billed as the biggest industrial relocation in the history of the nation occurred when the Chance Vought Aircraft Division of United Aircraft Corporation moved its entire facility to Grand Prairie from Connecticut. . . . With Chance Vought came its $25 million payroll.

Amid the thriving economy, Duncan found his niche in the business world. He took a job managing a Planter's Peanut store on Elm Street, in the heart of downtown Dallas near what was then the Palace Theater. Duncan concluded that the opportunity for growth was significant and purchased the peanut store from the Planter's company, renaming it *The Peanut Shoppe*. He continued to own and operate the business for some twenty years, until 1968, when he retired and moved with Kathryn to McAlester, Oklahoma.

Meanwhile, a few blocks to the north, at the R. M. Noblitt Cotton Company, Kathryn had become adept at the cotton trade. Reuben Noblitt was a cotton broker with a sixth floor office in the Dallas Cotton Exchange Building at the intersection of North St. Paul and San Jacinto. One day, he acknowledged that the bright, dynamic Kathryn had become an indispensable part of his operation when he reportedly boasted to another broker, "You know, I pay her three times what I could get a secretary for, but she's worth more to me than a half-dozen secretaries."

Carl Albert's son, David Albert, remembered visiting his Aunt Kathryn at the cotton exchange:

> It was an office with these big warehouse-like rooms and cotton bales all over the place. Her desk was right there in the middle of the cotton bales. . . . She booked the orders and did the accounting. . . . She was everything from a bookkeeper to a secretary. She would be called an executive assistant, today.

48

Kathryn, over time, became skilled at every facet of the business, from grading the quality of the cotton, to buying and selling it. And Reuben Noblitt eventually rewarded these contributions to his firm by sharing ownership of the company with her.

Now, bolstered by two good incomes, the Peacocks could afford to move to a larger home, this one on King's Highway in Oak Cliff, about a mile from Sunset High School. The duplex was owned by Alice White who was Kathryn's friend at the Cotton Exchange in Dallas. When she died, Alice White bequeathed the King's Highway property to Kathryn and Duncan notwithstanding the fact that years prior to Alice's death, the Peacocks had moved from Oak Cliff to University Park.

Kathryn and Duncan, by this time, also had the resources to realize some of their long-held dreams for Betty Jo. The most important was a college education. On that, everyone could agree. There was, however, disagreement about the choice of schools. Betty Jo had her own ideas: either The University of Texas at Austin, where a number of her friends would be going, or North Texas State College in Denton [now the University of North Texas], the school selected by her boyfriend, Chuck Stahl, and other Sunset graduates. But Duncan and Kathryn were set on Southern Methodist University in Dallas. Besides its Methodist affiliation, they liked the financial savings that would result from having Betty Jo live at home. Reluctantly, Betty Jo agreed to SMU.

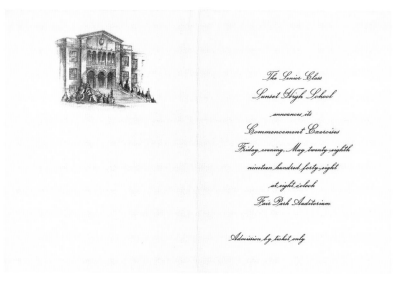

Commencement Exercise invitation.

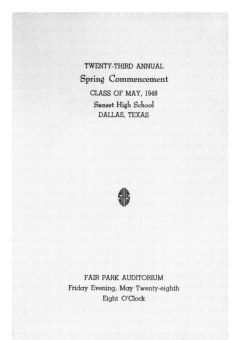

TWENTY-THIRD ANNUAL
Spring Commencement
CLASS OF MAY, 1948
Sunset High School
DALLAS, TEXAS

FAIR PARK AUDITORIUM
Friday Evening, May Twenty-eighth
Eight O'Clock

In May 1948, Betty Jo graduated with high honors from Sunset High School where she was a member of The National Honor Society and a Linz Pin recipient.

Betty Jo's high school graduation in 1948 concluded a formative chapter in her life. And though she had no way of knowing it at the time, the many honors she earned at Sunset High School set the pattern for future accomplishments. As she left Sunset, Betty Jo took with her the remembrances of many friendships. Among the most cherished was Rebecca Thayer—debate coach, mentor, guide, and good friend—whose parting words to her appeared on the last page of Betty Jo's 1948 yearbook, *The Sundial*:

Dear Betty,

You have a great future ahead of you—you have done a good job well. Your industry and ability—your unspoiled personality and cooperation are all assets to be admired. I have enjoyed working and playing with you—May Lady Luck always be your friend.

I love you,
Miss Thayer

■ ■

Words may outline and describe
Betty Jo Hay's life
as a daughter, wife, mother, grandmother,
public citizen, and friend.

But only photographs can enable one's
experience of her irresistible smile and only such
images can capture the vitality, joy and love of
life which defined her and enriched all those
who were touched by her grace and charm.
Those friends, in turn, had a profound impact
on her, and clearly helped shape the wonderful
person she ultimately became.

The photograph essays, presented sequentially
following each chapter of the text,
seek to depict this creative and reciprocally
beneficial interaction among
Betty Jo, her family, and her friends,
from which sprang the productive life
celebrated in this book of remembrances.

■ ■

PHOTOGRAPH ALBUM

1

HERITAGE

through

AUGUST 1948

52

Dr. Solomon Johnson Scott, great-great-great-grand-
father of Betty Jo, was born on March 6, 1798 and died
in October 1874. He is buried at Sherman, Texas.
Stacy Reeves Scott, the son of Dr. Solomon Johnson
Scott and Rebecca Reeves Scott, was born January 4,
1833 in Newport, Kentucky. He was great-great-grand-
father of Betty Jo.

Rebecca Reeves Scott, wife of Dr. Solomon Johnson
Scott, great-great-great-grandmother of Betty Jo.

Robert Carlton Scott, great-grandfather
of Betty Jo, was the son of Stacy Reeves Scott
and Sarah Ann Miller Scott, and was born
April 10, 1858 in Sherman, Texas.

Sarah Margaret Frantz Scott was the wife of
Robert Carlton Scott and great-grandmother
of Betty Jo.

Leona Ann Scott Albert, maternal grandmother of Betty Jo.
Circa 1900.

Ernest Homer Albert, maternal grandfather of Betty Jo.
Circa 1902.

Leona and Ernest Albert, Betty Jo's maternal grandparents,
with their baby daughter Kathryn Myrtle Albert,
Betty Jo's mother. 1913.

The grandparents of both Jess and Betty Jo were significant influences
in their lives. Jesse J. Roddy and Nettie Fleming Roddy. Circa 1925.

The old Bug Tussle school house in Bug Tussle, Oklahoma was the elementary school of three of the Albert children (Carl, Budge, and Kathryn). Betty Jo, Mary Albert, Vince Gleeson, and Kathryn Peacock are shown visiting the abandoned school in April 1997.

The Peacocks: Each child in his individual world on the Peacock farmhouse front porch, southeast of Sherman, Texas. Betty Jo's two uncles, Edgar, the fisherman, and Harry, the spear thrower; Nina, her grandmother; and Duncan Peacock, her father, the hunter. 1915.

Carl Bert Albert, with Noal Ernest Albert, later known to the family as Budge, and Kathryn Myrtle Albert. At the Albert farm in Bug Tussle, Oklahoma, also known as Flowery Mound. 1915.

Duncan watching, as Harry and Edgar Peacock feed a calf at the Peacock farm. Circa 1918.

A cold, winter's day was filled with excitement and the reward of rabbit stew.
Harry, Duncan, and Edgar Peacock home from rabbit hunting on the Peacock farm. 1919.

Betty Jo, one year old, with her mother Kathryn, at the Albert home in McAlester, Oklahoma in 1932.

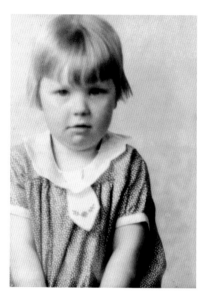

Betty Jo when she was 3 years and 10 months of age, living in Durant, Oklahoma. April 22, 1935.

A 1935 photograph of Duncan Peacock, father of Betty Jo. At that time he was living in Sherman, Texas.

Nina Peacock, grandmother of Betty Jo, with Kathryn and Duncan Peacock at the stairway entrance to Onyx cave, located in Eureka Springs, Arkansas. 1936.

Nettie Fleming Roddy, Jess Hay's grandmother, was an excellent cook. She passed recipes to Betty Jo which helped her become a much admired cook. Circa 1958.

Kathryn and Betty Jo at six years old, in Sherman, Texas. 1937.

Sam and Nina Peacock, Betty Jo's paternal grandparents at their home in Sherman, Texas. 1937.

Betty Jo and her parents, Kathryn and Duncan Peacock, in Sherman, Texas. 1938.

George Hay, father of Jess Hay. Circa 1955.

Myrtle Roddy Hay, mother of Jess Hay. Circa 1955.

600 South Brighton in Dallas, Texas, the first Dallas residence of Kathryn, Duncan, and Betty Jo from the Fall of 1943 to August 1945.

Betty Jo attended Greiner Junior High School in Dallas from September 1943 to May 1945.

Samye Peacock Newman, Betty Jo's aunt, with her husband, Rowe, and their daughter, Betty Jean, all of whom then resided in Sherman, Texas. 1945.

The Peacock family worshiped at Brooklyn Avenue Methodist Church in Dallas from the Fall of 1943 to August 1950.

Carl Albert and his brother, Earl Albert, in the Pacific Theatre,
World War II. 1944.

Betty Jo and her good friend and classmate,
Jimmie Dell Turner, on a church camping trip to
Turner Falls, Oklahoma. 1944.

Betty Jo, Kathryn, and Duncan Peacock when she was
a freshman at Sunset High School in Dallas. 1945.

Betty Jo as a sophomore at Sunset High School. 1946.

The Peacock residence at
1215 Kings Highway, Dallas, Texas.
From September 1946
to August 1950.

Betty Jo attended Sunset High School,
Dallas, from September 1945
to May 1948.

Betty Jo vacationing at the home of Betty and Budge Albert in
Wichita, Kansas. Summer 1947. She recently had completed her
junior year in high school.

Betty Jo dressed for a proper occasion alongside the family
automobile. She was a senior in high school in 1948.

CHAPTER
2

SEPTEMBER 1948
through
MAY 1955

Although Southern Methodist University wasn't Betty Jo Peacock's preferred school choice, her disappointment did not run deep, and in no time she discovered activities at SMU which captured her interest and enthusiasm. On the social front, she explored the Greek letter societies—sororities and fraternities—by going through the traditional week of rush. And in the fall of 1948, she accepted an invitation to join Sigma Kappa sorority, thus opening the door to a welcoming community and easing her entry into college life. A first-person glimpse into the sorority selection process, from being "rushed," at the onset, to the final step of pledging, appeared in *Sigma Kappa Triangle*, the sorority newsletter:

> "We'd like for you to be our sister in Sigma Kappa—will you?" Which one of us
> will ever forget these words—the starry-eyed acceptance—the maroon and lavender
> ribbons pinned next to our hearts? For weeks we had been rushed (both literally
> and figuratively) at parties, coke dates, open houses. . . . Mad pledge days followed.
> Our first pledge meeting, supper in the rooms and song practice with the girls—our
> sisters. . . . We went to parties galore—parties given by initiates—parties given by
> pledges. And always there were our *mothers* standing by to get us a date if necessary.

Betty Jo's outgoing nature was a perfect fit for sorority life. She put her energy into the many activities it offered and began to assume leadership roles, one of the earliest coming at a so-called "Frontier Party" hosted by her pledge class for the sorority's active members. A *Sigma Kappa Triangle* article describing the event noted: "'Emcee' for the stage show . . . was Betty Jo Peacock who really knows how to strut her stuff in a cowgirl outfit! She introduced Mrs. Caulfield, an alum, who awarded first, second, and third prizes for the best costumes." Betty Jo's performance and her ability to command center stage led to her appointment the following year as one of two Sigma Kappa social chairmen.

Amid the whirlwind of social activities in 1948, Betty Jo met and took a liking to Don Welsh, a member of the Lambda Chi Alpha fraternity. The attraction was mutual and soon the two began dating, appearing together at parties and other events, according to John Hamilton, a Lambda Chi fraternity brother. On one occasion, Hamilton—the Lambda Chi song leader—remembers socializing with Betty Jo when members of his fraternity serenaded the girls of Sigma Kappa. "She was a gorgeous little blonde lady who had a big smile and was active in her sorority," Hamilton said. "I could always recognize her at a distance, and she was easy to make eye contact and wave or say hello or 'How about that exam?'"

Betty Jo's decision to join Sigma Kappa, like most decisions in her life, was not haphazard. It simply made good sense. Because Sigma Kappa chose not to compete with sororities in the top tier—which often selected their members on the basis of social prominence and wealth—it enjoyed a reputation for quiet accomplishment and academic strength, making it a logical choice for an achiever such as Betty Jo. Sigma Kappa member Jane (Manton) Marshall, a 1945 SMU graduate, said the sorority was known for attracting a more intellectual group of young women:

> Sigma Kappa attracted a number of faculty daughters. . . . Each sorority had its own informal reputation and that was the flavor of Sigma Kappa. The coloration was more academic in its interests. They were the solid citizens group. Sigma Kappa girls were known for their high grade quotient.

Betty Jo's lifelong friend and fellow Sigma Kappa, M.C. (Patterson) Guilloud, agreed the sorority "did not march to the same drummer as the larger sororities. The kind of women that were in Sigma Kappa were more serious-minded," she said. Lou (Hirsch) Davison, who pledged Sigma Kappa the same year as Betty Jo said she found the emphasis on scholastics appealing. "One of the things they were looking for, which made the sorority attractive to me, was academics. I did have good grades, and they were very encouraging for you to maintain a high grade point average." Said John Hamilton about the Sigma Kappa women: "They were just good, solid girls. They weren't thought of as being flashy or spoiled millionaire baby girls . . . just solid citizens of the university who did good class work and participated in constructive activities."

Even as a college freshman Betty Jo had well-defined goals, many of which revolved around her enthusiasm for debate and public speaking. Within a short period of time she declared speech as a major, and not surprisingly—inspired by her friend and high school mentor, Rebecca Thayer—set her heart on becoming a teacher.

The degree to which her interest in the power of verbal communication was sparked in high school is revealed in written notes from an eleventh grade public speaking course which indicate the enormous value Betty Jo placed on the spoken word. So valuable, in fact, she bound sixty pages of those notes—as well as mimeographed course material—and kept it as a reference in her personal archive for more than fifty years. Quotations on the epigraph page reflected her firm belief in the importance of communication skills: "Words sink into the heart," read one, and "Oratory is all powerful," read another.

In addition, two of the "Course Objectives," appearing on page three of the document, stand out, particularly as they relate to Betty Jo, a young woman who would go on to devote much of her life to participating in the democratic process and who cherished the right to self-expression:

1. To aid the student in acquiring and developing the ability to communicate effectively in a democratic society. . . .

3. To develop speech as a tool which will enable the individual to present more effectively his ideas with confidence in whatever life situations he may face.

As would be expected, Betty Jo joined the SMU debate club and paired up with Lou (Hirsch) Davison, a member of Betty Jo's pledge class and an experienced high school debater from Highland Park and Hillcrest High Schools in Dallas. "Betty Jo was a gregarious, outgoing girl," said Davison. "We seemed to complement each other. I was a little more retiring than she was. . . . She was good at research. You have to be when you're debating at that level."

Betty Jo not only was known for mastering her subject and being well prepared with both pro and con authoritative citations, but she also had a knack for strategy. During one tournament, Davison recalls huddling next to Betty Jo listening to an opposing team's argument. After the team had made its point, Betty Jo scoured her note cards for just the right counter quotation, nudged Davison—her partner—and said, "Okay, now give them this one." With such a naturally extroverted personality, it was hard to contain the force that was Betty Jo Peacock, especially when she was competing. "She'd punch you or get all wiggly," said Davison. "She was just a little live wire." Helen (Prince) Furlong, another of Betty Jo's college debate team partners, remembers her as "a very forceful speaker," confident, and convincing. Furlong's father, a wildcat oil producer, felt the full effect of Betty Jo's verbal skills after dinner one evening when she decided to deliver a speech she'd been rehearsing for an upcoming class. As it happened, Helen Furlong had invited Betty Jo to stay the night at her home, and following a dinner prepared by her father, Furlong said Betty Jo got up and presented the speech to him:

> It was a declamatory kind of thing. He was just enthralled. He later told me, "That gal can really talk!" My father and mother were both quite fond of her. We would spend the night at each other's houses when we were preparing for debate tournaments.

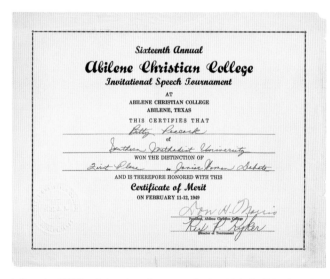

In September 1948 Betty Jo began her college career at Southern Methodist University, and that Fall joined the debate society. It was not long before her speech and debate skills were put to use. Abilene Christian College, on February 11-12, 1949, sponsored an invitational speech tournament where she and her partner, Lou Hirsch, represented SMU and won First Place in Junior Women Debate.

That type of extra effort paid off when, in February 1949, Betty Jo and Lou Hirsch won first place in women's debate at the Abilene Christian College Invitational Speech Tournament. Then, that same semester, came an even more significant and especially rare honor for a freshman team—Betty Jo and Hirsch were invited to participate in a national tournament at the University of Virginia.

Following the tournament, the SMU debaters, including a boys' team—Bill Nighswonger and Paul Morrell, two pre-theologues from Oklahoma City—spent a day in Washington, D.C., where

LOCAL NEWS
EDITORIALS . . . SPORTS
MARKETS . . . CLASSIFIED

Texas' Leading Newspaper

SMU coed Betty Peacock surveys the instrument panel of a new-look desk to be used by lecturers in Fondren Hall of Science. It has fifty controls and will do everything for a professor but give his lecture for him.

Betty Jo demonstrates that she knows which buttons to push.

they had the opportunity to experience some nuts-and-bolts lessons in the prerogatives of power, courtesy of Betty Jo's uncle, Congressman Carl Albert. In preparation, Betty Jo called ahead to her uncle, who welcomed them at the Capitol, and also had arranged for a tour of the Library of Congress. During the tour, Davison recalls a particularly attentive librarian and wondered, at the time, whether such eagerness might have had something to do with the fact Albert was a member of the subcommittee responsible for the library's budget. His influence was apparent again when the young debaters wandered inside the empty House chamber to have a look around. They quickly were spotted by a congressional page who sternly told them the chamber was off limits to them, but immediately was swayed when he saw their passes were from Carl Albert, after which he invited them to take their time looking around and asked if there was anything he could do to make their visit more pleasant.

Over the next two years the SMU debate club became the focal point of Betty Jo's college experience and provided her with a community of like-minded friends whose enthusiasm for political discussion matched her own. Every tournament—because of the preparation necessary—deepened her understanding of the day's issues and reinforced her interest in politics.

College debate gave rise to a level of confidence in Betty Jo that manifested itself in many areas of her life, including her life in the classroom. Never afraid to stand up to authority when justified—and skilled at countering a debate opponent—she one day challenged her freshman English teacher in front of the class after receiving a grade of C+ on an essay she'd written. In Betty Jo's mind there was no question an injustice had been committed, and, to her way of thinking, injustices demanded immediate correction. Her gutsy courage caught the attention of one classmate in particular who already had noticed Betty Jo in a casual sort of way as one of the more attractive girls in the class. But this incident elevated the feisty coed to a person of extreme interest to Jess Hay:

> She just stood up one day and raised Cain with the teacher. She got a C+ on an essay in which there were no grammatical errors. The teacher said, "Well, there's more to writing than just grammatical correctness." Betty Jo was . . . furious. It was the first C she had made, I guess. . . . It was the first time that I'd really focused on her. . . . She displayed considerable tenacity and willingness to be up front about her feelings, and she was cute. So all those characteristics attracted my attention. . . . I wouldn't have challenged a teacher at that time for anything in the world. . . . Her assertiveness was impressive to me, and I never forgot it.

Average grades, however, were not the norm for Betty Jo. On the contrary, she finished her freshman year with a solid record of success, in spite of a plate full of sorority and debate tournament activities. Excellent grades also secured her membership in Alpha Lambda Delta, the honorary scholastic sorority for freshmen women (now a coeducational organization at SMU). And along the way she earned an honor award from SMU that conferred upon her "the designation of UNIVERSITY SCHOLAR for outstanding scholastic attainment."

Many of Betty Jo's accomplishments in college had their source in her independent spirit, which served her well on most counts, but led her down a counterproductive path that would prove to be one of her greatest life challenges. Like many of her contemporaries, Betty Jo took up cigarette smoking, enticed perhaps by its depiction in films and magazines of the time as a glamorous and even romantic thing to do. Print advertisements featured such film stars as a smiling Rock Hudson—lit cigarette in hand—casually lounging above the words, "Rock Hudson agrees with smokers everywhere: 'I've tried 'em all—but it's Camels for me.'" Another seductive ad directly targeted the youth market: "These qualities tell why PHILIP MORRIS has made so many friends among younger smokers—with their fresher, unspoiled tastes. Follow young America's lead. Enjoy Philip Morris in the convenient snap-open pack." Sorority sister and debate partner M.C. (Patterson) Guilloud described Betty Jo as a "determined smoker." She remembers the two of them attending a debate tournament at Baylor University in Waco. "The school had a rule against smoking on campus," said Guilloud. "So, Betty Jo and I would walk out, step off the curb, and smoke." And there was the tournament at Abilene Christian College (now Abilene Christian University): "That's where we went into the girls' restroom to smoke." Among the college crowd, it seemed that flaunting the rules on smoking had as much appeal as the perceived chic of the cigarettes themselves. "Certainly, at the time we started smoking in the late 1940s and early 1950s, it was the sophisticated thing to do," said Guilloud, adding, "But it was addictive."

As a freshman at SMU, on May 4, 1949, at the end of the academic year, Betty Jo was selected to receive an Honor Award as a University Scholar for outstanding scholastic attainment.

By early fall of her second year at SMU, Betty Jo's personal relationship with Don Welsh took a serious turn when the couple became "pinned." Her acceptance of Welsh's Lambda Chi Alpha fraternity pin symbolized their commitment to a serious, exclusive dating relationship.

However, two months later Betty Jo met another boy at a weekend debate tournament in Natchitoches, Louisiana, from which grew a relationship that altered both of their lives. Jess Hay was that boy, first impressed by Betty Jo's encounter with their English teacher the previous semester, and now among the SMU debaters attending the tournament. Between rounds, the students socialized over soft drinks and discussed the tournament. Hay and his partner, John Reese, ended up spending much of their break time with Betty Jo and her partner Helen (Prince) Furlong comparing notes and exchanging information they hoped might strengthen their teams' arguments. As it happened, the two teams performed well and were required to stay late to finish their final rounds, while their adult chaperone and coach, Norma Jean Ballard, drove the eliminated SMU teams back to Dallas. When the debates ended, Bill Brice and Joe Stalcup, also finalists—Brice in oratory and Stalcup in after dinner speaking—joined the Hay and Peacock debate teams for the drive back home.

The friendly conversation and interaction at the tournament had engendered such a feeling of camaraderie between Betty Jo and Jess that they were compelled to sit together in the car. Stalcup remembers it being obvious the two had, in his words, "paired up." During the trip, they stopped for dinner in Shreveport at a restaurant which served alcoholic beverages, and swept up by feelings of fellowship and high spirits, the students ordered a round of cocktails. Reese remembers the group was feeling adventurous: "We drove back to Dallas through Shreveport, and these girls had to have a zombie. They had never had one before, and they wanted to try it. . . . It was a drink that was supposed to knock you off your feet." Jess Hay recalls Brice and Stalcup instigated the idea when they said they were going to have zombies and thought the girls should try them, too. "To Bill Brice and Joe Stalcup's credit, they both had zombies, and so did the girls with predictable results. . . . Betty Jo obviously was a little impaired." Continued Reese, "So the girls had those zombies, and they were zombied good. . . . My God, those poor girls were wobbling . . . . Betty Jo and Jess ended up in the front seat together. I think I was driving. . . .That's when the big move was made by Jess, and he put his arm around her and they started doing some smooching." Looking back, Hay said, "It got pretty intense."

Meanwhile, John Reese was torn between loyalty to his fraternity brother Don Welsh, who was pinned to Betty Jo, and his debate partner and friend, Jess, in whose arms

Betty Jo had fallen asleep on the drive back to Dallas. Reese remembers leaning over and whispering to Hay, "She doesn't know what she's doing." Blissfully pleased with the situation, Jess Hay whispered back, "Well, she may not, John, but she's doing it damn well."

The Natchitoches trip, and the resulting connection made between Betty Jo and Jess, marked the beginning of a meaningful new relationship. Hay later would credit the tournament with, as he put it, "tweaking Betty Jo's interest." For his part, he simply said, "I was smitten." Yet in spite of their obvious physical attraction, Hay said he didn't pursue that aspect of the relationship. Nor did he pursue even a dating relationship, since financially speaking, he said he really couldn't afford such an arrangement. "I was poor as a church mouse; so I didn't feel I was in a position to engage in a battle for her hand or anything like that." Instead, in what proved a clever and successful strategy, he initiated a low-intensity campaign to deepen their friendship. This allowed him to interact frequently with the girl of his dreams at little expense:

> We'd wind up at the student union together . . . between classes. We'd have a cup
> of coffee or a Coke. Usually, there were bridge games going on at the student
> union. Sometimes we'd pair up and play bridge for an hour or so between classes. . . .
> At night, we frequently met at the library to study for a while before she went to pick
> up her mother and daddy.

Their platonic arrangement suited Betty Jo, as well. It enabled her to continue dating Don Welsh, her Lambda Chi Alpha boyfriend, and attending his fraternity parties and all the other events that made up the busy SMU Panhellenic social calendar. At the same time, she was able to learn more about this interesting new person—Jess Hay—from the safe confines of a casual friendship.

What Betty Jo learned was that she and Jess shared strikingly similar backgrounds and many of the same interests. Jess Thomas Hay was born on January 22, 1931, in Forney, Texas, and was reared, as was Betty Jo, by a devoted mother and a loving adoptive father. Like Betty Jo, Jess's ancestry also had its roots in a rural, farming heritage. For many years, his maternal grandfather, Jesse J. Roddy, farmed successfully near Forney until the Great Depression wiped out most of what he had accumulated. Jess's parents, George and Myrtle Roddy Hay, were more fortunate when hard times hit. While their material circumstances were meager, Jess's parents at least had the steady income of a father who enjoyed continuous employment as an administrator employed by the federal government and a mother who, in addition to fulfilling her duties as wife and mother, also worked outside the home.

And though the finest details of their family lives may not have been identical, there was one important characteristic which Betty Jo and Jess shared equally—the love of their close-knit families, for which Hay remains ever grateful. "I always felt warmly nurtured by my family, and I count that as probably the overriding blessing and grace of my early life," Hay said. "My mother and grandmother, Nettie Fleming Roddy, and my aunts, Nora Roddy Bramblett, Jessie Roddy Dees, Mary Lee Roddy, Allie Roddy, and Hazel Hay Owen, were the affirming influences of my childhood days; and my father was the one who consistently challenged me to do better. Concurrently (and fortunately) my sister, Patsy, and my cousins, Richard Bramblett and Helen Jeanette Roddy, managed to keep me reasonably humble and to provide me with an embryonic appreciation of the importance and functions of communion with one's peers."

In 1942, the Hays moved to Orange, Texas just as an infusion of World War II defense dollars began to turn the sleepy, southeast Texas backwater town into an industrial shipbuilding complex that supplied the U.S. Navy with a steady stream of destroyers.

George and Myrtle Hay, both of whom were college-educated, encouraged scholastic excellence in their son, Jess, and his younger sister, Patsy. "Some fathers like their sons to be football players, and some fathers like their sons to be scholars," said childhood best friend and high school classmate Hubert Spradling. "Jess was directed toward learning."

And he did not disappoint. Jess responded to his parents' encouragement by diligently applying himself to his studies. In seventh grade, "an unusually gifted teacher" fostered his interest in history and debate, subjects which meshed well with his earlier decision to pursue a career in law. "Whenever Jess and I talked about the future, he always talked about going to SMU and becoming a lawyer," said former classmate Haskell Monroe. "That was my earliest recollection of what Jess wanted to do after high school— go to SMU and be a lawyer."

But Hay wasn't like many of his classmates. He distinguished himself from the others by his awareness of and interest in the world beyond school. Early on, he developed a passion for political participation, actively campaigning for his first candidate at the young age of nine. Influenced by his parents' admiration for Franklin Roosevelt and Harry Truman, Hay formed a strong allegiance to the Democratic Party as the political organization "most representative of social justice and fairness," he said. It was a political philosophy linked to his family's devotion to the Methodist church, which held, among its most important tenets, a commitment to the endless pursuit of a socially just world.

Hay experienced a dramatic reinforcement of that religious obligation during his senior year of high school when he and his high school buddy, Hubert Spradling, attended a national Methodist Youth Conference in Cleveland, Ohio. The remarkable event brought together ten thousand high school and first-year college students from around the country. "It was a powerful experience," Hay remembers. Richard Gelwick and Dick Wilke, who later—with their wives, Beverly and Julia—would become lifelong friends with Betty Jo and Jess, also participated in the conference when they were in high school and felt its transforming effect. "It had an enormous impact on us," said Gelwick. "We talked about race relations and world peace. That's where the emphasis was, and it was an exciting moment for us. We met a lot of world leaders who were working on those issues." Wilke recalls a ferment of liberal idealism infusing the conference:

> The mood in the church and the mood of the conference was one of . . . liberal Christian idealism. Now, we are going to work for peace all over the world, and we're going to feed the hungry, and we're going to have racial justice. This was before the country was ready for racial justice. . . . I think the conference put underneath Jess and me a liberal political sentiment. . . . Racial justice, food for the hungry, concern for the poor, peace for the world, make the world a better place— those were the moods. And . . . our political foundation was impacted by that.

"The impact on me was a conviction that our ethical calling as Christians was to serve our fellow man," said Hay. "Our responsibility was to love others as we would want them to love us. It was to do justice; it was to love mercy and to have a dimension of humility in our relationships with God and with other people. All of that was fundamental to Methodist tradition." And although Betty Jo did not attend the youth conference in Cleveland, years of Methodist education had instilled in her many of the same core convictions. To be sure, service to others was counted among the bedrock values she expressed throughout her life.

Eventually, what emerged from the games of bridge, the shared Cokes, and the study dates was a realization by Betty Jo that Jess Hay shared the interests that mattered most to her—religion, politics, debate, and intellectual inquiry. And while his affable personality certainly was pleasant enough, what drew her attention more than anything else was his seriousness of purpose. Jess had goals. Become a Dallas lawyer. Redirect SMU student politics toward qualified leadership and more widespread involvement. Actively participate in mainstream politics. Fulfill his ethical commitment to the Methodist tradition by better serving others.

Meanwhile, Don Welsh, Betty Jo's steady boyfriend—an engaging young man, but one whose interests, at least from Betty Jo's perspective, were more narrowly focused than Hay's—would suffer from the comparison. Finally, in January or February 1950, Betty Jo told Welsh about her friendship with Jess, and although the information wasn't offered as a threat, Welsh took little pleasure in learning he had a potential rival. No longer able to ignore the other person in Betty Jo's life, Welsh expressed his concern to fraternity brother John Reese, who was Hay's debate partner. Apparently, Welsh's complaints about Hay didn't elicit as much sympathy from Reese as he would have liked:

> He [Welsh] knew something was going on and it wasn't in his favor, and he was asking me about it because Betty Jo was drifting away. . . . We would talk and so on and finally I told him, "Well, Don, if you can't hold on to your woman, don't blame Jess. I mean, she's making the choice. . . . He's just another guy looking for a girl-friend, like all of us, and she's choosing him over you." I didn't say it quite that way. But I said, "Don, you've got to hold on to your woman."

Reese characterized the pairing of Don Welsh and Betty Jo "as the kind of relation-ship where you go out with someone. You have a good time. You go out with them some more, and then it moves into something a little more serious, even though you may not have had all that much in common."

It didn't take long for Betty Jo to recognize she had more in common with Jess Hay than she did with Don Welsh. "They were almost like soul mates," said Reese. "They just didn't know it, initially, because they didn't know enough about each other." But, by late spring 1950, Betty Jo had it figured out. She'd come to the conclusion that, given the choice between Hay and Welsh, Hay's friendship offered more substance and a deeper level of connection and commitment.

■

As for Jess, there was no doubt about his desire to advance the relationship to the next level, a goal he achieved by devising a strategy of some ingenuity. First and foremost, he knew that in order to pursue his relationship with Betty Jo he had to remain in Dallas during the summer, but for that to happen he needed a legitimate reason and some financial assistance. The upcoming election for Dallas County district attorney provided both. On his own initiative, Hay co-founded an organization known as the Youth Council for Better Government made up of his politically active SMU friends, including Betty Jo,

Richard Gelwick, Joe Stalcup, Bill Brice, Bob Desmond, and Phil Palmer, Jr.:

I do remember with absolute clarity . . . that I was going to start pursuing Betty Jo
in a very serious way. . . . I knew Betty Jo would not be in school; I would not be
in school. So there would be a different kind of freedom. Now my problem was I
had to figure out a credible rationale for remaining in Dallas during the summer
and some way to make enough money to live on. . . . Creation of the Youth
Council for Better Government provided the means through which both objectives
were accomplished.

In advance of the primary election, the Youth Council decided it would evaluate
each district attorney candidate, select one for endorsement, and then work for his election.
To that end, it invited the candidates to present their experience and plans to the Youth
Council's board, and unbelievably, each of the three contenders accepted the invitation.
When the presentations were over, the youngest candidate—Henry Wade—had come away
with the Youth Council endorsement. Wade represented a wave of reform that had been

Youth Council to Fire Barrage
At District Attorney Candidates

About seventy-five young Dallas
voters Friday night will put the
three District Attorney candidates
on the spot.

They are members of the newly
organized Youth Council for Better
Government, made up largely of
SMU students.

Between 6:30 and 9:15 p.m. the
group's 11-member steering committee will quiz each candidate on
his platform. The meeting will be
held at the SMU student center.

Each candidate will be asked how
he intends to promote "honesty, efficiency and economy" in the office
he is running for. The candidates
are Andrew Patton, Henry Wade
and Al Templeton.

"In a week or ten days, we'll announce the man we will actively
support in the race," said Jess Hay,
activities co-ordinator of the council.

Campaign support will range all
the way from ringing doorbells to
button-holing friends to vote for
their champion. The youths have
divided the city into five districts
and will have 300 persons working
in teams for the candidate.

"Each election year, from now
on, we intend to pick out what we
believe the most important race
and support one of the candidates –
the one whom we think is most interested in good government," explained Bill Brice, president.

Ages of the group's members
range from twenty to thirty years.
Members of the steering committee are Bob Desmond, Joe Stalcup,
Bob Robertson, Mary Jeanes, Harold Griffin, Homer Koliba, Betty
Peacock, Danny Hitt, James Slat-
ton, Phil Palmer Jr., and Lee
Weber.

In late May 1950, the
Youth Council received
a page one notice in *The
Dallas Morning News* that
it was going to evaluate
each district attorney
candidate.
Courtesy The Dallas Morning News.

building in Dallas, and although he played the part of a country boy, he undoubtedly had the credentials of an attractive candidate, not the least of which was he'd graduated first in his law class at The University of Texas at Austin. Smart and youthful, Wade also happened to be a former FBI agent and war veteran, giving him even more of an edge over his two older opponents who were tainted by what Hay describes as "some warts from the past."

Hence, the Youth Council joined the so-called "Wade Parade" and began volunteering its services to his campaign. Jess Hay accepted the offer of a semi-professional position within the campaign organization, made by John Plath Green, Wade's campaign manager. With the position came the use of a car—furnished by W.O. Bankston, a Wade supporter and the owner of one of Dallas' largest car dealerships—and a small stipend to cover expenses, with a little left over. By living with his grandmother in Forney, just outside of town, Hay had what he needed to make it through the summer in Dallas.

With the financial side of things taken care of, he now was free to focus full-time on the Wade campaign. And in doing so, Hay worked with and encountered a number of civic leaders, thereby advancing another of his agenda goals:

Wade Gets Backing Of Youth Council

After quizzing all three District Attorney candidates, the newly organized Youth Council for Better Government said Sunday it would support Henry Wade.

Joe Stalcup, chairman of the steering committee, said "our selection was made on the basis of qualifications, integrity, future plans and program" of each candidate.

At the Southern Methodist University student center Friday, the group, made up largely of SMU students, individually questioned Wade, Al Templeton and Andrew Patton.

The council intends to pick a candidate to support with doorbell ringing and stump speaking each election year.

A few days later *The Dallas Morning News* published that the Youth Council had given Henry Wade their support.
Courtesy *The Dallas Morning News.*

I had known as long as I can remember that I wanted to go to SMU, I wanted to become a lawyer, and I wanted to live in Dallas. . . . I knew I needed to begin getting acquainted in Dallas, so the Wade campaign contributed to my introduction to the broader community. That was the beginning of the expanded horizons of Betty Jo's Dallas citizenship, and of my becoming a citizen of Dallas.

To garner more young supporters and momentum, the Youth Council's handful of college members—acting primarily through Joe Stalcup and Bill Brice, both former Adamson High School debaters—recruited a group of debaters from Adamson, thus giving the Wade campaign a respectable number of student workers. Led by Hay, the students concentrated not on stuffing envelopes, but rather on direct campaigning which involved, among other tactics, a series of rallies that took Wade's message out to the small towns of Dallas County. Hay's group soon found it wasn't hard to attract a crowd among rural residents who were hungry for entertainment and political oratory. "During those days," said Richard Gelwick, "campaigning was still done by loudspeaker from the back of a pickup truck with music and a microphone." In fact, organizing the rallies required a fairly simple formula, recalls Hay:

> Every little community had a town square or something comparable to a town square. The first thing you'd do was have a group go out during the day and pass out leaflets that said, "Come to the town square tonight for music and political speechifying." Then you'd get a small country band to perform on the back of a flat-bed truck and the crowd would assemble. Not only would they stay to listen to the music, but they were interested in the political speeches as well.

But it was music that made the difference. A band with good command of Texas swing fiddle music could draw anywhere from 100 to 200 people. Add to that, Wade's proxy speakers—Betty Jo, Jess, and Joe Stalcup—and chances were good the crowd would be sufficiently stirred up. Often attending the rallies was Ann Morton, Wade's campaign headquarters manager, who recalls being pleasantly surprised by Betty Jo's ability. "I was amazed at how smart she was," Morton said. "She knew how to express herself. She grasped the situation and knew how to respond to people."

According to Hay, the students' campaign work caught the eye of *The Dallas Morning News* and *The Daily Times Herald*, and drew an editorial round of applause from *The Herald.* This recognition may be what prompted Wade's principal opponent, Al Templeton, to beef up his own staff with a contingent of young campaigners dubbed, "Al's Pals," recruited from the Woodrow Wilson High School debate team. In the end, Templeton's last minute attempt at countering Wade's masterful Youth Council fell short and Henry Wade won the election.

While Wade was quick to credit his youthful supporters for the victory, Hay, even decades later, flatly dismissed such acclaim, though he did acknowledge, "We were a factor. We made an impact. We were his surrogates all over Dallas County, making speeches and passing out literature. It was really fun."

Hay's campaign to win the affection of Betty Jo also met with success. On June 6— with a car at his disposal—Jess invited Betty Jo to dinner and then to Fair Park's Starlight

Operetta for a musical comedy performance of *High Button Shoes*, an invitation she accepted with enthusiasm. "Unknown to me at the time," said Hay, "June 6, 1950, not only was the day of our first 'formal date' but also Betty Jo's nineteenth birthday. . . . The entire evening was terrific and it triggered the commencement of a deep and loving relationship which persisted without interruption for nearly fifty-five years."

Betty Jo and Jess welcomed the evolution of their relationship from one of platonic friendship to romantic involvement. The previous months had led Jess not only to appreciate Betty Jo as a person who shared his Methodist faith and political affiliation, "but mostly I learned that I really liked her, and we got along well. I think we complemented one another in obvious ways. She was outgoing and very comfortable in her own skin. . . . So by the time we started dating in June we were ready to go. Both of us, apparently, were ready for a . . . serious dating relationship starting that day."

Joe Stalcup and his fiancée Nancy Vaughn, who would marry in September, were among Jess and Betty Jo's closest friends during the summer of 1950. The couples had worked on the Wade campaign together and now shared frequent double-dates to the movies or picnics at White Rock Lake. "Betty Jo was very much falling in love with Jess," said Nancy. "They liked to kiss in the backseat when we were together. They were very much in love. One of our big entertainments that summer was the Starlight Operetta. We double-dated to see *Brigadoon*, then afterwards we rode the roller coaster. We went to several musicals that summer."

Kathryn and Duncan Peacock graciously accepted Betty Jo's new boyfriend and were able to get to know him through Sunday dinner invitations. Later that fall, as Jess and Betty Jo's relationship intensified, Hay remembers "more frequently than not, I would have Sunday lunch with the Peacocks. It was a pretty regular routine."

That summer, Kathryn and Duncan bought a house in University Park near SMU. The decision to leave Oak Cliff and purchase their first home in the upscale neighborhood came about as a result of more prosperous circumstances. Duncan's business, The Peanut Shoppe, had done well. In addition to a bustling stream of retail customers, he expanded it to include a dependable wholesale clientele. At the same time, Kathryn applied her considerable business acumen to the cotton brokerage industry and became an essential part of R. M. Noblitt's cotton company, which he rewarded with added responsibilities and commensurately higher compensation. Ever the astute businessperson, Kathryn also applied her skill as a cotton market analyst to investments on her own account. Lou (Hirsch) Davison, Betty Jo's debate partner, remembers Betty Jo mentioning once "that her mother had made some speculative buys that came out real good."

Still, in spite of their good fortune, Duncan and Kathryn were not given to extravagance and responded to financial success in careful, measured ways. This down-to-earth manner was reflected even in the purchase of their new home—a modest, cottage-style residence at 2715 Milton Avenue in University Park, which perfectly suited their unpretentious lifestyle.

■

Meanwhile, Jess and Betty Jo's relationship deepened in the fall of 1950, and what followed was a relatively expensive show of devotion, especially for a young man working his way through college. Nevertheless, in an effort to express his feelings for Betty Jo, Jess used what limited funds he had to surprise her with nice gifts. Richard Gelwick, Hay's roommate at the time, remembers registering a certain amount of shock and surprise when he saw a platinum watch Jess planned to present to Betty Jo. No matter, said Hay. "I was smitten. There was no question that I was deeply in love with Betty Jo. That watch cost fifty dollars . . . which then was a lot of money for me . . . but it was an appropriate symbol of my deep feelings for her." On another occasion—and as a further statement of his growing commitment—Hay presented Betty Jo with an opal ring.

While Betty Jo may have reciprocated the love felt by Jess Hay, it wasn't blind infatuation. Like her mother, Kathryn, Betty Jo called them like she saw them. M. C. (Patterson) Guilloud remembers an example of this in the fall of 1950 during her freshman year at SMU when she first met Jess. At the time, he was recovering from a cracked vertebra following an automobile accident. Betty Jo had told Guilloud about Hay's many fine attributes but prefaced her remarks with, "he isn't much to look at." And when she met him, Guilloud agreed, but said it wasn't that simple. "I thought, she's right. He's very nice, but kind of funny looking. At the time, he was in a body cast from his neck down to his hip line and he weighed 135 pounds, tops. . . . He had this red hair and rather prominent-looking ears and kind of a hawk-like nose." But Jess Hay also was enchanting, said Guilloud. "He was polite; he was generous; he was gentle. He clearly knew where he was going and what he wanted to do. I think that's always impressive in a young man."

For Betty Jo's part, she fared well at her first meeting with Jess's parents, George and Myrtle Hay. They met in Waco at a football game between SMU and Baylor University:

It was my family's first opportunity to meet Betty Jo, and they were impressed, and I believe Betty Jo was as well. After we parted, my mother (who apparently sensed my feelings) told my dad they probably had met their future daughter-in-law. . . . Both of them really liked Betty Jo, but my father was particularly enthralled with her. It was mainly because it comes across very quickly that Betty Jo is for real. She didn't pretend to be who she wasn't. She was as far removed from a snob as you could get.

Myrtle Hay's prescient comment about a "future daughter-in-law" was not misplaced. By late November or early December of 1950, Betty Jo and Jess were talking about making their relationship permanent, and on New Year's Eve the moment of truth came. During a party hosted by Bill Brice at his home on Richmond Avenue in the Lakewood area of Dallas, Betty Jo and Jess found a quiet corner where they discussed their future. Forty-five minutes later they had concluded they "were ready to move to the next level. . . . We knew we were going into something that was going to be difficult, but we decided nonetheless that we wanted to go ahead and do it. So we decided then and there we were going to get married sometime before the end of August 1951."

When they announced their decision to the Peacocks a few days later, all hell broke loose, but not surprisingly. The young couple had expected opposition to their plan from Betty Jo's parents and they got it. Duncan was appalled. Kathryn broke into convulsive sobbing. In short, the Peacocks were stunned and crushed. To them, it meant the derailment of their dreams and aspirations for Betty Jo. They wondered whether all their years of loving involvement and soaring hopes had been for nothing, not to mention Kathryn's personal agony at having to relive the nightmare memory of her disastrous first marriage and thwarted dream of higher education.

The Peacocks insisted getting married at such a young age was a reckless, irresponsible course to take. With Betty Jo a year-and-a-half away from graduating and Jess four years from a law degree, they felt the couple had no economic basis on which to build a successful marriage. And while Betty Jo and Jess didn't dispute those realities, they held fast to the belief that their "love for one another trumped all those logical arguments." Admittedly, they knew life would be difficult, but like other idealistic young couples before them, thought they could handle whatever adversity might lie ahead. Such fanciful notions did not sit well with the Peacocks and eventually Betty Jo and Jess were forced to negotiate a compromise. Disconcerted by the vehemence of parental opposition and Kathryn's emotional reaction, they agreed to postpone the wedding until Betty Jo graduated in May of 1952.

It took only a few weeks for Betty Jo and Jess to regret that decision. After all, they longed for the intimacy in their relationship which only marriage would allow. But that wasn't possible given the puritanical attitudes dominating the general moral climate of middle-class America in the 1950s. Few challenged what Hay well remembers as the inflexible code of virtues at the time. "It was never considered an option that you could live together or even have a more intimate kind of relationship outside of marriage." Nancy Stalcup remembers, too. "It really wasn't acceptable then to live with someone before you were married. So that did promote early marriage." Lou (Hirsch) Davison recalls Betty Jo putting a lighter spin on the issue when the two girls were discussing the marriage plan. "Betty Jo said they had to get married because she and Jess were both tired of staying up so late at night." Whatever the motivation, the sense of urgency surrounding their decision to renege on the postponement is palpable when Hay describes the couple's state of readiness:

> Although our youthful hormones may have been a factor, our determination to proceed with our wedding plans was much deeper than mere desire for sexual release. We were ready to get married and to become a couple, a married couple, united in that sense. We didn't want to wait. We were *ready* to be united, and that was it.

So one month after their initial discussion with the Peacocks, Betty Jo and Jess returned for another, and this time they were not asking for consent or agreement. Hay characterized it as a unilateral "announcement that we're going to get married and we hope we can do it with your blessing and with your participation, but whether we do or not we're getting married sometime before the end of next summer. . . . This time Duncan was mad. There wasn't any question about that. He was really upset."

Kathryn, on the other hand, got on board "real quick. I guess she knew the way Betty Jo said it that it was over." With no further discussion necessary, a wedding date of August 3, 1951 was set, and Duncan's anger gradually subsided.

■

In spite of having a wedding to plan, Betty Jo still was able to keep up with her busy schedule at SMU. She continued to seek leadership positions in Sigma Kappa, serving as social chairman, pledge master, and first vice president. Other campus activities reflected her commitment to scholastics, campus leadership, service, speech, debate, drama, and public affairs. In the fall of 1951, a profile on Betty Jo appeared in *Sigma Kappa Triangle—*

ion 3   THE DAILY TI

n's News   DALLAS, TEXAS, THURSDA

—The Times Herald Staff Photo

WAVING GOOD-BYE to friends as they departed Thursday are three members of Sigma Kappa
Sorority who are to attend the group's national convention in Swampscott, Mass., June 25-30.
Left to right are Miss Bobbie Iris Rickard, president of the local active chapter at Southern
Methodist University and official delegate to the sorority's 75th anniversary meeting; Miss Betty
Jo Peacock, pledge trainer, and Miss Mary Jo Autrey, rush captain. Pre-convention plans in-
clude a visit to New York City where the girls will attend a house party with a group of Sigma
Kappas. Parents of the girls are the R. R. Rickards, 5711 Redwood Lane; Mr. and Mrs. Dun-
can Peacock, 1213 Kings Hwy., and Mr. and Mrs. W. B. Autrey, 3032 Milton Ave.

Future Mrs. Bill W—

Betty Jo Peacock, Bobbie Iris
Rickard, and Mary Jo Autrey of
the Sigma Kappa Sorority at
SMU, board a plane for the
group's national convention June
25-30, 1950, in Swampscott,
Massachusetts.

CHAPTER 2

■■

Page 4 · SIGMA KAPPA TRIANGLE

Jayne Hodge, One of Our Newest Alumnae

Becoming a Rotunda Beauty is a cherished dream of almost every girl. Sigma Kappa's Jayne Hodge was one of the deserving girls to see this dream come true. Jayne, with her beauty, brains, lovely voice, and cute Southern drawl, has been winning honors for herself, S.M.U., and Sigma Kappa since she entered college and we feel sure that she will continue to do this even though she has graduated.

She is a past president and vice president of Sigma Kappa. Jayne was president of the Dolphin Club, club, organized for swimmers, a member of Kirkos, for outstanding women on the campus, member of the Choral Union, and was on the staff of S.M.U.'s Coordinating Council. She was Sigma Kappa's representative for Homecoming Queen and was a runner up for Rotunda Beauty in 1950.

Other honors that have won her campus-wide recognition are an appearance in the Pigskin Revew in 1950 and her selection as S.M.U.'s representative to the Cotton Bowl in 1951.

All of the members of our chapter of Sigma Kappa will miss Jayne but we know that with all of her attributes she will live a full and happy life.

Betty Jo Peacock, A True Sigma Leader

Being secretary of the Student Body is a big job, but not too big for Betty Jo Peacock, one of Sigma Kappa's outstanding members. Having been social chairman and pledge trainer, Betty Jo will again take her place of leadership as first vice-president of the sorority for the coming semester.

Betty Jo is a member of Alpha Lambda Delta, freshman honorary, Zeta Phi Eta, speech honorary, Tau Kappa Alpha, debate honorary, and is a University scholar. She is a member of the S.M.U. Debate Club, and represented this organization in twenty-six Inter-Collegiate Speech Tournaments while serving as secretary. She is now serving as president of the Arden Workshop.

Betty Jo has beauty as well as brains. She was Sigma's nominee for Engineer's Queen in 1950, nominee for Debutramp Queen, and was chosen Miss Popcorn of 1951.

S.M.U. has recognized Betty Jo's ability in making her a member of Mortar Board, the organization for outstanding young women on the campus.

Sally Sutton Elected to Pledge Trainer

Recently elected to the post of second vice-president of Sigma Kappa is Sally Sutton. Her chief duty is that of pledge trainer.

Aside from the responsibilities involved in her being Sigma Kappa's second vice-president, Sally is a representative of the Arts and Science School to the Student Council, vice-president of the Student Rally Committee, treasurer of the Campus League of Women Voters, and a member of the "Y" Cabinet.

As if this were not enough, Sally found time to do an excellent job as chairman of S.M.U.'s "Hey Day" activities last semester, and also to be Sigma Kappa's song leader. She is a past secretary of the "Y" program committee of the Student Union, and a past chairman of the House Committee of the Student Union.

These are not all of Sally's activities, however. She is into most everything on the campus. Her ability and charm make her one of Sigma's outstanding members.

SIGMA KAPPA SORORITY
Southern Methodist University
Dallas 5, Texas

In the *1951 Fall Rush Edition* of the *Sigma Kappa Triangle,* Betty Jo Hay (née Peacock, she was married on August 3) is acknowledged as being secretary of the SMU student body as well as being an outstanding member of Sigma Kappa. Sorority sisters Jayne Hodge and Sally Sutton, future wife of Bill Brice, also are acknowledged.

84

written in summer 1951 between her junior and senior years—which highlighted many of her accomplishments:

> Being secretary of the Student Body is a big job, but not too big for Betty Jo Peacock, one of Sigma Kappa's outstanding members.
>
> Betty Jo is a member of Alpha Lambda Delta, freshman honorary, Zeta Phi Eta, speech honorary, Tau Kappa Alpha, debate honorary, and is a University Scholar. She is a member of the S.M.U. Debate Club, and represented this organization in twenty-six Inter-Collegiate Speech Tournaments while serving as club secretary. She is now serving as president of the Arden Drama Workshop.
>
> Betty Jo has beauty as well as brains. She was Sigma's nominee for Engineer's Queen in 1950, nominee for Debutramp Queen, and was chosen Miss Popcorn of 1951.
>
> S.M.U. has recognized Betty Jo's ability by making her a member of Mortar Board, the organization for outstanding young women on the campus.

You are invited to become a member of Decima of Mortar Board

Pledge Service   Faculty Women's Lounge
Wednesday, April 25   Dallas Hall
1 a. m.   Fee $13.20

On Wednesday, April 25, 1951, the day before the campus elections, with a somewhat lackluster hand written envelope and invitation, Betty Jo, in her junior year, was invited to become a member of the prestigious Mortar Board Honor Society at Southern Methodist University.

Mortar Board, Inc.

Honors

Betty Jo Hay

Upon the 50th anniversary of your initiation into Mortar Board National College Senior Honor Society at

SOUTHERN METHODIST UNIVERSITY

You are honored for your contributions to Mortar Board, to society, and for your commitment to scholarship, leadership and service - qualities that were the foundation of your distinguished selection into Mortar Board.

On February 15, 2001, Betty Jo Hay was recognized on the 50th anniversary of her induction into Mortar Board National College Senior Honor Society at Southern Methodist University.

National President   *February 15, 2001*
                              Date

The article, however, did not mention Betty Jo's membership in Kirkos, an honorary women's service society that promoted campus community service. In October 1951, Kirkos sponsored a career day event, and based on a description in the 1952 *Rotunda*—the SMU yearbook—it would have been just the kind of program to receive Betty Jo's enthusiastic support:

> Kirkos, a woman's service organization on campus, gave a program for the freshmen showing them the various methods of choosing a career. The girls gave examples of the various careers and presented different ways of attaining these goals while in college. Even though the advice given was valuable and very serious, the Kirkos members seemed to have a good time putting on the show!

Betty Jo's involvement in an organization such as Kirkos was a good match, considering what friends described as one of her trademark characteristics: the ability to have a good time while maintaining a seriousness of purpose.

And that is exactly what she and Jess derived from their political activism at SMU—enjoyment and purpose. It was serious work for which they felt great passion. Jess preferred working in the background, and in spite of having served a term as president of the Independent Students' Association as a sophomore, he said his temperament was better suited for behind-the-scenes persuasion and strategic planning. "I've always been a little more comfortable trying to accomplish political objectives through other people," Hay explained. Betty Jo, on the other hand—though not without strategic talent of her own—favored direct public engagement, utilizing her debate and theater skills to influence others.

When the two paired up in the spring of 1951 to help elect a slate of student association candidates, Jess already was a seasoned veteran of SMU student politics. An opponent of the Greek-dominated political scene, independents such as Jess and a cadre of his politically active friends were determined to create a more inclusive, genuinely democratic process. John Reese recalls the group Jess joined was comprised of older, more serious students:

> There was a group of older guys, some of them were World War II veterans, and Jess was drawn to that crowd like a bee to honey. . . . They were interested in something other than just out-and-out fraternity politics for the sake of prestige and building the fraternity's resume. . . . A lot of the people elected by the fraternity crowd weren't good in office. Some didn't really know what they were doing or care. They wanted to party.

Jess and his friends operated first as the Committee for Representative Student Government [CRSG], but later adopted the name Association for Individual Action [AIA]. As such, they assembled a coalition of independents, fraternities, and sororities that rejected what they saw as the narrow focus of some Greek organizations driven by self-interest and a preference for limited participation. The AIA was determined to bring positive change to the campus. Hay said it "was a matter of picking good candidates. What you try to do is put everything on a higher plane and say, 'Our purpose is not to elect from this group or that group but to elect the best qualified candidates.'"

With Hay's support—and a solid record of service and achievement—Betty Jo won their party's nomination for secretary of the student association. Campaign posters

emphasizing her qualifications were plastered around campus featuring an attractive photograph and the words: ABILITY—INTEGRITY—ACHIEVEMENT. John Hamilton
said by the time Betty Jo ran for office, she had high campus visibility and was, by his
estimation, among the top ten outstanding female student leaders at SMU. Nancy Stalcup
remembers how the campaign absorbed Betty Jo and Jess:

> We [Nancy and Joe Stalcup] had an apartment, and Betty Jo and Jess would come
> over, and we would eat together and then spend hours planning political strategies
> for getting elected. I just remember laying out strategies and planning specific
> campaign tactics—how the campaign should go.

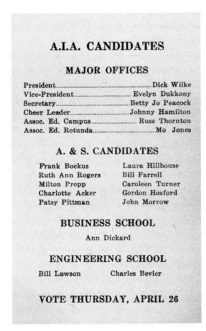

Betty Jo was nominated by the Association for
Individual Action ("AIA"), one of the two political
parties then active at SMU, to the office of secretary
of the student body. She and most of the other
AIA candidates were elected on April 26, 1951,
and then served as student body officers during the
1951-1952 academic year.

As a student at SMU, Betty Jo was secretary for various college and politically
oriented organizations while working in the Dallas community. All aspects of her
work showed her very impressive credentials for the position she was seeking.

A key tactic required the intense presence of campaign workers at the Student Union, the principal gathering place for most SMU students. "We worked the student union," said Richard Gelwick, a campaign worker. "I don't think many students got in or out of that place without being approached by somebody in our campaign. I mean, we worked that hard."

Gelwick said the central campaign theme was designed to appeal to individual student interests, and sought to educate the electorate by asking such pointed questions as:

> Do you know how much of your money student government spends? Do you know whether or not you have any input into that? Don't you think your student government should try to find out what you want? It was a wake-up call to most people who didn't know how their money was being spent.

In other words, the AIA offered a well-defined alternative—a public-spirited group of students which was not interested in fraternity back-scratching. The strategy worked. Betty Jo, Jess, and their cohorts succeeded at mobilizing a winning coalition that swept the AIA slate into office in the spring of 1951. Serving alongside Betty Jo in her capacity as secretary were fellow student body officers Dick Wilke, the group's president, Evelyn Dukkony, vice president, Jim Raetzman, treasurer, and Richard Vann, who—having been elected as associate editor under the CRSG banner in April 1950— automatically became editor of the student newspaper, *The Campus*.

■

Over the summer months, school-related triumphs and concerns subsided as Jess, Betty Jo, and their families prepared for the couple's wedding. The first formal event was reported on July 1, 1951 in one of the major Dallas newspapers. It contained a photograph and story with a headline that read, "Dinner Begins Parties Honoring Future Mrs. Jess Thomas Hay." The accompanying text described a celebration that was both formal and traditional:

> Mr. and Mrs. Duncan Peacock, 2715 Milton Avenue, announced the engagement of their daughter, Betty Jo, to Jess Thomas Hay at a dinner given Saturday evening at their home.

The table centerpiece displayed a miniature bride and bridegroom approaching an altar banked with pink rose buds. On either side were blue satin ribbons inscribed with the names of the couple and their wedding date, August 3.

As for details about the wedding itself, Hay said he remembers few, but the same could not be said for the feeling of impatience he experienced at wanting the formalities, at long last, to be completed. That memory, he said, remains vivid:

> The anticipated event occurred, as planned (and from our perspective, not a day too soon) on August 3, 1951, in the Sanctuary of University Park Methodist Church in Dallas. Reverend Lance Webb (then senior pastor of the church and subsequently a Methodist Bishop) officiated. Betty Jo was at her radiant best, her mother was proud, her father was a reconciled participant, and I was a happy young man.

Their nuptials received prominent newspaper coverage in the Women's section of the Dallas newspaper, which portrayed the event as elaborate, and displayed a large, formal photograph and detailed description of Betty Jo's wedding gown:

The Dallas Morning News
JUL 1 1951

—Laughead Photo.
MISS BETTY JO PEACOCK

Miss Betty Peacock Engaged to J. T. Hay

Announcing the engagement of their daughter, Miss Betty Jo Peacock, to Jess Thomas Hay, Mr. and Mrs. Duncan Peacock entertained Saturday night with a dinner in their home, 2715 Milton.

The centerpiece of the table displayed a miniature wedding scene, with blue satin ribbons bearing in gold letters the names of the couple and the wedding date, Aug. 3. The wedding will take place at the University Park Methodist Church with Dr. Lance Webb officiating.

The bride-elect has named Miss Mary Catherine Patterson of Houston as her maid of honor and Misses Barbara Ballard, Cynthia Cargill, Jan Davison and Joan Turner as bridesmaids.

Hubert Spradling of Orange will be best man. Groomsmen will include John Reese, Colorado City; Richard Gelwick, Bristow, Okla.; Richard Bramblett, Houston, and Joe Stalcup.

Ushers will be Richard Vann of Belton and Bill Brice. Ruth Ellen Peacock of Sherman, cousin of the bride-elect, will be flower girl, and Bill Morton will be ring bearer. Judy Albert and Anne Albert of Wichita, Kan., cousins of the bride-elect, will light the candles.

Miss Peacock has attended SMU for three years and will continue her studies this fall. She is student body secretary, Youth Council for Better Government secretary, president of Arden Workshop, secretary of Tau Kappa Alpha, forensic honorary fraternity, and secretary of the Debate Club of SMU. She is a member of Mortar Board, Alpha Lambda Delta and Zeta Phi Eta, honoraries, and Sigma Kappa, social sorority.

The prospective bridegroom, son of Mr. and Mrs. George Hay of Orange, also is an SMU student. He serves as executive secretary of the Youth Council for Better Government and belongs to Beta Theta Pi. He is past president of the Independent Students Association and served as publicity chairman of the Association for Individual Action.

At a New Year's Eve party on December 31, 1950, Jess Hay and Betty Jo Peacock formalized their mutual intentions for each other and became engaged. After agreeing with her parents to wait until Betty Jo graduated from SMU, they realized they couldn't. The engagement was publicly announced in a July 1, 1951 newspaper article with an August 3 wedding date of the same year.

90

A white imported Swiss organdy gown was selected by the bride. It was designed with a deep portrait neckline edged with rows of pleated embroidered organdy which extended to softly puffed sleeves. The bouffant skirt was topped with an apron effect edged with pleated embroidery and was worn over old-fashioned hoops and swept into a formal-length train.

The veil of illusion, which was attached to a crown of shirred organdy edged with pearls, fell fingertip-length.

The wedding ceremony ascribed to the same attention to detail, drawing on wide participation from family and close friends to secure and bless Jess and Betty Jo's union from the beginning. Jess Hay notes this aspect of his wedding in considerable detail:

Our wedding participants included one Maid of Honor, four Bridesmaids, one Best Man, four Groomsmen, one Flower Girl, one Ring Bearer, four members of the House Party, two candlelighters, two ushers, and two vocalists. The group included four cousins (Ruth Ellen Peacock, Richard Bramblett, Judy Albert, and Anne Albert), my sister (Patsy Hay), and some of our very best friends. Specifically, they were:

Maid of Honor	Mary Catherine Patterson (now M. C. Guilloud)
Bridesmaids	Barbara Ballard
	Cynthia Cargill
	Jan Davison
	Joan Turner
Best Man	Hubert Spradling
Groomsmen	Richard Bramblett
	Richard Gelwick
	John Reese
	Joe Stalcup
Ring Bearer	Skip Morton (the son of Ann and Steve Morton)

Flower Girl	Ruth Ellen Peacock	(the daughter of Ruth and Edgar Peacock)
Ushers	Bill E. Brice	
	Richard T. Vann	
Candlelighters	Anne Albert	
	Judy Albert	
Vocalists	Barbara Cowley	
	Sue Bates	
House Party	Patsy Hay	
	Wanda Maness	
	Sylvia Shultz	
	Nancy Stalcup	

For all the pomp and circumstance, though, what impressed groomsman Richard Gelwick most about the wedding had nothing to do with ceremonial trappings. Rather, during the exchange of vows, he remembers being struck by the genuine feeling of love and commitment Betty Jo and Jess—just barely out of their teens—had for one another.

> They were truly in love. That was very clear from standing there and watching them say their vows. I recall that Jess was more emotional than I expected he would be. . . . He was so emotionally caught up that his voice almost left him. His voice was barely a whisper. . . . There was nothing about the ceremony that was perfunctory. . . . It was a very religious service and it conveyed their sense of full commitment, full sincerity, and very great happiness that they were being united by the church in the eyes of God.

On the lighter side, Betty Jo took care to observe a number of traditional wedding customs, in hopes she and Jess might receive their promise of good luck. One such superstition—which warns the bride not to be seen on the wedding day by the groom before the ceremony—is mentioned in Betty Jo's wedding book:

August 3, 1951—I stayed home all day. M. C. helped me pack and open presents. Jess came over and I had to hide in the back room. Edgar took M. C. and me to the church to dress. We lost the car keys. Finally found them but they were bent. At last we made it to the church where we dressed in the bride's room. I was very nervous and excited.

Moreover, like generations of brides before her, Betty Jo heeded the customary Victorian good luck rhyme, "Something old, something new, something borrowed, something blue":

My shoes were old;
My dress and veil were new;
I had a borrowed penny in my shoe,
Little flowers under my dress were blue.
(Edgar Peacock loaned me the penny.)

In contrast to the wedding, the honeymoon was exceedingly modest. Betty Jo and Jess spent their first night at El Sombrero tourist court in Dallas before driving to Orange, Texas with Jess's best man and high school friend, Hubert Spradling and his wife, Margaret. The newlyweds later managed to get away on their own to Galveston, where they spent a couple of nights at the Hotel Galvez, known as the "queen of the gulf." Built in 1911, the historic hotel offered old-fashioned Edwardian elegance. Unfortunately, the years had taken their toll, and not only had the queen lost some of her sparkle, but she stubbornly refused to make any concessions to modernity and, therefore, did not provide air-conditioning. And although it was impossible not to notice the heat—it was, after all, August in Texas— Hay said he and Betty Jo were undaunted:

It was humid and hotter than Hades, but we had a good time. We didn't have any money. . . . We went to a grocery store and bought some lunch meat, bread, potato chips, and went down to the beach, tried to play some movie scene, I suppose, and had a picnic in the sand. We got eaten up by mosquitoes. But anyway, we enjoyed it as a young couple would. We enjoyed everything about it, but we remembered the heat, the mosquito bites, and how stifling the room at the Galvez, without air-conditioning, was at that time.

Then, as a final concession to economy, the couple rode the bus back to Dallas. Betty Jo, meanwhile, continued documenting her early days as a newlywed in her wedding book, which included this entry upon their return from Galveston:

> Mother and Daddy met us at the bus station. We went to the grocery store and bought our first supply of groceries. Jess went back to work (Jas. K. Wilson) the next day. I stayed home and began straightening our apartment. Our first address was 3113 Fondren, Apartment 4.

Apartment number four actually was a small efficiency across from the SMU campus, which might have been described by a real estate agent of the day as "cozy" and "convenient." Betty Jo later would joke about her father's terse comment regarding the degree of convenience the efficiency offered. Duncan had said: "You could sit on the john and scramble your eggs at the same time." Hay fondly recalled additional details of his first home with Betty Jo:

> The unit featured a hide-a-way bed, a tiny kitchen, a small kitchen table, a couch for two, one regular and four kitchen chairs, and a seating area which at most would accommodate four or five people on folding chairs. But it was home, and we were delighted to be sharing it as a happily married couple.

Earning the income they needed to meet their living expenses became the couple's primary non-academic goal, but even with the efficiency's affordable rate—about $70.00 a month—Betty Jo and Jess continued to require financial support from both sets of parents. For their part, George and Myrtle Hay subsidized Jess with full tuition and $40.00 a month. Likewise, Duncan and Kathryn Peacock covered all of Betty Jo's college costs, including tuition, sorority fees, and other expenses, as well as periodic "ad hoc monetary gifts."

In addition, the couple obtained a steady source of income from Betty Jo's skill as a typist, which she put to good use in her job as part-time secretary for Dr. Ellis Shuler, Dean of SMU's graduate school. But even more lucrative was the steady stream of typing assignments from professors who were revising textbooks and publishing journal articles, not to mention the Ph.D. candidates who needed immaculately-typed dissertations. In fact, doctoral candidate manuscripts had to be so carefully done as to contain no mistakes, no corrections, no erasures. This meant retyping an entire page in the event of one errant strike of a key, which was particularly unnerving if the mistake came on the final line. Nevertheless, it was a task the hard-driving Betty Jo was up to.

Jess, meantime, cobbled together three small jobs. He was the Student Union business manager and night attendant at SMU's science library. "The library duty was a godsend because it was a place to study," Hay said. "All the students were serious, and they were there for a purpose. They knew more about the library than I did, so I was seldom burdened with requests for help of any kind." And on Thursdays and Saturdays, Hay worked as a salesman at Jas. K. Wilson, a men's clothing store in downtown Dallas.

Meager though they were, the combination of small jobs provided the means by which Betty Jo and Jess could meet their financial obligations. But still, some constraints to their lifestyle remained necessary and, to their credit, were managed with typical cleverness:

> We would allow one another one dollar each day for food away from home and for transportation and for miscellaneous stuff, and anything we had left over at the end of the day we'd put in this little . . . jar or whatever. These residual deposits would build up until enough had been accumulated to enable our going to a movie and occasionally even out for dinner. That was our entertainment budget.

Regardless of the economic pressures, Jess Hay's response to married life was unmistakably positive. From his perspective, the strength and soundness of his marriage to Betty Jo was clear from the beginning. In fact, a college term paper entitled *The Quadruple Wedding*—written under the supervision of Dr. John O. Beatty in November 1951— reflects Jess's deep satisfaction with his status as Betty Jo's husband. Excerpts from the essay include the following affirmations:

> I have found marriage to be the grandest experience of my young life. Since August 3, I have found a new type of friend—a friend in whom there can be placed absolute, uncensored confidence. . . . (With guidance from Dr. Lance Webb, Betty Jo and I) have come to view marriage as one of life's great ventures and as the union of our physical, social, intellectual and spiritual selves. (From Dr. Leland Foster Wood's *Harmony in Marriage* and from our own intuition) we realize that "although a wedding is a happy and sacred event, it is significant mainly as a promise of what is to be." In other words, "Marriage is a creative journey which can be as fine as the

two participants make it." (After four months of marital experience) I personally think marriage is the best thing that can happen to a man and a woman if—but only if—they share (as we do) one vital and indispensable feeling for one another—love. With love, marriage enriches, enlarges, and expands the scope of two lives. . . . With love as a base, a union of the body, character, mind, and spirit of two people can be realized, and the greatest of all American institutions—the home—may be soundly built and continuously fostered. . . . I have enjoyed every minute of the first four months of my union with Betty Jo, and I look forward with limitless anticipation to our sharing of the next fifty years or more.

By February 1952, Jess and Betty Jo's financial circumstances had improved to the extent that they were able to move into an unfurnished, one bedroom apartment on Airline Road near SMU at a cost of $95.00 a month. In an effort to furnish it, they scoured the classified ads and discovered a bargain—an Oak Cliff store offered five rooms of furniture for only $425.00. "U-G-L-Y" describes what Hay said they found upon inspecting the advertised furniture, after which the salesman immediately steered them toward an attractive upgrade for $710.00:

> Compared to the first offering, the upgrade appeared to us fit for a king and queen. 24-month financing with minimal interest was offered, and we decided then and there to purchase the double bed, two bed-side tables, chest of drawers, couch, two chairs, coffee table, lamp, two end tables, a kitchen table and chairs, and a Duncan Phyfe dinette set. . . .When the furniture was delivered the next week, we moved into our new home and felt that we had all the room we ever would need. Betty Jo made some drapes from material furnished by her mother, thereby giving the apartment a more finished appearance.

Shortly after the move, Betty Jo—not quite twenty-one—learned she was pregnant and, though she had the luxury of parents nearby for support, she and Jess soon began to experience a part of life they would come to know well and appreciate—the value of good neighbors:

> Three older couples were occupants of the other three units of the fourplex, and all were very nice and supportive as we moved through Betty Jo's pregnancy to Debby's birth on December 8, 1952. These couples included Mr. and Mrs. Wyatt Jones.

Wyatt was a graduate of the University of Tennessee where he had achieved
distinction as an All-American football player. He also was a great fisherman, and
he kept us supplied with fresh fish (typically bass from a nearby lake). Mrs. Jones
was of Italian heritage, and she frequently brought us pasta dishes and other
varieties of Italian cuisine. They were all great neighbors.

Undoubtedly though, the prospect of becoming parents so early in their marriage
took Betty Jo and Jess somewhat by surprise, given the fact Betty Jo had planned to teach
while Jess attended law school. "She did not intend to get pregnant right away," remembers
Nancy Stalcup. "She already had a teaching position at Sunset High School that fall."

In fact, six months earlier—about the time of Betty Jo's wedding—the bride-to-be
felt close enough in her friendship with Stalcup to inquire about pregnancy prevention:

I remember Betty Jo asking me about birth control. We . . . discussed intimate
things. She thought, as a married woman, I would be knowledgeable, which I
wasn't. I suggested she go to her doctor.

As did many women of the 1950s, Stalcup used a diaphragm as a means of birth
control and recalls passing along to Betty Jo one sage piece of advice her doctor had given
her: "It won't protect you if it's in the dresser drawer."

Young and inexperienced though they were, Betty Jo and Jess did their best to heed
the advice they'd received and attempted to practice contraception, "but . . . obviously,"
said Hay, "we didn't do it consistently." In the end, it hardly mattered. Betty Jo's
announcement that she was expecting a baby was welcome news. "We didn't plan on
Debby, but we were absolutely elated when it happened," Hay remembers. And few people
were more thrilled than Kathryn and Duncan, according to Nancy Stalcup. "If they were
opposed to the marriage, they were doubly joyous when Debby came."

While the pregnancy didn't affect Betty Jo's university graduation goal, it did alter
her plans for a career in teaching. After careful consideration, she came to the conclusion
that nothing was more important than teaching her own children and creating a loving
home for them and her husband. That decision, acknowledges Jess Hay, resulted in some
profound blessings:

Betty Jo decided (and I agreed) that her primary role in the immediate future would
be that of mother and homemaker and that her plans for a career as a high school

97

teacher would be deferred or canceled. Viewed retrospectively, it was a great decision and one which contributed immeasurably to the nurturing of our children, to the warmth of our home, and to the depth and strength of our marriage.

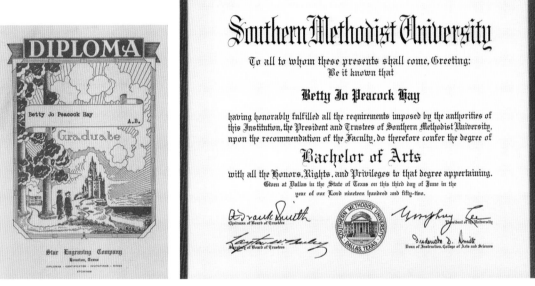

"Diploma" on the envelope signified much. Inside this magic thing was the evidence of years of dedicated work and effort: A Bachelor of Arts Degree from Southern Methodist University, conferred on June 3, 1952.

As planned, during the spring of 1952, Betty Jo graduated from Southern Methodist University, and no one celebrated with more pride than Duncan and Kathryn Peacock. Years of loving parenting and carefully laid out plans had paid off, the visible results of which now were many. Among them was Betty Jo's designation as a University Scholar at SMU, which status was reflected in her final school record. Furthermore, her prominence as a campus leader was acknowledged in the 1952 *Rotunda* through her inclusion—along with thirteen other students—in a yearbook section entitled, "the *Rotunda* salutes." The caption beneath her photograph read:

BETTY JO HAY, secretary of the Students' Association. Betty Jo is a member of the Mortar Board and has served as secretary of the Debate Club and Tau Kappa Alpha.

Unfortunately, Jess had to postpone his graduation briefly until he could make up the credits he had lost after being forced to sit out one semester while recovering from his earlier automobile accident. It didn't take him long, though. He earned the credits quickly during summer school, thereby allowing him to remain on his planned academic path and enter SMU Law School in the fall of 1952.

The Peacocks, meanwhile, continued to offer their daughter and son-in-law material support. Late in the summer of 1952, they bought a new Chevrolet and generously gave their older 1947 model to Betty Jo and Jess, allowing them a means to visit Hay's parents and sister. "We enjoyed the visit," Hay said, "and the relationship between my folks and Betty Jo deepened discernibly during our brief stay in Orange. Both of my parents—and particularly my dad—thought Betty Jo truly was an outstanding woman."

After one year of marriage, the couple's own relationship showed evidence of strength, so much so that Betty Jo made a note of it in her wedding book on August 3, 1952, the date of their first anniversary:

One year has passed and with it there have been many happy times. Jess and I both went to school and worked too. We moved the first of February to 6510 Airline Road and bought our own furniture. By April (1952) a newcomer was on the way. We expect this little blessing in January 1953. If all the years are as happy as the first, I know that there will never be two happier people.

Several months later, on December 8, 1952, marital bliss reached new heights when Deborah (Debby) Anne Hay was born at Baylor Hospital in Dallas. Looking back, Jess can still recall the pleasure Debby's arrival brought:

Debby's advent as a healthy and beautiful baby was a joyous occasion for us, and our lives thereafter were focused first and foremost on her nurturing and care. . . . Seventeen days after Debby's birth, we celebrated our first Christmas as a family of three. All was right with our world, and our love for one another was more fulfilling than ever.

On their own, and with an infant to care for, Betty Jo and Jess undertook the hard work of learning to become good parents. Among the many new routines they established was a bedtime ritual of rocking Debby to sleep each night, but after nine months, their pediatrician, Dr. Doris Spegal, suggested putting an end to the practice in hopes Debby would begin to fall asleep on her own. Reluctantly, Betty Jo and Jess agreed to follow their doctor's recommendation and made a first attempt at putting Debby into her crib without the benefit of rocking, but as babies sometimes do, Debby had other plans. While Betty Jo and Jess retreated to their adjoining bedroom, they were followed by Debby's howls and screams. Minutes later, after hearing a distinct thud and a fresh crescendo of piercing screams, they ran into Debby's room to find her on the floor. Somehow, in her frenzy, Debby had hoisted herself over the crib railing, but managed not to get hurt. She did manage, however, to put a prompt end to her parents' new get-tough policy at bedtime, and as a result, continued being rocked to sleep for the next three years of her life. The same routine followed the birth of Jess and Betty Jo's second daughter, Patty, who was rocked to sleep for four years. Unapologetic about not taking the medical advice they were offered, Hay said he felt the benefits of the decision to continue rocking their toddlers to sleep outweighed conventional medical wisdom on the subject, adding, "It was a therapeutic practice benefiting both parents and both daughters."

The Hays significantly improved their living conditions in May 1953 when they accepted an offer to lease a three-bedroom home at 2709 Milton Avenue—next door to Betty Jo's parents—at an affordable $105.00 per month. "For the next two years," Hay said, "we lived very comfortably as neighbors to Kathryn and Duncan Peacock, who were great parents to Betty Jo, supportive in-laws to me, and doting grandparents to Debby." During those years, the bond between Kathryn and her granddaughter, Debby, grew particularly strong. In fact, on one occasion in 1954 when the Hays left Dallas for a few days, Kathryn expressed her feelings about Debby's absence in a letter to her brother, Carl Albert. "I surely do miss Debby when I go home in the evenings," she wrote. "It is really quiet around home without her."

Close family connections were crucial, because Betty Jo and Jess needed all the support they could muster. Jess was maintaining a grueling schedule of law school classes and long hours of study, while continuing to work three jobs. The responsibilities Betty Jo shouldered were equally fatiguing. Rearing a child, homemaking, working as a partial breadwinner, and typing a large chunk of her husband's law class notes required enormous energy and organizational skill. Betty Jo also expanded her typing business to bring in more income. While textbook revisions and academic journal articles from Dr. Edwin Foscue—chairman of SMU's geography department—provided a reliable source of funds, typing Ph.D. dissertations represented another vital revenue stream. Even so, it could be frustrating work, said M.C. (Patterson) Guilloud, Betty Jo's friend, who also earned money typing doctoral candidate manuscripts:

> In those days, of course, we had manual typewriters, and you beat yourself to death because you had to make something like five carbons, and you were not allowed to make mistakes. You got to the bottom of the page and if you made a mistake, you had to do the whole stinking page over again. . . .

> After she had Debby, Betty Jo typed when she could. You wait for nap time or you stay up late at night or you rock the cradle with one foot and type with two hands. You do what you have to do, and that's what she did.

Jess remembers after Debby could sit up, Betty Jo would put her in the stroller beside her typing table "so she could move the stroller a little bit and keep Debby happy while she typed. It was multitasking in its most fundamental sense."

Still, what the days on Milton Avenue lacked in tranquility for a young mother with a new baby and a husband in law school, was more than offset by the comfort of close friendships. One of the closest at the time was Virginia (Sammie Harwell) Carrey, who had three young children of her own. "We established a good friendship and visited everyday. . . . Betty was busy, busy, busy day-and-night, typing and helping Jess get through law school. . . . She had a lot of pressure on her at that time, but we were such good friends. She always had time to stop for a cup of coffee and visit."

The strain Betty Jo experienced surfaced on one occasion in a piece of correspondence to her uncle. In February 1954, Betty Jo typed a letter on behalf of Kathryn, who was writing to Carl Albert about a family business matter. Betty Jo's personal note at the bottom of the letter reveals a mother close to the point of exhaustion:

> Dear Uncle Carl,

> I was the typist—late at night and tired as I don't know what—pardon the errors but Debby runs one ragged! She is over all of her sick spells now but has been exposed to the chicken pox. I have that to look forward to next week.

> Love, Betty

And yet, the burden of responsibilities didn't prevent Betty Jo and Jess from nurturing friendships, especially with their neighbors, the Harwells. They grew especially close to Virginia (Sammie Harwell) Carrey, her husband, Joe Harwell, and their three small children, Robin, Janey, and Rodger. Carrey remembers her family's Easter egg hunts and how much the Hays enjoyed those occasions. "We'd hide the Easter eggs and Jess and Betty would stand there at the fence and absolutely collapse with laughter at watching those two little kids run around collecting Easter eggs." Likewise, Hay recalls three-year-old Rodger's egg-gathering technique:

> Rodger was particularly cute. . . . He had his little basket, but he didn't understand the concept of picking up the eggs and putting them in the basket. He'd pick them up with his free hand. He'd get maybe two and try to pick up a third one, and then two of them would fall out of his hand.

Jess's love for children inspired him to buy a football for Rodger when the little boy got older. "Jess was the sweetest guy in the world," said Carrey. "He would get out in the front yard and throw the football to Rodger. . . . I think Rodger still has the black and white football Jess bought him."

The Hays' natural sociability led Betty Jo to take an active role in the SMU Law Students' Wives Club, which was responsible for organizing picnics and other events throughout the year. With these activities came new friendships and informal social gatherings, the cornerstone of which was the game of bridge. "Most of our bridge playing at that time was with other law students and their wives," Hay said. "We enjoyed having friends over on Saturday nights for a country meal and for games of bridge, '42', or canasta." One such friend, M.C. (Patterson) Guilloud—who dated, and then married Lewis Sweet, Hay's law school study partner—recalls playing a lot of bridge with Betty Jo and Jess because "we didn't have any money to do anything else." Other frequent guests for dinner and sometimes games during Jess and Betty Jo's undergraduate and law school years included: Barbara Ballard, Sue Bates, Henry Baer, Bill Brice, Cynthia Cargill, Barbara Cowley, Jan Davison, Ann and Bob Desmond, Ken Dippel, Richard Gelwick, Patsy Lynn and Hubert Gentry, Mary Anne Hein, Shirley and Bill Jones, Patsy Matheny, Bill Nighswonger, Virgil Olson, John Reese, Billie Lee and Bill Rippey, Russell Smith, Nancy and Joe Stalcup, Molly and Robb Stewart, Sally Sutton, Joan Turner, Richard Vann, Barbara Wall, Rae and Ronnie Wiess, Dick Wrangle, Nancy and Walter Zivley, and a number of others. Each enriched Jess and Betty Jo's lives, and all remained cherished friends throughout the next half century.

When close friend and neighbor, Virginia Carrey, thinks back to the days with Betty Jo and Jess, abundant friendships come to mind as a defining feature of their lives. "They had so many friends and associates. Betty was such a warm, friendly lady. . . . They had tons of friends."

And though they had little money at the time, that didn't stop the Hays and the Harwells from splurging, so to speak, on a budget mini-vacation now and then, an infrequent luxury Hay remembers as a welcome break:

> Neither the Harwells nor we had anything approximating enough money to have a vacation in the sense that you would have one today. On two or three occasions we went with our families to a Dallas motel on Samuell Boulevard for Friday and Saturday nights. The motel had a swimming pool, and each time we had a fun and relaxing weekend.

■

As for Jess Hay's academic progress, his ability to master the SMU law school curriculum secured him an enviable scholastic record, and for three consecutive years he finished at the top of his class. Accordingly, the school recognized his first-year accomplishments by awarding Hay the scholarships he needed to attend the following two years of law school at no cost.

Fortunately, the rigorous discipline which was required to maintain a stellar grade point average didn't entirely prevent Hay from participating in politics and extracurricular organizations, and in the spring of 1952—just before Hay entered law school—the Youth Council for Better Government endorsed the candidacy of W. L. "Lew" Sterrett for Dallas County Judge. "For the first two months of the summer of 1952 I was engaged substantially full-time in Sterrett's successful campaign," Hay said. "Betty Jo was involved to the extent her schedule permitted." During the campaign, Hay persuaded his friends, the Harwells, to host a cookout for young Sterrett supporters, a purposeful event which Virginia Carrey—the former Sammie Harwell—remembers vividly. "Politics was so big in Jess's mind," she said, "and he was involved as much as he could possibly be. . . . We organized a backyard party for Lew Sterrett, and I remember the throngs of people that came and how excited Jess was about it."

Then, in the spring of 1953, Bill Brice ran for the office of SMU student association president, asking Hay to serve as his campaign manager. Hay took on the responsibility and, subsequently—as was becoming his pattern—orchestrated a victory for his good friend. At the same time, Hay also served as a member of the Student Union Governing Body and was appointed to the Student Court where he presided, first, as Associate Chief Justice and later as Chief Justice. In addition, he sat on the Student Bar Association's executive board, participated as a member of the law school's Moot Court team, and served on the editorial board of the *Southwestern Law Review*. Near the end of his second year of law school, and in recognition of his academic record and his service activities, Hay was selected for membership in Cycen Fjodr, which is the oldest honorary on the SMU campus and is composed *each year* of the ten outstanding men chosen from the next graduating classes of the university.

The year 1954 marked the occurrence of two other notable events. During the spring Betty Jo announced she was pregnant for the second time, and in the fall Jess was recruited by one of Dallas' most prestigious law firms. The latter occurred in November 1954 when Hay was invited to meet with Eugene M. Locke, one of two senior partners from the firm of Locke, Locke & Purnell (later Locke, Purnell, Boren, Laney & Neely, and subsequently Locke, Liddell & Sapp). At the conclusion of the hour-long session, Hay was told simply that the firm would be in touch. However, by the time he arrived home shortly afterwards, Betty Jo informed him Locke already had phoned, requesting that Hay return the call as soon as possible. With that phone call came an offer from Locke asking Hay to join the firm as an associate, starting at a salary of $350.00 a month. Considering law firms in New York City at the time were starting their young attorneys at $400.00 a month, Hay realized the opportunity before him, and accepted the job. He was to begin part-time work January 2, 1955, but, on receiving his first paycheck discovered—to his surprise and delight—he was being paid at full salary though only working half time until June of 1955.

The Locke, Purnell job and sudden boost in income transformed the couple's financial fortunes. From January 1955 forward, Betty Jo and Jess enjoyed a new kind of prosperity, which gave rise, first, to a more comfortable lifestyle. Then, as Jess proceeded to build a spectacularly successful career in law and business, the door to economic affluence opened.

The satisfaction that came from securing a good job was enhanced by the joyful expectation of a second child. But as fate would have it, Jess and Betty Jo's euphoria would be fleeting, and within a day of their son's birth, would turn to anguish:

On February 12, 1955, Betty Jo delivered a beautiful baby boy. We previously had decided to name our first boy Jess Richard, which we did at our son's birth. To our immense sorrow, the baby soon developed lung difficulties. . . . The day after his birth, Jess Richard Hay, our only son, died as a result of the illness and then was buried in a shroud of faith and hope.

"I remember terrible grief," said M.C. (Patterson) Guilloud. "I can remember going to see Betty Jo in the hospital. When I got there, Nancy Stalcup was with her. It was just very sad." Virginia Carrey said the memory of that moment still "puts chills all over" her, even with the passage of time. "It was the saddest, most devastating thing in the world, because she had carried this baby for nine months, and it was born, and it died," Carrey remembers. "It just tore us all to pieces." Said Hay: "Betty Jo and I were heartbroken, but we muddled through it by talking to one another and talking to our minister. . . . After a while, we picked ourselves up and went on with our lives."

The pace of life accelerated in the spring of 1955. After passing the Texas bar examination in March, Hay became a state-licensed attorney, and in May, he graduated from SMU Law School with high honors. That same month, he and Betty Jo bought a 1700-square-foot brick home at 6560 Fisher Road in Dallas which—with its purchase price of $15,250—may have been something of a stretch from what they thought they comfortably could afford. And, yet, they bought it anyway, choosing not to exercise the more prudent option of a $10,000 smaller home in the Casa View area of Dallas. It was a decision that reflected among other things, Jess and Betty Jo's desire for more space, a location closer to downtown Dallas, and above all, a feeling of optimism about the future.

Indeed, if the first four years of marriage were any indication, there was ample reason for the Hays to believe in a beneficent future. They had avoided the dire consequences predicted by those who cautioned they were too young to marry, and instead—through their focused determination and ability to overcome difficulties as a mutually supportive team—effectively rendered the naysayers mute. The young couple—Jess, now twenty-four, and Betty Jo, nearly the same age—took satisfaction in their accomplishments: graduating from college with honors, budgeting their financial resources through diligence and sacrifice, and working together to create a loving environment for their daughter. "We were happy campers," Hay remembers, "and we faced the future with unabashed confidence and with limitless anticipation."

PHOTOGRAPH ALBUM
2

SEPTEMBER 1948

through

MAY 1955

Betty Jo in the Fall of 1949, then a sophomore
at Southern Methodist University, Dallas.

Bill Nighswonger, Betty Jo Peacock, Lou Hirsch, and Paul Morrell represented SMU on the debate
trip to the University of Virginia campus. Winter 1949.

M.C. Patterson and her date, Rick, Betty Jo Peacock and Jess Hay, Barbara Wall and John Reese, at a Sigma Kappa party. Fall 1950.

Betty Jo Peacock and Jess Hay at the SMU Sigma Kappa Christmas dance held at the Dallas Country Club. 1950.

Betty Jo being called out for Mortar Board by D.A. McReynolds Brown at SMU. Spring 1951.

THE WEDDING OF BETTY JO PEACOCK AND JESS HAY
UNIVERSITY PARK METHODIST CHURCH
AUGUST 3, 1951

The wedding of Betty Jo Peacock and Jess Thomas Hay was solemnized August 3, 1951. She was given in marriage by her father, Duncan Peacock.

The union of the families Peacock and Hay. From left to right: Duncan and Kathryn Peacock, Betty Jo and Jess Hay, and Myrtle and George Hay.

University Park United Methodist Church, Dallas, where Betty Jo and Jess Hay were married, was the Peacock family church from August 1950 to June 1955.

The wedding party. Bridesmaids: Joan Turner, Barbara Ballard, Jan Davison, and Cynthia Cargill. Maid of honor: Mary Catherine Patterson. The bride Betty Jo Hay and groom Jess Hay. The best man: Hubert Spradling. Groomsmen: Joe Stalcup, Richard Gelwick, Richard Bramblett, and John Reese. Flower girl: Ruth Ellen Peacock. Ring bearer: Skip Morton.

The house party for the wedding: Nancy Stalcup, Patsy Hay, Wanda Maness, Sylvia Shultz, and Barbara Cowley. Not pictured are ushers Bill E. Brice and Richard T. Vann; candle lighters Anne Albert and Judy Albert; and vocalist Sue Bates.

The kiss.

Cutting the wedding cake.

The newlyweds were off to Galveston after the wedding for their honeymoon.

SMU living quarters at 3113 Fondren, apartment 4, was the newly weds'
residence after their marriage, from August 3, 1951 to February 1952.

SMU living quarters front entrance. Apartment 4 is on left.

Residence quarters, apartment 4, rear
entrance. After the Fondren apartment, they
moved to another apartment at 6510
Airline Road and lived there from
February 1952 to May 1953.

Betty Jo as a Senior standing in front of Dallas Hall on the SMU campus. 1951.

Betty Jo graduated from SMU in May 1952.

Betty Jo and Jess at their residence at 2709 Milton, next door to her parents, who lived at 2715 Milton. They lived here from May 1953 to May 1955.

Photograph taken in 2005 of 2709 Milton, depicts improvements made some years after Betty Jo and Jess moved to Fisher Road.

Sammie Harwell, with her daughter Janey and Deborah Hay, affectionately called Debby, who is about one year old. At the Harwell home on Milton in Dallas. The Harwells were good friends from and after 1951.

Debby at the Christmas tree with her proud mother, Betty Jo, for Christmas 1953 celebrations. She was born December 8, 1952 in Dallas, Texas.

Betty Jo and Debby, 30 months, dressed for church at the Hay home on Fisher Road. 1955. At the time, Jerry and Ross Pittman and their first two daughters, Susan and JoEllen, resided next door to the east; and Flo and Frank Loper lived in the home immediately to the west of the Hay home. Both families became nurturing and lasting friends of the Hays.

Betty Jo and Jess resided at 6560 Fisher Road from May 1955 to June 6, 1961. They took pride in the fact that the house was purchased, neither rented nor leased. They installed central air-conditioning at the house in the Spring of 1957. This 2005 photograph shows the house to look much as it did when they moved in.

CHAPTER
3

JUNE 1955
through
SEPTEMBER 1965

T he move to 6560 Fisher Road represented a major milestone in Jess and Betty Jo's fourth year of marriage, and one Hay recalls with great satisfaction. "We thus became 'freeholders' for the first time," he said, "and we were very pleased." Not only did it give them a stake in the American dream of home ownership, but the move also brought to a close their lives as students, signaling their entry into the adult world of middle-class family life.

Adequately supported by Hay's starting salary as an attorney, Betty Jo now was able to concentrate full-time on childcare and home management, an understandable desire given her upbringing with Kathyrn, who believed wholeheartedly that family came first. "When Betty Jo married and had children, that was the focus of her life," said friend M. C. (Patterson) Guilloud. "She was very dedicated to home and family." Later calling herself a "professional homemaker," Betty Jo embraced the role and brought to it that familiar seriousness of purpose which had come to define her. By this time, she had established a pattern of excelling at the things she valued, and now—applying the same strengths and talents that had brought her success in school—Betty Jo devoted herself to what had become the most valuable of all: the Hay family.

In October 1956, additional responsibilities came her way with the birth of a second daughter, Patty, whose arrival was not without some anxious moments. During the final weeks of pregnancy Betty Jo had begun to experience cramping, which—in light of the painful loss of Jess Richard in 1955—prompted the doctor to take the necessary precaution and order continuous bed rest. As would be expected, Betty Jo and Jess heeded the recommendation and remained vigilant in the decisive three months leading up to Patty's birth. Meanwhile, with Betty Jo in bed, three-year-old Debby needing care, and a home to maintain, help arrived in the person of Patsy Hay, Jess's sister. In a meaningful show of support for her brother and Betty Jo, Patsy volunteered to take a semester leave from North Texas State University in Denton where she was a student at the time. Her assistance at such a crucial moment made all the difference, Hay said. "Betty Jo was so grateful she thought we should name Patty for her. Neither of us particularly liked the name Patsy, so we chose Patricia." And so it was that Patricia Lynn Hay was born in good health on October 26, 1956.

Three months later in January 1957, Jess lost his father, George Hay, who died in San Antonio at the age of sixty-five. Jess went immediately to San Antonio to comfort his mother and sister, and to help with funeral arrangements. Betty Jo soon followed, making the trip by passenger train while toting four-year-old Debby and their strong, healthy newborn, Patty. "She was a beautiful baby with a modest showing of strawberry blond hair and a light complexion," Hay recalls proudly.

Unfortunately, Patty's fair complexion did not stand up well to the brutal Texas summer of 1957, and as did many babies around the sweltering state that year, she suffered from intolerable heat rash. To bring relief, Betty Jo and Jess did the only thing they knew to do, and fortunately could afford to do. "The result was a blessing to our entire family: the installation of a central air conditioning unit at 6560 Fisher Road," Hay said. "We thus joined thousands of other families in the 'Sun Belt' of the United States benefiting from the miracle of central cooling."

The widespread use of central air conditioning reflected the growing affluence of 1950s America. The Hays, along with millions of others, experienced the good fortune of living during one of the most prosperous eras in the nation's history, as unprecedented numbers of families achieved middle-class status. And with those growing numbers came a heightened emphasis on home and family life. Images of thriving, happy families dominated the mass media during this time, particularly on television, where so-called sitcoms— such as 1954's *Father Knows Best*—depicted the iconic, mythical American family. Popular culture promoted feminine domesticity as a primary goal for young mothers of the period. Indeed, in 1955, while addressing the graduating class of Smith College—a private liberal arts college for women in Massachusetts—Democratic presidential candidate Adlai Stevenson urged his female audience to participate in politics through their roles as wives and mothers, and not to define themselves by a profession. These and a barrage of similar messages, while seeming to place limitations on the role of women in 1950s American society, nevertheless lent a high level of respect and admiration to their status as homemakers.

And like millions of postwar suburban women, Betty Jo, at the time, found significance, meaning, and pleasure in that role, the effects of which left a lasting and positive
impression on her daughters, said Debby Hay Spradley:

> Mother was the quintessential 1950s housewife. She was very focused on the home.
> She kept a nice home, she provided tasty and nutritious meals, and sewed almost all
> of our clothes. . . . She made beautiful dresses for us. The one that stands out in
> my mind was an Easter dress with tulips appliquéd on the front. She sewed. She
> cooked. She was a gracious and welcoming hostess to our friends. I mean, she was
> the ideal mother of the 1950s.

In addition to her vital role within the home, Betty Jo also was an integral part of a
vibrant group of neighbors, remembers younger daughter Patty Hay:

> Mom was very much a full-time mom. Our house was a meeting place for all the
> neighborhood kids. It was a different time. It was a time of neighborhood schools.
> The kids in your neighborhood went to school with you, they went to church with
> you, and all the parents knew each other.

One of those neighborhood kids was Patty's close friend, Michelle McCormick who
would go on to become a doctor of clinical psychology, and carry with her vivid memories
of Betty Jo and the days on Fisher Road. "She was the most active, involved mother I had
ever known," McCormick said. "Their home was always open. They welcomed you into
their family. . . . I felt like I was one of their kids."

Fellow homemaker Juanita Smotherman, a friend and neighbor, regarded Betty Jo's
approach to child-rearing with admiration and respect:

> I liked her mothering very much, in that she would try to get her point across to
> Debby and Patty by talking to them. She was my kind of mother. She didn't spank
> them or do a lot of harsh things. . . . She also had a good sense of humor, and kept
> her perspective when some of the childish pranks occurred. She wouldn't become
> irate and go into a rage and fall apart. She was able to remain cool and maintain a
> sense of humor about some of Patty's pranks. . . . Patty was more of a handful.
> Debby was more serious.

118

But perhaps it is her husband, Jess, who knows best the full extent of Betty Jo's impact on the lives of their daughters, Debby and Patty:

Betty Jo's primary focus was on the nurturing of our children, which involved at-home mentoring and participation in virtually every activity of either of our two girls: home room mother, PTA, church, Blue Birds, Camp Fire Girls, birthday parties, school programs, drill teams, school elections. Whatever the need, whatever the interest, whatever the activity, Betty Jo was there. . . . She was a superb mother, a great teacher, a kind redeemer, and a rational judge who always encouraged our daughters to be the best they could be. . . . Along the way, she also produced in each of our girls a keen sense of public responsibility and a dedication to community service and to the pursuit of social justice.

In addition to meeting those obligations, Betty Jo made certain her daughters—and husband—were well fed. To be sure, when it came to her many skills as a practitioner of the domestic arts, none found more favor than her proficiency in the kitchen, and no one could take more credit for passing down those skills than her mother. It was Kathryn—with her long-standing reputation among family and friends as a "fantastic cook"—who equipped Betty Jo with the bulk of her culinary know-how. But there was an additional source as well, said Hay. "Betty Jo's cooking prowess derived primarily from on-the-job training at her mother's side, and later, with respect to a few specialties including cornbread dressing, homemade rolls, and a few country dishes, at the side of my grandmother, Nettie Fleming Roddy." The guiding influence of Hay's grandmother came to an end in the fall of 1961 when Mammy—as she was called—died in her East Texas hometown of Forney, the place where she had resided throughout her eighty-six years.

With a heritage so steeped in the rural, southern tradition of East Texas and Oklahoma's "Little Dixie" region, it wasn't surprising then that Betty Jo regularly put on her table what daughter Patty fondly remembers as "comfort food," including at various times everything from savory pot roast, chicken-fried steak, and meat loaf, to turkey and dressing, fried okra, and biscuits. And as a sweet ending, one could always count on Betty Jo's delectable cream pies—chocolate, banana, lemon, and coconut, to be precise—which, according to Jess, "were the tastiest to be found anywhere in this part of the world."

In these many and varied ways Betty Jo succeeded at bringing an air of professionalism to her role as a 1950s homemaker, while Jess dedicated himself to learning the legal profession at Locke, Purnell, Boren, Laney & Neely, where he quickly caught the eye of

Gene Locke, one of the firm's senior partners. To acknowledge that fact, and to bid the Hays a proper welcome, Locke and his wife, Adele, invited Betty Jo and Jess to be their guests for dinner at one of the city's premier private establishments—the Dallas Country Club. It would be a pivotal occasion for both couples. "Dining with a senior partner and a grand lady, particularly at the Dallas Country Club, was an exciting experience for the two of us," said Hay of that February evening in 1955. "It led to a lasting friendship with Adele and Gene, and it was the first of many acts of kindness and guidance which the Lockes extended to us over the years."

For her part, when thinking back to that initial get-together with the Hays, Adele (Locke) Seybold remembers experiencing the same feeling of friendship:

> We enjoyed Betty Jo and Jess very much as a couple, admiring their great devotion to each other and their children. Our friendship deepened as we included them in many of our activities and dinners at our home and with friends and associates in many fields. They were an important part of our lives.

As it turned out, the country club dinner marked more than just the beginning of a new and cherished friendship between the Lockes and the Hays. It also served as Jess and Betty Jo's introduction to the city's elite social stratum. In fact, the trajectory of the Hays' lives followed a path similar to that of their distinguished mentors, and eventually led them in 1971 to membership in the Dallas Country Club.

Meanwhile, with his legal acumen, dedication, and dependability, Hay was proving a compatible associate for Gene Locke, who shared many of the same qualities. These common character traits, according to an attorney who knew them both, led to an instant rapport between the two, as each possessed great powers of concentration, the ability to process large volumes of information, and a combined positive outlook which rendered nothing impossible.

In short, it appeared that this cohesion and sense of mutual respect had the potential to yield good results, and may have been in evidence early on when Locke asked young Hay to help him prepare an appeal to the Texas Supreme Court. Lewis Sweet, a former Locke Purnell associate, remembers the case:

> Jess and Gene sat for hours bouncing theories back and forth. Both had extremely creative minds. Finally, they decided on what legal route to take, worked together on the brief, and were successful. It was a great piece of legal work. From that

120

point forward, I'm sure Gene had total confidence in Jess.

Sweet's take on the matter was, in fact, correct. Adele (Locke) Seybold confirms it didn't take long for her husband to recognize he had someone special in Jess Hay:

When Gene started working with Jess, Gene realized that he could handle any case he gave him. Jess instantly grasped the whole concept . . . so, that's when Gene increased Jess's responsibilities, and Gene depended on him more and more to help with legal matters and then later with business matters.

According to former SMU classmate and friend, John Reese, Hay responded aggressively and effectively to the opportunities afforded by these increased responsibilities. In recognition of his commendable performance, the firm rewarded him with fast-track promotions and substantial salary increases. Finally, in 1961—capping his rapid rise at Locke, Purnell— Jess Hay, at the age of thirty, accepted partnership in the firm.

LOCKE, PURNELL, BOREN, LANEY & NEELY

ATTORNEYS AT LAW

ANNOUNCE THE ADMISSION INTO THE FIRM OF

JESS T. HAY

MAURICE E. PURNELL	JOHN D. HARRIS
EUGENE M. LOCKE	HAROLD B. PRESSLEY, JR.
BENJAMIN N. BOREN	JOHN LOUIS SHOOK
JAMES J. LANEY	CHARLES G. PURNELL
STANLEY E. NEELY	WAYNE O. WOODRUFF
GORDON FOGG	ALBERT E. AIKMAN

1900 REPUBLIC NATIONAL BANK BUILDING

DALLAS, TEXAS

JANUARY 1, 1962

Following six and one-half years as an associate, Jess was admitted as a partner of Locke, Purnell, Boren, Laney & Neely in December 1961.

Jess's vocational success, in conjunction with the warm, satisfying home life created by Betty Jo's continued dedication to "professional" homemaking stood as two significant pillars of the Hays' early years as a couple. A third, critical cornerstone was their belief in the importance of community, a principle that would guide them throughout the rest of their lives. "Community to me involves commitment to some common cause, and hopefully a worthwhile cause," said Hay. "You do things together, and that's how you build friendships and you build meaningful and positive relationships."

The building of these vital relationships took a significant turn about a week after Betty Jo and Jess moved into their new home on Fisher Road. That's when community, literally, came knocking at their front door. The caller was none other than The Reverend William T. Stephenson, who'd served as associate pastor at University Park Methodist Church—where the Hays had been members—and now was presiding over Ridgewood Park Methodist Church, a brand-new church in their neighborhood and one in search of members. At Stephenson's asking, Betty Jo and Jess joined the congregation, setting in motion the very sense of community they were looking for, said Hay:

> We had known and admired Bill and his wife, Alyce, during our years as members of University Park Methodist Church . . . and readily accepted his invitation to join the fledgling new church. That decision resulted in our being a part of a vital community which was central to our lives for the next fifteen years, from 1955 through 1970. Indeed, the friendships made during those years are among our closest relationships and most persist to this day.

Intent on building a strong, religious community, these like-minded parents of baby boomers flocked to the new suburban church. Many of them, including Brownie and Bob Shytles, saw church affiliation as a means of putting down "strong roots" for their families. "It was the beginning of our married life and all our children were about the same age," remembers Brownie. "It seemed to be really meaningful to us. Our faith and our social life and everything centered around the church." Reverend Stephenson, himself, remembers well how Ridgewood Park, in his words, "jelled around . . . a group of young couples with young children. . . . We had about as many babies on Sunday in the nursery as we did adults in the sanctuary when we got our first building." For most of the young families, involvement in the church seemed the next logical step in the progression of their lives. "I guess everybody who joined the church was kind of in the same boat," said LeAnn (Harris) Solomon, one of Betty Jo's closest Ridgewood Park friends. "We were all just kind of starting out. We had completed our schooling and now it was time to raise our families, and we wanted the church to be a part of that in a very important way."

Fortunately, a few slightly more mature folks also became members and helped guide the younger crowd and the new church to an encouraging commencement. These relatively senior members initially included, among others, Geraldine and Willard Brown, Jeanette and Jack Dolph, Mildred and Ray Ferguson, Margaret and Zeb Freeman, Charlotte and Joe Graham, Mary Sue and Reed Hoover, Russie and Ellwood Jones, Edna and Bob

Lancaster, Jean and Lonnie Leeper, Hazel and Roland Lewis, Juanita and Fred McCord, Sue and James Mason, Agnes and Otto Morris, Tommie Lee and J. C. Rhodes, Irma and J. W. Runyon, Hazel and Paul Silliman, Vada and Oscar Shucany, Lila and Arthur Thomas, and Billie and Reed Yeager. "Their wisdom and leadership during the church's earliest days contributed much to its successful launch," said Hay.

Others made equally significant contributions during the church's formative years. Lannie and Dave Arant, Connie and Henry Amlin, Beth and Don Averitt, Margaret and Harold Baxter, Peggy and Carl Blanchard, Sandra and Corky Bridgeman, Claudia and Irwin Carroll, Barbara and Steve Clay, Bernice and Ben Christopher, Kathy and Charles Dees, Patsy and Ken Dippel, Bobbie and Ross Dixon, Margaret and David Fagin, Iva Marie and Lindsay Fleck, Elsie and Homer Flewharty, Betty and Bill Gillespie, Nancy and Lloyd Gilmore, Joy and Jim Goyen, Lee Haggard, Ann and Bruce Hallmark, Isla and Jerry Harvey, Margaret and Doug Jenkins, Gwen and Al Krutilek, Mary Frances and Paul Luther, Norma and Bob Mathis, Sue and Bill Nail, Hope and Joe Nelson, Ann and Dave Newman, Dewena and Bill Powell, Caribel and Gene Rutherford, Martha and Charles Squibb, Sue and Al Stockard, Lucille and Gene Tilley, Joanne and Malcolm Turner, Jeannine and Bob Verinder, Billie and Spike Webb, Ora and Gorman Webb, and Joan and Charles Wisler were among the pioneers who gave much to the early thrust of Ridgewood Park Methodist Church and epitomized the warmth and thoughtful nature of its embracing community.

Fueled by what several former church members recall as Stephenson's caring and challenging ministry and his superb organizational and administrative skills, the Ridgewood Park neighbors involved themselves at all levels of church business. Many answered Stephenson's call as he worked to get the church on firm footing, and to that end, he found in Betty Jo and Jess two of his most active and capable participants. "Betty Jo excelled at training children and youth," said Stephenson. "And Jess was a convincing, well-organized leader who provided good direction as a board chairman. They helped move the church forward in its earliest years." Yet, in spite of the time and effort Stephenson put in, he did not stay for long. After only four short years, he and Alyce moved on to minister to a different congregation, but not before overseeing the construction of Ridgewood Park's first building—a combination sanctuary-fellowship hall and classroom wing. With the completion of that structure, and a cluster of vigorous lay leaders in place, it seemed the church's departing first pastor had all but guaranteed that his dynamic church community was well-positioned for the future.

Enter The Reverend Wallace E. Chappell, Stephenson's successor. Wally, as he was known, arrived in 1958, bringing to Ridgewood Park a major shift in emphasis from recruiting, organization, and infrastructure—a necessary focus of the church's formative period—to theological renewal and social action. Indeed, in Wally Chappell, Ridgewood Park church members would discover a most extraordinary man of God. Chappell—a Dallas native with a degree in chemical engineering from Rice University in Houston and a graduate degree from Perkins School of Theology at SMU—brought intellectual rigor to the study of religion, and challenged his congregants to think about their faith in more penetrating ways. He introduced what Hay called "a dimension of theological daring to the pulpit." In addition, Hay said of Chappell, "He was a great wordsmith and an inspiration to almost everyone who heard him preach. He also had an intellectual depth and agility that attracted a number of intellectually gifted people—primarily faculty members from SMU and Perkins School of Theology."

Those drawn to the church—*some as members and others as program participants*—included Dr. Richard Bush and his wife, Mary; Dr. George Crawford and his wife, Jeanette; Dr. Howard Grimes and his wife, Johnnie Marie; Dr. Morton King and his wife, Joan; Dr. Paul Minton and his wife, Mary Frances, known as "Massie"; Dr. Joe Matthews; Dr. Shubert Ogden; Dr. Albert Outler; Amanda and Gilbert Finnell; Roger Ortmayer; Alice and Rex Stultz; and Ruth and Bob Turner. This intellectual powerhouse of gifted lay persons and distinguished theologians succeeded not only at bringing about a deepening of the church's theological perspective, but as Hay recalls, they also opened the door to "a broadened understanding of and commitment to our faith and to the pursuit of just and fair treatment for all within our society."

Chappell's style clearly challenged—and sometimes rattled—the members of his flock. But at the same time, many of them came to realize the value of being pushed to think more deeply about issues of faith than perhaps they ever had done before. Said Brownie Shytles: "My husband always said that Wally helped him firm up what he believed. Even though he didn't agree with him all the time, Wally helped him realize what he did believe." However, for those members of the congregation who were accustomed to old-time, Bible-thumping, revivalist religion and strict word-for-word literal interpretation of the biblical drama, Chappell represented a wrenching change. One member, LeAnn (Harris) Solomon, admits she had difficulty adjusting to the ministry of a man she remembers as being "pretty far out," and "on the edge":

124

He was much more liberal than most of us had grown up being. It was a problem and yet it was a challenge. He had a number of unusual ideas about the faith, some of which in my opinion were not very scriptural. I think one of the best things Wally did was make us crystallize our own beliefs. . . . When Wally would come out with things that were pretty far afield, we would have to think about why we disagreed with that. It made us think. We learned a lot about ourselves and our faith from Wally even when we did not agree with him.

In fact, Ridgewood Park's new pastor was responding to deepened ways of viewing traditional Christianity. The theology, of the type Chappell presented in the early 1960s, was a product of its time and part of a larger trend that not only questioned misunderstandings of tradition, but also challenged many notions of the nineteenth and early twentieth centuries which, in effect, made God a bit player supporting man's assumption of inevitable movement to enriched individual comfort and universal progression to an imagined utopia.

Chappell's approach, however, was far from a rejection of the core beliefs of the Christian faith. His message at the time was being honed and profoundly influenced by Biblical study; by process theology; by the writings of Schubert Ogden, Charles Hartshorne, Albert Outler, Reinhold Niebuhr, Paul Tillich, Rudolph Bultmann, and other twentieth century theologians; and by the sermons and various writings of two outstanding ministers, Harry Emerson Fosdick (of the Riverside Church in New York City) and Marshall Steel (of Highland Park Methodist Church in Dallas). Fosdick and Steel were exceptionally gifted preachers and both regularly proclaimed and promoted the "Social Gospel," an important component of Methodist tradition. This linkage to the heritage of Methodism clearly is evidenced by the following excerpt from the Methodist Social Creed of 1940:

> We believe that all persons have supreme value in the sight of God, and ought to be so regarded by us. We test all institutions and practices by their effect upon persons. Personality is oppressed in many parts of the world, and we seek its emancipation and those things which will enrich and redeem it. Since Jesus died for the redemption of human life, we believe we should live to help save man from sin and from every influence which would harm or destroy him.

The commentaries and insights of these Biblical scholars, and of the quoted portion of the Methodist Discipline, stood in contrast to the nineteenth and early twentieth centuries' popular theological views which believed in inevitable progress through the application of man's seemingly endless ingenuity. The new theology began in 1919 with Karl Barth's commentary on the Book of Romans which saw afresh the depth of sin in the human condition and humanity's resulting need for God's saving grace.

The First World War had crushed the optimism that humanity alone could make a perfect world. This point was the beginning of the rediscovery of the biblical message reclaimed by the protestant reformation in its emphasis on justification by faith and the priesthood of all believers. To many, this notion—as reasserted by Barth—placed squarely on the backs of the individuals within the proclaimed "priesthood" the clear responsibility to act as such by reaching out in love to those in need or in pain. The insights of Barth, and of those theologians influenced by his work, led to a whole generation of new theological development which, while affirming the faith's core principles, sought to make those principles relevant to our twentieth and twenty-first century experiences.

Wally Chappell was among those attracted to and inspired by this fresh approach to the Christian faith. Building on a foundation of years of Methodist tradition, he taught social responsibility by showing its basis in the Bible, particularly in the life and teachings of Jesus Christ, and in the prophetic imperatives presented in the Old Testament. He replaced unexamined biblical literalism with historical, literary, and theological understanding of the scripture, thus leading Ridgewood Park's members beyond emotional and "feel good" religion to commitment with their minds as well as their hearts.

Anglican Bishop John Robinson similarly was a product of and a contributor to this theological renewal. His book, written in 1963 and entitled *Honest to God*, became a best seller and a thought-provoking alternative to many of the narrow religious perceptions in vogue during the waning days of Victoria's reign as Queen of the British Empire. Described as "radical" and "heretical" when it first appeared, the book ignited controversy that raged for several years during the mid-sixties. Its popular success and unconventional message guaranteed it a top spot on Ridgewood Park adult study group reading lists. The same was true of Anglican Bishop James A. Pike's *Doing the Truth*, of Dr. Howard Grimes' *The Church Redemptive,* and of many works written by Paul Tillich, Soren Kierkegaard, Dietrich Bonhoffer, Reinhold Niebuhr, and a number of other theologians and philosophers, "each of whom in his or her own way," according to Jess Hay, "contributed to the Ridgewood Park congregation's continuing search for deeper understanding of the Christian faith."

Robinson's particular critique sought "to relocate God deep in the human experience rather than above and beyond the world." The idea of "heaven," by which is meant a separate supernatural dimension, was, Robinson suggested, "the greatest obstacle to an intelligent faith." As one essayist explained:

126

Whereas traditional theistic concepts placed God above the world . . . Robinson places God deep in the human experience (so that we have to look within to find God). . . . Whenever we pray we are not speaking words into the heavens (which can exonerate us from action) but are allowing our prayers to change us so that we will act. Whenever we act ethically, lovingly, and compassionately towards another, we are reaching towards God. . . . The close marrying of God with ethics, morality, and compassion leads one to emphasize this world rather than anything beyond this world.

For many faithful folks, these insights represented a reasonable extension of the Methodist Social Creed, and moved them a step closer to linking the Biblical message with the realities of our age.

And for a significant number of Protestants, the new perspective—far from freeing Christians from individual responsibility—in fact called for intense renewal of one's sense of personal accountability, and for steadfast commitment to the Biblical challenge to love others and to serve the broader interests of our society. For those Christians, affirmation of one's faith meant responding positively and creatively, and in gratitude for God's redeeming grace, to the call to service and sacrifice. It did not mean—as some televangelists have suggested—that prosperity inevitably and magically would follow in the wake of one's declaration of belief and accompanying contribution to the particular televangelist's financial coffers.

It was a theology that connected with Betty Jo and Jess and resonated strongly with their understanding of the Methodist traditions of personal and institutional responsibility and dedicated service to others. From the Hays' perspective, there was nothing "other-worldly" about their core spiritual perspective, as Jess explains:

The main driver is a commitment to the fundamental notion that the Christian calling is about caring for one another, about serving others, and about being reasonably humble in relationship to other people and certainly in relationship to God. . . . The extension of kindness, caring, service, and love to others, paradoxically, contributes to one's personal glimpse of noble purpose and shifts life's focus from nervous preoccupation about whether you're going to heaven or to hell toward a quest for a sense of fulfillment in the here and now.

That having been said, there's no question that Betty Jo's faith embraced a very deep commitment to the idea that we are mystically related to a loving God who has given us some guidance as to how we ought to live . . . in relationship with others. She and I shared the view that the life, teachings, death, and destiny of Jesus Christ constitute, *not exclusively but for us,* the supreme manifestation of God's nature and of His aspirations for our lives. This core conviction, in turn, led the two of us to believe that since our ultimate fate resides in the care of a redemptive and loving being whom we call God, we need not be anxious as to the specifics of that destiny. Such detail, we realized, is beyond our knowing. Nonetheless, each of us found peace in the faith that, regardless of the specifics, in the end all would be well or, as Paul proclaims in Chapter 8 of the Book of Romans, we were (and I remain) "sure that neither death, nor life . . . nor anything else in all creation ever can separate us from the love of God."

While this degree of moral clarity might have stirred in some people an overpowering urge to lecture others, Betty Jo was not one of them. Never given to sermonizing, she lived her life content with the deeply private nature of her faith, secure in her understanding of God's will in her life. "She didn't go around preaching to people," said Hay. "Her outreach was, to a remarkable degree, by example." Over time Betty Jo would touch the lives of more and more people, driven by an increasingly prominent moral grounding that eventually encompassed every aspect of her existence.

■

Theological leanings aside, Ridgewood Park provided an environment which allowed many of its congregants to achieve a deep level of personal connection. In fact, some members—Betty Jo and Jess included—found this notable feature to be one of the most rewarding aspects of their affiliation with the church, as it gave rise to important and enduring friendships. "Regardless of the nuances of your particular theological views, there was a strong sense of belonging to a community of love and caring," said Hay.

Among several particularly active church couples, there developed a special bond that went beyond formal church events and ended up lasting a lifetime. Affectionately known as "the group," this collection of church friends initially was comprised of Betty Jo and Jess, Jerry and Ross Pittman, LeAnn and Ned Harris, Ina and Mac McCormick, Brownie and Bob Shytles, Juanita and Harold Smotherman, Martha and John Binion,

Frances and Jimmy Thomas, Charlene and Buddy Miller, Bobbie and Al Hopkins, Peggy and Ken Smith, Marjorie and Wayne Harmon, and Shirley and Lee McVey.

It was, without question, an impressive line-up of adults, particularly from a child's standpoint. Michelle McCormick remembers them all, and the role they played in her early life:

> There was a group of some ten to twelve families that we called "the group," and we still call it "the group." Until I got out of high school we were like an extended family. We vacationed together and every Christmas we gathered for Christmas carols either at the Harris's or the Hays' house. . . . The kids grew up together. We were in and out of each others' homes. It was an incredible experience.

Like McCormick, Patty Hay also remembers the unique closeness that developed between the Ridgewood Park Methodist Church families, and acknowledges the mark it left on her:

> When I was little, the church was the center of our lives. Our vacations were spent with people from the church; most of my best friends went to that church. I consider it the "village" we grew up in. Those people seemed to me to be the core of that church.

And though the summer vacations taken over the years may not have been elaborate, they were exceedingly special, made so by the shared sense of fellowship among the families. Typically—as a means of escaping the oppressive Texas heat—various members of "the group" would head for the cool Rocky Mountains of Colorado. On several occasions their journey took them to the YMCA camp near Estes Park in the northern part of the state, but the families also vacationed in the southwest corner of Colorado, and on those trips they stayed in a large log home owned by Jo and Roy Guffey, Jerry Pittman's parents. Nestled alongside the Rio Grande River in the town of South Fork, the home provided the perfect mountain getaway, not to mention a scenic place for Betty Jo to do what she loved best. "No matter where we were, Betty Jo played bridge," said Hay. "That was her favorite activity, vacation or otherwise. There also was horseback riding, hiking, fishing, and hayrides, which usually concluded around a campfire with a sing-along that was particularly enjoyable if you had someone leading it like Bob Shytles or Jim Harmon, each of whom at different times had directed the choir at Ridgewood Park Methodist and each of whom had a great singing voice."

Closer to home was the frequent weekend destination known as *Greentrees*, located in the country near Sanger, Texas, just north of Denton. *Greentrees* belonged to Ned and LeAnn Harris and other members of Ned's family and, with its ranch-like feel, made for a perfect playground. "They had a lot of cattle," recalls McCormick. "An older guy and his wife ran it. We would go up almost every weekend; so, we grew up riding horses and playing in the creek and hiding in the hayloft. I remember Betty Jo and Jess being a part of that. I remember Betty Jo would wear her cute, little Western outfits." The weekends at *Greentrees* left Patty Hay with a bundle of memories, too, especially "the horses and the camaraderie":

> Ned was such a hoot. He and daddy—it was just one joke after another. "The group" would get together there on weekends and everybody would bring food and we'd cook burgers or hotdogs. Never could spit a watermelon seed as far as the boys, which was a great disappointment. It was a fun place.

No doubt "the group" had a knack for enjoying life, but the good times are hardly an indication of how deeply these families cared for one another. Rather, it was when families hit a rough patch—as they would from time to time—that the true extent of love and support within this informal community was most evident. The Hay family experienced just such a moment of crisis in 1957 when four-year-old Debby contracted rheumatic fever. Though signs of serious illness began on the last day of summer vacation with the Pittman family in South Fork, Colorado, it wasn't until the Hays' return to Dallas several days later that a diagnosis was made. Once home, Betty Jo quickly phoned Dr. Doris Spegal, the Hays' gifted and trusted pediatrician who, on hearing Debby's symptoms, said she suspected rheumatic fever. Medical tests the next day confirmed Spegal's diagnosis, and the doctor prescribed treatment. "She immediately started me on antibiotics," remembers Debby, "and then I was bedridden for six months." The long, slow recovery of their daughter—and the outpouring of love from friends—remain vivid memories for Jess Hay:

> The illness required Debby to remain perfectly still in bed for the next five or six months. During this . . . period, our friends responded with frequent visits to relieve Betty Jo. Bill Stephenson, Jerry Pittman, Susan Pittman, Mary Bush, Nancy Bush, Frances Thomas, Ned and LeAnn Harris, Brownie Shytles, Martha Binion, Ina McCormick, Charlene Miller, and our next door neighbors, Flo and Frank Loper were particularly attentive.

A FAMILY VACATION WITH
RIDGEWOOD PARK METHODIST CHURCH FRIENDS
ESTES PARK, COLORADO, SUMMER 1964
PHOTOGRAPHS BY JAMES W. THOMAS

From back to front,
left to right:
Wayne Harmon,
Susan Pittman,
Susan Harmon,
Debby and Betty Jo Hay,
Frances Thomas,
Spence Shytles,
Margie Harmon,
Bob Shytles,
Ina McCormick,
Terry Wimberly,
Ned and LeAnn Harris,
Jess Hay,
Julie Thomas,
Beth Harmon,
Bob Thomas, and
John Harris.

Betty Jo, Ina McCormick,
and Frances Thomas taking
a spin on their go-carts.

Jess and Julie Thomas having fun on a go-cart.

Buddy and Charlene Miller share a moment
of togetherness.

From the top: Jess, Brownie Shytles, LeAnn Harris, Betty Jo,
Ned Harris, Frances Thomas, Bob Shytles, Mac and Ina McCormick,
Margie and Wayne Harmon.

From the bottom, left to right: Bob and Julie Thomas,
Michelle and Kimberly McCormick, John Harris, Debby and
Patty Hay, Mac McCormick, Spence Shytles, Neil Harris,
Susan Pittman, Bruce Harris, Jess, and Ned Harris.

Frances Thomas and three young wranglers about
ready to depart on an early morning ride.

"We all took food, drove her, or ran errands if she needed it, and did whatever we could," said LeAnn (Harris) Solomon. Charlene Miller even rolled Betty Jo's hair since she couldn't get to the beauty shop during those homebound days of caring for Debby. "We'd sit there and talk afterward," Miller recalled, "and then I'd take her hair down and fix it."

Young Debby, meanwhile, faced her own set of challenges, including the boredom that came from having to spend months in bed. To help alleviate the monotony, Betty Jo, among other measures, enlisted the help of Debby's friends. First, there was Susan Pittman, Debby's best friend and next door neighbor, who did her part by paying frequent visits. In addition, said Debby, "Another friend, Nancy Bush, who was a few years older than me, walked home from school and would stop by every day and play with me. Mother lined up lots of things like that, including craft projects and other activities." By February 1958—with the help of proper medication, Debby's acceptance of the need to remain still, and Betty Jo's tender and attentive care—Debby made a full recovery from rheumatic fever.

Less than two years later, though, the Hays suffered another painful shock at the end of Betty Jo's fourth and final pregnancy. On January 14, 1960, she gave birth to a baby girl, Mary Kathryn, who, like Jess Richard in 1955, was born prematurely and suffered similarly from respiratory distress syndrome, a common lung disorder in premature infants. Tragically, just as Jess Richard had died one day after his birth, Mary Kathryn died one day after hers. And though losing the baby was traumatic for both Betty Jo and Jess, Hay concedes the death of Jess Richard five years earlier had left him with an instinctive need to, in his words, "hold back some dimension of hope and expectation as the birth of our fourth child approached. For that reason, although the loss of Mary Kathryn produced deep and profoundly-felt grief, in my case it was not as totally devastating." Sadly, the same could not be said for Betty Jo. "I know it was something that upset mother until the day she died," said daughter Debby Hay Spradley, who was seven when Mary Kathryn was born. "She had dreams about it later in life. I know it was upsetting to her as long as she lived."

As was his hope, The Reverend Bill Stephenson had indeed left his fledgling church community well-positioned for the future. Within two years of his departure and under the stewardship of Wally Chappell, Ridgewood Park Methodist Church had become the heart of the neighborhood, and its members the driving force. They were dedicated adults—many of them good friends—whose sense of caring and personal responsibility extended well beyond the borders of their Ridgewood Park neighborhood. "The community seemed not only always to be there for each other during good times and bad times, but they also reached out to those less privileged," remembers Patty Hay. "It was a very active, motivated community that cared a lot about others."

At the forefront of this community outreach, according to Michelle McCormick, were the rich traditions of Methodism, "which included pursuit of social justice and emphasis on redemptive social action," furthered, she said, by a view of Christianity that was:

> less about Jesus dying on the cross for our sins because we're bad people and more about accepting God's abiding grace and going out into the world and taking care of the marginalized, and otherwise contributing to our common good. Respond to God's presence by loving His world. Build and sustain hospitals and orphanages. Sponsor and support institutions of higher learning. Feed the hungry. Tend the needy. Care about the young. Visit the infirm. Nurture and care for our families. Embrace others. And, working together, do your best to make the world a better place. All such outreaches are a vital part of our Methodist heritage, and all are reflections of the church's responsibility to enhance the general quality and caring nature of our society.

Betty Jo was among those who took their Methodist heritage seriously and, thus, devoted herself wholeheartedly to the service of others, wherever they might be. Her volunteer work took her to Bethlehem Center, a Methodist mission in poverty-stricken south Dallas, whose executive director was Mary Cameron, a fellow member of Ridgewood Park Methodist Church. At the same time, Betty Jo's close friend, Brownie Shytles, volunteered as a delegate to the mission. Brownie clearly remembers the mark left there by Betty Jo, and particularly the affinity she had for the needs of children in a place of such great despair and meager hope. "I remember the little kindergartners were about to graduate and move on to first grade," said Brownie. "Betty Jo sewed little graduation uniforms for them to wear and walk across the stage to get a diploma. She made every one of them a cap and gown. She wanted to give them a feeling of importance and a sense that having achieved completion of their preschool work, they could go on to bigger and better things if they stayed in school." It was this level of compassion, and her regard for the feelings of others, that—during Betty Jo's lifetime—characterized her volunteer service and her personal relationships with adults and children.

Even older children had a chance to experience the emotional lift that came from working with the Hays, whether through Sunday school classes at Ridgewood Park—taught by Betty Jo and Jess—or through the Methodist Youth Fellowship, a church youth group which they advised for ten years. During those years, according to Erin Barger Orgeron, Betty Jo and Jess formed many "strong and lasting relationships" with young people, herself among them:

> The great thing about Betty Jo in our lives was her kindness and caring and her attention to us. That was out of the ordinary. So often as a child, you're treated like you don't count. Maybe when you get to be an adult you'll count, but you don't count, now. Betty Jo and Jess's philosophy was you count, now. In Sunday school they wanted to know our reaction to Bible verses and stories and to related doctrines of the church. . . . They cared about what we thought. What we thought mattered . . . and that was pretty wonderful.

Though the circle of people within the scope of Betty Jo's community service widened, she continued to bring to the lives of her own daughters the same sensitivity she displayed in her work with other children and young adults. There was a period in Patty's life, for example, when she—like nearly every five-year-old girl—had a longing to feel special about herself. This problem, reasoned Betty Jo, was nothing that a little extra mother-daughter time couldn't fix, so on Fridays when the kindergartners were released early from school, she and Patty had their moment together. This single act of understanding directed at her little girl opened the door to what became not only a weekly ritual, but more important, one of Patty's most treasured memories:

> Mom picked me up every Friday at 11:30, and we would go to Cabell's [convenience store] . . . where we bought chopped barbecue beef sandwiches and Sprites. . . . I thought the green glass bottle was really cool. They had little dots on them. We would go home and Mom and I would eat lunch and watch re-runs of *Father Knows Best* on Channel 11—just the two of us. I love my sister, but when you're the second child you're never the only child; that was my time with Mom. I remember it so clearly, having those Fridays with her and how great that was. She always took the time to do it. She never missed.

In the meantime, Betty Jo was gaining recognition and respect for her volunteer work at Ridgewood Park, due in large part to the magnitude of her talent, and the skill and competence she brought to each project. "She commanded . . . admiration and inspired confidence because whatever she did was good," said Stell Chappell, the pastor's wife and an active member of the congregation. "Whatever you needed, she knew how to do it."

For one project, Betty Jo and her close friend Charlene Miller decided it was time to rid the Methodist Youth Fellowship room of what they considered its bleak and institutional appearance, and in the process, make it more appealing to the church's younger members. With that goal in mind—and equipped with their time-tested sewing skills—Betty Jo and Charlene successfully undertook the task of outfitting the room with bright, new, red and white striped awnings. "It looked like a carnival midway," remembers Miller. "Jess and [my husband] Buddy hung them for us. It helped make the youth room more palatable for the kids. That was a big project."

It seemed no matter the size nor the complexity, Betty Jo was up to the task. This was particularly evident at the church, where she was responsible for several high-profile activities, each of which, according to Jess, she managed with signature proficiency:

> Betty Jo served a number of years as chairperson of the Commission on Missions. She was president of the Women's Society of Christian Service. She also was on the official board and hostess for scores of church functions. And she was active every year, either as a teacher or director of our church's summer vacation bible school program.

In all of these activities, Betty Jo volunteered alongside numerous other hard-working women, several of whom, in looking back, say they were struck by their friend's remarkable ability and dynamism. "She was always an extremely well-organized person," said LeAnn (Harris) Solomon, "very efficient." Mary Bush recalls Betty Jo "was very comfortable speaking, and made other people comfortable. She knew how to prepare and had things well in hand when she spoke." She was "a very good study leader, and very good speaker," Jerry Pittman remembers. Indeed, these traits—thorough preparation, focus, and public speaking skill—had propelled Betty Jo through her days at SMU, and now were being drawn upon in her work as an effective adult leader. A sense of her style can be gotten by reviewing the minutes of the first meeting of the Commission on Missions held in January 1964 "at the home of Chairman, Betty Jo Hay." Betty Jo began that meeting by immediately directing the attention of the members to the committee's purpose:

> Betty Jo opened the meeting with a prayer and began the business by reading from *The Methodist Story* an article concerning the work of Missions and the points to keep in mind as to what our work will be.

But serious though Betty Jo could be, she was by no means all business, as surely her involvement at SMU could attest. Rather, Betty Jo was that rare sort who, at an early age, mastered the art of being able to stay on task while having a good time of it. This unique quality carried over into her adult life, where her gift for wit and humor spared many a committee meeting from the inevitable monotony that often characterizes such gatherings. "Betty Jo had a fun streak in her," said Mary Bush. "Whatever the activity was she would make it a fun experience."

Betty Jo did have a way of achieving weighty goals through enjoyable means, and nothing gave her more enjoyment than performing in front of an audience. So it came as no surprise when, as chairperson of the Commission on Missions in 1965, she responded to a funding request from Methodist missionaries in Hong Kong by organizing a church talent show. And though this method of fund-raising was not novel—musical revues, under the direction of and in response to encouragement by church member Gwen Krutilek, had by the mid-sixties acquired some vogue at Ridgewood Park—Betty Jo was among those who embraced the shows with particular fervor.

And on at least two occasions, it could be said with certainty, she took the stage to great effect. One performance was a satirical revue called, "Specifically South," which featured parodies of songs from the musical *South Pacific*. It was in this show that—to Jess Hay's recollection—Betty Jo and Jimmy Thomas performed a memorable dance number that featured a no-holds-barred version of the Charleston. "Of course, Jimmy is a very good dancer," said Jess, "and Betty Jo was a very, very good dancer. So, they had a fun time."

But it was another performance, a solo dance number, which garnered the most acclaim, and left an indelible mark. In a moment that Ridgewood Park friends recall as shoot-the-lights-out terrific, Betty Jo portrayed the one and only Broadway character, Mame. "She *was* Mame," those who truly knew Betty Jo said, and she could play the part with ease, they concluded, because something deep inside her connected with the brassy, uninhibited stage character who proclaimed, "Life is a banquet, and most poor sons-of-bitches are starving to death." Given Betty Jo's own zest for life, Jess said her kinship with Mame made perfect sense. "Mame was a free spirit who wasn't bothered by a lot of rigid social rules. Betty Jo wasn't, either," he said. David Farr agrees. Farr, who several years later would serve as Ridgewood Park's youth minister and form a close friendship with the Hay family, remembers Betty Jo's face lighting up "when she talked about being Mame." Trained in personality theory and psychology, Farr was one who truly could appreciate the deeper meaning behind what he saw as an exhilarating experience for Betty Jo:

That was one of her star moments. . . . It was almost as if she'd gotten to do something she always wanted to do, something that really expressed who she was. And, Mame really did express Betty Jo very well. . . . Mame was a very strong woman, who was not very diplomatic, but she lived life fully. . . . Mame was a gal who had broken out of some shackles and really cut loose on the world. . . . Betty Jo was not prim and proper. She enjoyed being a wee bit wicked.

That is to say Betty Jo had no hang-ups about portraying her character's naughty side, and in this dance number, according to Farr, she effortlessly revealed Mame's unconstrained, lusty persona. Considering the audience and the venue, the artistic decision to portray the character with such unabashed honesty was more than a little daring, especially for the times. "From what I understand Betty Jo's performance was pretty sexy at times," Farr recalls. "There was some choreography and movements and love stuff going on that I don't think was very acceptable for most church groups at that time." But for the bold Betty Jo, breaking conventional norms was precisely the point, and those in her path couldn't help but be mesmerized.

Even observant youngsters were moved by her free spirit and fierce independence. Michelle McCormick, Patty's good friend and a frequent visitor to the Hay home, recognized early on Betty Jo Hay was not your standard-issue mom and she remembers with great clarity the qualities that set her apart from other mothers:

Betty Jo was not afraid to be herself. . . . She was different from the other mothers. She dressed impeccably with her hair and nails and wardrobe like the rest of the North Dallas women . . . but she sometimes was a little rough around the edges and, thank goodness, because a sense of authenticity came through with her. She spoke her mind, she smoked, she drank, she cussed—rarely but effectively—and it made her so alive and so real and so different from the other mothers I grew up with. I had a sense of her strength. Even when we were kids and she was doing PTA like the other moms, she was different. I had a sense that this was an outstanding person in her own right, that she was an equal with her husband, that she had a voice.

■

Her intense interest in politics and national affairs—as opposed solely to concerns on the domestic front—provided yet another contrast between Betty Jo and the typical 1950s housewife. Martha Binion, a close friend from Ridgewood Park, would drop by the Hay home occasionally and visit with Betty Jo over a morning cup of coffee. Those visits, she said, were anything but typical:

> I always enjoyed those conversations. . . . We talked about issues in life and what's going on in the world. They were deeper than just chitchat. . . . She was up on things, and she certainly had her own opinions. . . . She wasn't afraid to let people know where she stood.

Likewise, Juanita Smotherman, another church friend and member of "the group," recalls the degree of Betty Jo's intellectual involvement in public affairs and how this outside interest added a dimension to her life not shared by other housewives:

> She was not typical. When you were a housewife back then, you got caught up in the cleaning and the diapers and other household activities . . . and most women were content to do that. Betty Jo, on the other hand, was always thinking and reading. . . . She didn't quit thinking just because she became a mother. . . . She knew what was going on in the world and was interested in things the average woman of the 1950s wouldn't be.

Advancing the cause of social justice was one of those interests, and while Betty Jo and Jess remained as committed to it as ever through their work in the church, they realized during those years that any significant progress was going to take a combination of their moral values *and* politics, between which they saw a strong connection. In other words, meaningful change would be possible only through the reform of public policy, and only then—if they were to remain true to their primary values—on the condition that Judeo-Christian ethical principles be considered in the development of that policy. They viewed political activism, specifically within the Democratic Party, as the means to that end. Thus, just as they had with the Methodist Church, Betty Jo and Jess committed their lifelong allegiance to the Democratic Party and its principles.

To their satisfaction, and within the context of their firm and relentless commitment to preserving the constitutionally-mandated separation of church and state, the Hays found mainstream, moderate-to-liberal Democratic politics to be comfortably compatible with their Methodist heritage. In the early 1960s this view was reinforced to no small degree by the leader of the Democratic Party—newly-elected president, John F. Kennedy— who seemed to take a page from the Hays' hymn book when he uttered the following words during his January 20, 1961, inaugural address:

> With a good conscience our only sure reward, with history the final judge of our deeds, let us go forth to lead the land we love, asking His blessing and His help, but knowing that here on earth God's work must truly be our own.

Locally, Jess Hay was spreading a similar message in sermons he delivered to church and civic groups. In 1964, an Oak Lawn United Methodist Church newsletter announced the upcoming visit of "Mr. Jess Hay, one of the most brilliant young attorneys in the Southwest. . . ." It noted: "He is a dynamic, exciting speaker very much in demand for all occasions. The subject of his message to us is *The Call to Radical Commitment*." Many years later Hay would describe the sermon as a "call to conscious and positive response to the demand that we serve social justice and that we relate in love to those most in need, and that we do so without the expectation of accolade or reward."

This activist spirit—engendered in part by the Kennedy presidency—led to growing support around the country for the administration's economic and social programs, dubbed the "New Frontier." The Democratic Party in each state eagerly promoted Kennedy's agenda at the grassroots level by organizing Operation Support, an initiative of volunteer committees "designed to increase citizen backing of legislation proposed by the Kennedy administration." Betty Jo was one of a handful of party stalwarts who served on the Dallas committee and whose involvement at a Wednesday evening program "in the French Room of the Hotel Adolphus" attracted the attention of the local media. The newspaper story went on to say the speakers, including "Mrs. Jess Hay . . . will discuss four fields of legislation: education, jobs and economic growth, foreign affairs, and health care for the aged. An informal social hour will follow the program."

Jan Sanders, another party activist who participated in Operation Support, and wife of Judge Barefoot Sanders—former Chief Judge of the United States District Court for the Northern District of Texas—saw the committee's work as a "response to the spirit that was sweeping the nation following the Kennedy-Johnson victory. It was a local reply to   the young president's inaugural clarion call to the country, 'Ask not what your country can do for you; ask what you can do for your country.'" Sanders said she and other dedicated Democratic women such as Betty Jo understood full well the need to maintain the momentum of the presidential victory. "There was a high level of awareness among Democratic women that voting wasn't enough; we needed to become advocates. . . . Betty Jo was the kind of woman who was willing to step up. Public service was important to her."

Certainly, local Democratic Party politics in the 1960s was nothing new to the Hays. Since their role in Henry Wade's successful 1950 campaign for Dallas County District Attorney, they had supported numerous other political candidates. Among them was Barefoot Sanders. And although Sanders failed to unseat Republican Congressman Bruce Alger in 1958, Betty Jo and Jess were there, doing what they could to promote his candidacy. "To stimulate support for Sanders among our friends," said Hay, "Betty Jo organized coffees and hosted them in our home. She also organized work crews to get out mailings and to do telephoning and that sort of thing. She probably was more active in that campaign than I was."

During the hard-fought 1960 presidential race between John F. Kennedy and Richard M. Nixon, the Hays threw their enthusiastic support behind the candidacy of Kennedy and his running mate, Lyndon B. Johnson. "We were just two of the worker bees," Hay modestly proclaimed of the role he and Betty Jo played in the campaign. But as it was, they were more than simply worker bees, and in fact by 1960, had become the beneficiaries of the close friendship that had developed between Gene Locke and Lyndon Johnson. "Because of Gene Locke, who was very active in the campaign as a result of his relationship with LBJ, Betty Jo and I probably had a slightly larger involvement than we otherwise would have," Hay said. And that was only the beginning. The ripple effect of this powerful association would be felt by Betty Jo and Jess, in one way or another, for years to come.

One such occasion was two years later when Johnson protégé John Connally was running for Texas governor, and the Hays found themselves with a noticeably higher campaign profile. Again, it was Locke's influence which led to their increasing level of responsibility, said Hay:

> Governor Connally's campaign in 1962 was chaired by Gene Locke. . . . As a result, Betty Jo and I had rather significant roles in the Dallas County portion of the campaign. Together with Cliff Cassidy, Robert Strauss, Ted Strauss, and a number of others, we served as active members of Connally's Dallas County Steering Committee. In addition, I assisted Gene to a small degree in fundraising efforts on behalf of the campaign.

Over the next several years, Jess and Betty Jo's close ties to Gene Locke would lead to a dramatic elevation in their political stature and eventually to their influential participation at the highest levels of state and national Democratic Party politics.

An early indication of that emerging stature came in July 1963 when the Hays set out on a three-week vacation to Washington, D.C. As would be expected, they toured the capitol and enjoyed a visit with Betty Jo's aunt and uncle, Mary and Carl Albert, and cousins, Mary Frances and David. "While there, we spent several days introducing Patty and Debby to many of the great features of our nation's capital city," Hay remembered fondly. But beyond typical sightseeing, the Hays' vacation included an opportunity to experience Washington in a way unimaginable to the average citizen. "Among the trip highlights was a brief visit with President Kennedy and a continental breakfast at the White House. . . . Our admiration for the president was enhanced by our brief meeting, and we left firmer than ever in our support of his leadership of the country and of the Democratic Party."

Four months later on November 21, 1963, President Kennedy, the elegant first lady Jacqueline, Vice President Johnson and the much-loved Lady Bird, made a trip to Texas, with initial stops in San Antonio, Houston, and Fort Worth. At their final destination in Dallas on November 22, 1963, the president was to deliver a luncheon speech at the Dallas Trade Mart, where an exuberant crowd—each of whom had paid $100 a plate—anxiously awaited his arrival. Surely, it would have been hard to find any among them more excited to see the president and hear him speak than Jess, Betty Jo, and her mother, Kathryn. Twenty years later, in 1983, journalist Bryan Woolley described the scene in a *Dallas Times Herald* news story:

> At the Trade Mart, the luncheon guests were showing their tickets to the door guards and filing to their seats. . . . Inside the atrium hall, parakeets flew freely from tree to tree. A fountain splashed. An organist was practicing "Hail to the Chief." Dozens of yellow roses adorned the head table. The presidential seal had been mounted on the rostrum.

At 12:30 p.m. as the president's motorcade slowly made its way through Dealey Plaza in downtown Dallas, Kennedy was fatally wounded by gunshots and rushed to nearby Parkland Hospital. Governor Connally—riding with his wife, Nellie, in the forward seat of the president's limousine—was hit in the back, but survived. At the time, they had been less than five minutes away from the Trade Mart. Announcement of the president's death at

1:00 p.m. brought a sudden end to an administration that had achieved mythical status almost overnight. Indeed, the Kennedy White House had become known as Camelot for the charismatic, stylish couple living there. But the events of November 22, 1963, changed all that, and in the end, 1600 Pennsylvania Avenue would be their home for only three short years. "Gentlemen," a weeping Texas Senator Ralph Yarborough told reporters, "this has been a deed of horror. Excalibur has sunk beneath the waves." And with the demise of that uniquely enchanted era, came this remark from Jackie Kennedy: "There'll be great presidents again . . . but there'll never be another Camelot."

At the Trade Mart, meanwhile, a security guard who knew Jess told him what had happened:

> He came up and whispered to me that Kennedy had been shot. The blood drained out of me. I don't remember the details but once the news spread through the crowd, a pall settled over the room, and we all left. . . . We then joined the rest of the nation, first in shock and then in deep mourning.

Betty Jo was so stunned and shaken by the news of Kennedy's death that while driving home from the Trade Mart she decided to give up her self-imposed, rigidly-enforced prohibition against smoking in front of Kathryn. Although a smoker since college, she had refrained from the habit while in the presence of her parents and other relatives. It was no secret. Everyone knew she smoked. But out of respect for her mother and father, Betty Jo had maintained a pattern of restraint. However, under the searing trauma of the day's events—and in a moment Hay remembers well—discretion and pretense simply withered:

> She never, ever smoked in front of her parents or in front of my parents or in the presence of any uncle or aunt. She was very guarded about that until Kennedy was assassinated. Her mother was with us at the luncheon. Once we got in the car and began driving home, Betty Jo lit a cigarette, and that was the end of her avoidance of smoking in the presence of senior family members.

Children around the country absorbed the impact of the assassination in their own way. Patty Hay was a second grader at the time, and holds vivid memories of that most unforgettable day in November 1963. She remembers sitting in her classroom at Dan D. Rogers Elementary School when the school's science teacher, Mrs. Peel, walked into the room crying, and asked Patty's teacher, Mrs. Fowler, to step out into the hall. Minutes later, the school principal announced the news that something terrible had happened:

> Robbie Lee Williams comes on the intercom and says, "The president has been
> shot, and teachers who would like to are free to turn on the televisions for the news
> reports, and parents will be coming to pick up students." I remember some kids
> whose parents had been for Nixon and were really right wing started laughing.
> The teacher stopped that very quickly. I remember being picked up at school and
> getting home and mom cried and cried. I knew my parents were really upset. It
> was a horrible time.

That evening the Hays turned to the one place they knew they could find strength
and reassurance—Ridgewood Park Methodist Church. Along with other grieving church
members, they gathered in the sanctuary for what Juanita Smotherman remembers as a
particularly moving service conducted by Wally Chappell:

> We were all so distraught. Wally did a masterful job of talking about the event and
> our nation and reconciliation and love. At the end of the service, there was one
> candle that was blown out. It was very dramatic; very effective. I'll never forget it.

■

It was during this period of sharpened political interest and activity that Jess Hay,
in 1962, entertained the idea of seeking the 1964 Democratic nomination for Congress
with the primary purpose of defeating Republican Congressman Bruce Alger. Hay was
encouraged to run for public office by fellow attorneys Joe Stalcup and Bill Brice, his two
good friends from SMU. Stalcup, who had served as president of the Young Democrats of
Dallas County, felt he had a firm grasp on the political landscape of the community and
thus put together a committee to bolster Hay's candidacy. That step brought significant
backing, including the "enthusiastic endorsement and generous offer of support" from
Trammell Crow, a gifted Dallas businessman whose success in real estate development
eventually would bring him international acclaim.

Still, Hay remained reluctant about the prospect of squaring off with Alger, and in
the end, declined the suggestion, writing to Stalcup on December 31, 1962, that his decision had been a difficult one considering his "inborn love of politics" and "genuine desire to
do battle against Dallas' leading exponent of fanaticism and negative reactionism." But he

144

had come to the conclusion, after an "objective evaluation of the current political climate," that the success of his candidacy would be unlikely. In addition, Hay cited his lack of economic independence, ongoing interest in his law career, and "love of family and friends" as the most "compelling arguments for the status quo."

At the time Hay made the decision not to seek public office, family and friends figured more prominently in his life than ever before. Specifically, where family was concerned, years of encouraging and nurturing close ties between relatives in Texas, Oklahoma, and Kansas had resulted in a deep bond of friendship among cousins. Betty Jo's Uncle Budge, his wife Betty, and their daughters Judy and Anne paid frequent visits to the Hay home during the late 1950s and early 1960s, as did the two children of Mary and Carl Albert—Mary Frances and David—and Jess's cousins, Ruth Ann and Mary Lee "Sister" Roddy, the daughters of Mary Lee and Perry Roddy. The Roddy girls often would stop in Dallas along the way from college to their parents' home in Lubbock, Texas. During those years Sister was a student at Radcliffe College in Massachusetts, while Ruth Ann attended Barnard College in New York City. After graduation, Ruth Ann married Albert Shapiro, an assistant movie director, and headed to southern California, where she still resides with her husband and daughter. Sister, meanwhile, graduated from Radcliffe and also got married. She lived for a time in Wichita, Kansas before moving back to Dallas with her two children and husband, Dr. Brad Reeves, a physician specializing in radiology.

Earl and Doris Albert and their daughters, Kathy, Nancy and Polly—all of whom then lived in McAlester, Oklahoma—had grown particularly close to Betty Jo, Jess, and their two daughters. "I have lots of memories of Dallas," said Polly Albert Crawley, "because my parents thought it was really important that we all love each other and grow up close to each other. The Albert group was like that." The cousins were able to remain close by trading regular visits with each other—a favorite family activity. "Betty Jo and her family visited frequently," said Polly. "Whenever there were any important family events, she was always there, and if they had important events in Dallas we always came for those."

These exchange visits took on a heightened sense of importance for the cousins, and in fact, became prized summertime rituals, said Patty Hay. "Polly, Kathy, Nancy, and Debby and I would go back and forth during the summer, always crying when they came to separate us. 'Oh, *please*, let us stay one more week!' We had a lot of fun with family game nights, playing Monopoly and other board games."

And from that fervent game-playing came many endearing memories. "I remember playing jacks in the Hays' entry hall," said Polly. "We did that for hours. That was really fun. We would play Monopoly and Patty and I would stay up until the wee hours of the morning playing Monopoly, and sometimes Jess would stay up with us, and then Betty Jo would come out, 'It's three in the morning. You all have to go to bed.' I'm telling you, we loved it."

Edgar and Ruth Peacock and their daughter Ruth Ellen—residents of Sherman, Texas at the time—also enjoyed a close relationship with the Hays. "They were part of our lives and part of our family for as long as I can remember," said Ruth Ellen Leever, who was the four-year-old flower girl in Jess and Betty Jo's wedding. And although Ruth Ellen has no specific memory of their 1951 wedding ceremony, there is plenty more about Betty Jo and Jess that she does remember:

> We frequently would go to Dallas for Thanksgiving or Christmas. During the summer I would spend a week or so with Aunt Kathryn and Uncle Duncan, and I would spend a lot of time at Jess and Betty Jo's and play with Debby and Patty.
>
> One of my fond memories was when I was thirteen or fourteen and Betty Jo took me shopping downtown with her. Of course, downtown Dallas, then, was quite the thing. She took me to lunch at the Zodiac Room [Neiman Marcus]. I thought that was just about the most exciting thing that had happened to me. I remember it so well. The Zodiac Room was all decorated in turquoise and silver and white and green, and they had a fashion show.

There were other attractions in Dallas, as well, including Betty Jo's father's Peanut Shoppe, a visit to which no out-of-town cousin's trip was considered complete without. "We'd get to go see Uncle Duncan at the peanut store and that was such a treat," remembers Polly. "To this day, I love chocolate-covered peanuts. You could go behind the counter and get whatever you wanted. He was the kindest, gentlest man, and we all loved him dearly."

Ruth Ellen Leever has equally vivid memories of Uncle Duncan's peanut store:

> It was small, long, and narrow. It had a big plate glass window in front, and you could smell the peanuts roasting before you ever got there. . . . Uncle Duncan always wore a long-sleeved white shirt and tie. He took his tie and tucked it inside his shirt so it wouldn't get caught on anything. His sleeves were usually rolled up. I remember as a younger girl, he would give me peanuts to take outside to feed the pigeons.

"To go to his store, was like a child's dream," said Nancy Albert Lane. "You could go in there and get whatever candy you wanted, and toward the back of the store you could sit down and get a frosty root beer. It was just wonderful."

For cousin David Albert, mere mention of The Peanut Shoppe stirs rhapsodic recollections:

> It was like an old-fashioned candy store, and he had these roasting machines. Oh, the smell of roasting peanuts! It was just a kid's heaven. I'd spend all day there eating candy and peanuts and drinking sodas. There were people coming in all the time buying bags of hot-roasted peanuts or popcorn. Uncle Duncan had all different kinds, hot-roasted peanuts in the shell, out of the shell, sugar-covered, chocolate-covered, caramel-covered, you name it. It was absolute heaven!

While the quiet, reserved Duncan counted on The Peanut Shoppe to captivate his nieces and nephews, Kathryn needed no props. Her dynamic personality naturally commanded attention, and her warmth and caring drew people to her. Those qualities—and the cooking skill she began honing as a teenager—left a lasting impression on Polly, the daughter of Kathryn's brother, Earl:

> Aunt Kathryn liked to cook, especially on Sundays after church. . . . I remember mashed potatoes and fried chicken, all those normal comfort foods. And you never went to Aunt Kathryn's house for dinner that she didn't have homemade dessert. . . . She made a blackberry cobbler that was the best thing, and she baked a coconut cake that only Debby and Patty have mastered since. When you spent the night with Aunt Kathryn, you always got biscuits and gravy for breakfast. She was an excellent cook.

Being part of a close-knit family undoubtedly presented many opportunities for celebration, but the Hays realized that inevitably there would be other times when family members would encounter some of life's most painful and jarring experiences, and truly need each other. Such was the case with Jess Hay's cousin, Richard Bramblett, who suffered the bitter breakup of his marriage in 1959, but found—to his great comfort—that he could lean on those closest to him, and particularly on Betty Jo. When the dust settled,

Bramblett had custody of the couple's four children, but no independent means of caring
for them, so he quit his job and moved from Houston to Forney to live with his mother,
Nora Roddy Bramblett. Recalling her as a "strong woman, good person, and excellent
mother," Bramblett said she and a maid cared for the children while he drove to Dallas
every day in search of work. Despite his diligence, though, he endured two months of dead
ends and discouragement before finally landing a job, and remembers that if not for Betty
Jo's friendship and support during that dry spell, he might very well have fallen into even
greater despair:

> I would get through looking for a job about 2:00 or 3:00, and almost every day
> I'd go by Jess's house. Jess and I were, and still are, very close, good friends; we kind
> of grew up together. So, on the way back to Forney, I'd stop off and chew the rag
> with Betty Jo. She was a great sounding board and sympathetic to what the hell
> happened and was a very, very receptive, honest, down-to-earth friend, and that
> was a great relief to me during that period of time.

Even after Bramblett found work he continued to see Betty Jo and Jess on a regular
basis, making no secret of the fact he now was interested in dating. Taking the cue, and
in a further show of support for Bramblett, Betty Jo embarked on a search for women she
thought might be suitable for him, including her cousin Judy Albert, who spent a good
deal of time at the Hay home in the 1950s. But though they enjoyed a number of dates
together, Judy and Richard were not destined to be, and in due course Patty Platt came
along. "For about that first year," said Bramblett, "Betty Jo introduced me to every available girl she knew in this town and Patty was the last one." Patty, as it happened, was a
close friend of Bill and Sally Brice. Sally and Patty were colleagues at DeGolyer and
McNaughton, a Dallas-based consulting firm serving the oil and gas industry, and Patty
was indeed eligible. It didn't take long for Betty Jo to arrange a blind date, and shortly
thereafter, in December 1961, Richard and Patty were married. Judy Albert, meanwhile,
went on to marry Ernest Hooter and, after brief stays in Dallas and Atlanta, she and her
family moved to Houston.

The Bramblett-Platt union wasn't Betty Jo's first foray into matchmaking, nor
was it her only success. She actually had been instrumental in bringing Sally Sutton and
Bill Brice together not long after Brice's first marriage ended in divorce. Sally had been
Betty Jo's sorority sister, and Brice was a good friend to both Betty Jo and Jess. Hay said
it was while he and Betty Jo lived on Milton Avenue in University Park that Brice called

148

one evening and suggested a game of bridge at the Hays' home, provided they could find a fourth player:

> Betty Jo said, "I've got just the person." She called Sally who knew Bill had been married. Sally was very much a Victorian, and so she said, "I'd love to play bridge, but I'm not going to have a date with Bill Brice. He's older and been married, and I'm just not going to do it." I said, "Betty Jo, let me talk to Sally." So I said, "Sally, this is just a bridge game; it's not a date. I'll pick you up, and I'll take you home, if you wish." She said, "Fine, on that basis I'll come." So, we played bridge and about halfway through the game that evening Bill and Betty Jo got up to go to the restroom and Sally leaned over to me and said in a very low voice, "You don't need to take me home tonight." From that moment on, she and Bill were an item, and it wasn't long thereafter when they were married. And then they became our close friends as a couple.

Some of the most vital friendships the Hays formed during this period came from the tight-knit community at Ridgewood Park Methodist Church. Besides "the group," Hay fondly recalls the fellowship he and Betty Jo shared with scores of other church members, and particularly with the young adults of the church who were part of their Sunday school classes and youth groups. "We developed very strong and typically lasting relationships with many of the church's young men and women, including Erin Barger; Becky and Eric Binion; Jean Charles; Annie and Bill Dippel; Terry Graham; Beth Ann and Susan Harmon; Bruce, Neil, and John Harris; Jan, Susan, and Larry Hopkins; Ellwood Jones, Jr.; Betty Kenner; Alicia Lancaster; Linda Lefan; Mack Lewis; Kimberly and Michelle McCormick; Ron and Sheree McVey; Diane, Russell, Jim, and K. C. Miller; Jane and Otto Morris; Susan, JoEllen, and Mary Frances Pittman; Ilona Rakentine; Wick, Spence, Priscilla, and Susanna Shytles; Leslie and Kevin Smith; Randy Squibb; Sarah and Dan Stultz; Julie and Robert Thomas; Karen Wisler; Jim Yeager; and a host of others who were active in one or more of the church's youth programs," said Hay. "Together with our daughters and their other delightful friends, this outstanding group of teenagers added a zestful spirit to our lives, and all of them reinforced our instinctive optimism and faith in the future."

But there was one young man in particular—Dennis Barger—who stood out among the crowd. "Dennis was very precocious," his twin sister Erin Barger Orgeron remembers, "and he was very intelligent. He was a National Merit Scholarship Finalist." Betty Jo and Jess first met Dennis when he was in the seventh grade, and even at that young age, Hay said they noted and appreciated his unusual qualities:

> He was . . . the brightest star in an outstanding group of kids who were active in the youth program. . . . Dennis, even then, was the one on whom you always could depend. He was a leader. He was bright. He loved people and people loved him.

The Hays' admiration for the brightest star in the youth group's constellation led to an enduring friendship. "During his high school years Dennis and Jess bonded quite a bit . . . and Betty Jo, also," said Erin. "They felt Dennis was like a son to them; the son they didn't have. So, their relationship got closer." When Dennis graduated from high school and moved to New Hampshire to attend Dartmouth College, his relationship with the Hays did not diminish. If anything, it deepened. "Every Christmas when Dennis and I came home for the holidays from school, we'd go see Betty Jo and Jess," said Erin. "Dennis, more often than I did, because they became closer and closer." She said a dinner invitation to the Hays' home invariably included long "discussions with Betty Jo and Jess about the things Dennis was studying and how he felt and how they felt. So they bonded even more closely." Likely on the table for discussion during those days would have been Dennis's college philosophy courses, which, Erin said, had prompted her brother to examine and reconsider his religious convictions. They also wrestled with the fundamental questions of existence, recalls Hay:

> I remember his trips home and his sharing with us his deepening struggle with questions of life, death, and destiny. His doubts, his faith, his unfaith, his hopes, his despair, and, again, his faith.

Over the next several years, Dennis's quest for answers would continue, as would the Hays' affection and admiration for this young man whom they considered quite remarkable.

The nature of Jess and Betty Jo's relationship with Dennis Barger reflected their ability to establish and maintain a wide array of friendships. Their welcoming, non-judgmental ways attracted a broad spectrum of associations and enabled them to engage effectively in compassionate outreach and up-close, personal, one-on-one philanthropy throughout the rest of their lives.

But as much as Betty Jo and Jess valued family and friends, their core commitment was to each other. "One thing I always knew about my parents," said Patty Hay, "which was obvious to me and Debby and also to our friends, was that they were very much in love and very affectionate." It was true, said Patty's close friend, Michelle McCormick—the uniqueness of Jess and Betty Jo's relationship was indeed noticeable, and did set them apart from other couples she knew:

> Their relationship was different from most other parents. . . . They truly were soul mates; they loved each other and they were affectionate and they played together. I noticed that my parents and many of the other parents of my friends had very stereotypical . . . gender relationships, where the men were in charge and the women didn't say that much; they took care of the kitchen and the kids and the laundry. . . . But Betty Jo and Jess were different. . . . They had an egalitarian relationship as lovers and friends during a time in history when couples didn't relate that way, not where I came from.

Evidence of that relatively rare relationship surfaced on many occasions, but one moment, in particular, has remained with McCormick since it happened years ago on one of the many nights she spent at the Hays' home with Patty. The two girls were watching television in the den while Betty Jo and Jess were eating a late dinner in the kitchen. "At one point, the lights were turned off in the kitchen, and we heard them coming down the hall," said McCormick. "As they walked by the den, we could see them holding hands and giggling like kids. They had a champagne bottle with them, and they were heading back to their bedroom."

These playful moments not only were manifestations of a truly loving relationship between two people, but they also added an uncommon dimension to Jess and Betty Jo's world. That is to say, they experienced a sense of genuine togetherness, a phenomenon Hay describes as "a meshing of our lives. . . . What I wanted to accomplish in life was richly and deeply enhanced by my relationship with Betty Jo. And I think the same probably was true of her. It was a matter of learning together and doing together. There is strength in community, and we discovered that *together*, as well. . . . I did not perceive any limit to what we might accomplish."

Jess and Betty Jo's love for one another expanded the boundaries of their lives, allowing them to function at a visibly higher level, and providing an example, perhaps, of what Chinese philosopher Lao Tzu meant when he said: "Being deeply loved by someone gives you strength, while loving someone deeply gives you courage."

During these years, Jess Hay was directing large amounts of energy toward his legal career and getting equally good results. Under the guidance of and with encouragement from his firm's law partners, Gene Locke, Maurice Purnell, Ben Boren, Jim Laney, Stanley Neely, Harold Pressley, Jack Harris, Wayne Woodruff, Charles Purnell, Gordon Fogg, John Louis "Tiny" Shook, and Al Aikman; aided by the sage advice of Frank McCullough (Locke, Purnell's senior associate); and of Myrtle Satterfield (the firm's office manager and unofficial keeper of its cherished cultural, professional, and intellectual traditions); and patiently assisted by Barbara Skinner, Roberta Mullinix, and Doris Halliburton, three very dedicated and experienced legal secretaries, Hay quickly developed into an attorney with a particular affinity for and proficiency in matters related to eminent domain, real estate, contract, corporate, and securities law.

In 1958, with prompting from Locke, twenty-seven-year-old Hay accepted a job as corporate secretary and legal counsel of Dallas Tank Company, a steel tank manufacturer, where Locke served on the board. Later that year, when the company merged with the slightly smaller Trinity Steel Company, Hay prepared the necessary legal documentation and stayed on as the merged company's corporate secretary and legal counsel, and later as one of its directors. The end result for Hay was an intensive education in corporate governance and exposure to a wide range of corporate legal matters, not to mention access to important business and social friendships. Among those friendships was Trinity Steel's young CEO, W. Ray Wallace, and his wife, Virginia, as well as other members of the Trinity board and their spouses. The company eventually would change its name to Trinity Industries, Inc. and be remembered by Jess as a crucial stepping stone in his career:

> My corporate practice began to broaden our relationships, and it was fun. I seem to
> have had an aptitude for that kind of work, and I really enjoyed it. . . . That led to
> my doing a number of securities transactions . . . which prepared me for the advent
> of Wallace Properties, and thereafter, that corporation became the focus of much
> of my legal work.

Indeed, Hay's opportunities increased substantially in 1959 when he was asked by Locke to help prepare the legal structure for a company Locke and other prominent Dallas businessmen were organizing. The new venture's principal focus was to be three-fold: land development, investments in and management of commercial real estate, and short-term real estate lending. Former Republic National Bank senior vice president E. E. (Gene) Wallace—*no relation to W. Ray Wallace*— was chosen to serve as president and chief

152

The November-December 1959 cover of SMU's alumni magazine, *Mustang,* featured the Hays, a family in progress: "Former and future Mustangs . . ." Jess, Debby, and Betty Jo. At the time, Jess was applying his legal education as a practicing attorney, and Betty Jo was experimenting and expanding her skills as mother and professional homemaker.

executive officer, and Gene Locke was designated as the first chairman of the company, which initially was named Wallace Properties, Inc. As for Hay, by this time he had earned the unqualified confidence of Gene Locke—and of many of the other investors as well—thereby securing for himself a place on the board and the role of legal counsel and corporate secretary.

One of Hay's early 1959 assignments was to prepare a public offering of securities for Wallace Properties, which called for him to make his first—and never to be forgotten—trip to New York City:

> New York was so different from anything I previously had seen, and the quality of the hotels and restaurants was beyond my imagining. I was awestruck by the theater district and the thousands of people who gathered there each evening. The city had a vibrancy I had not encountered before. . . . Not only did it open new vistas in terms of experiences but, more importantly, it expanded our circle of relationships.

From that point forward, Hay traveled frequently between Dallas and New York and consequently began developing business friendships with prominent New York-based investment banking executives, as well as attorneys from prestigious firms.

And because he often included Betty Jo in his travels, she, too, was able to join what fast was becoming an urbane, cosmopolitan adventure. She accompanied him to New York for the first time in March 1960, and over the next forty years, to their great delight, they took many such trips—either by themselves, or with friends, business associates, their daughters, or other family members.

As for the dynamic New York City itself, it goes without saying that a first-time visit is nothing short of wondrous, but to experience one of the most fascinating cities in the world as the Hays did—from a five-star perspective—gave new meaning to their notion of opulence:

> We normally stayed either at the Pierre or the Carlyle. Both provided grand accom-modations and both . . . left Betty Jo and me literally overwhelmed by the incredibly high quality of their facilities and services. We particularly enjoyed the entertain-ment offered at the Cotillion Room of the Pierre (in our opinion, by far the finest nightclub in New York at the time) and the bar at the Carlyle, which featured Bobby Short at the piano. Other favorite haunts included the Persian Room of the Plaza; the "Upstairs at the Downstairs" and the "Downstairs at the Upstairs" both of

which offered critically acclaimed political satire; the Copacabana, at which we first heard Paul Anka sing some of his great compositions; the Monkey Bar which was a bit raunchy but fun; any one of perhaps ten or fifteen first-class French and Italian restaurants . . . although one of our favorite places was not upper-end at all . . . Mama Leone's in Lower Manhattan. . . . It was a happy time, and for a young lass from McAlester, Oklahoma and a young lad from Forney, Texas, it was high cotton indeed. Ours was emerging as a grander life than either of us ever had anticipated.

From its commencement in early August 1959, the organization and funding of Wallace Properties took about eleven months and finally culminated on June 29, 1960, with the closing of the company's underwritten public offering of securities consisting of common stock and 6-1/2% convertible subordinated debentures.

The company's successful launch was the product of extraordinary efforts by Gene Wallace, A. B. Cass, Jr., Eugene Locke, Trammell Crow, Henry C. Beck, Jr., and Ed Hoffman (six of the company's founders); and in addition to Jess Hay, by a number of others, including DeWayne Wommack, John Sexton, Lanelle Latendresse, Pete Scarborough, and Harold Crossen (the company's initial officers); Joe Stalcup (who by then was a Locke, Purnell associate and who assisted Hay on related legal matters); Ned Harris (who arranged insurance coverages required in connection with the offering); Hope Hamilton (at the time, Trammell Crow's principal accounting officer); Bill Tucker and Sam Pryor III of Davis Polk (the New York law firm which provided legal counsel to Harriman, Ripley and Co., Incorporated, the investment banking firm which underwrote the company's public offering); and Stuart Silloway and Procter Winter (president and senior vice president, respectively, of the underwriter).

The closing was celebrated "Wallace-style." That is, lavishly. It took place in New York City, where, at Wallace's invitation, the named participants and some of their spouses—including Betty Jo, Nancy Stalcup, and LeAnn Harris—attended the closing and participated in the related fanfare. True to character, the colorful Gene Wallace acknowledged his colleagues' hard work in grand fashion, freezing in time a moment in Jess and Betty Jo's life best described as an expansive encounter.

"Gene Wallace provided . . . the largest suite at the Pierre Hotel for Betty Jo, LeAnn, Ned, and me," said Hay. "The suite, which included three bedrooms, a dining room, a large living room, a grand piano, and a large balcony overlooking Central Park, had been used by Elizabeth Taylor just prior to our arrival." When asked about their accommodations years later, Ned Harris could barely contain his utter astonishment:

My God, the entry hall was as big as my office! The living room was huge. The bedrooms were fabulous. The dining room and kitchen were unbelievable. And the patio overlooking Central Park—God almighty! We *were* in tall cotton.

During their five or six days in New York on that occasion, Betty Jo and Jess enjoyed sharing evenings at the theater and at various night spots with Nancy, Joe, LeAnn, and Ned. It was, remembered Nancy Stalcup, "great fun and very exciting."

Soon Betty Jo and Jess found the good life of New York spilling over into Dallas and presenting them with a fresh, new reality. "We began to realize," said Hay, "that we were moving into a dimension of life that we had never even thought about." With Hay's increasingly lucrative legal career, he and Betty Jo now had the financial resources to upgrade their standard of living. However, they responded to prosperity with reasonable restraint and in 1961, when they decided to move to a larger home, Hay said they intentionally selected one in the same general neighborhood—on Annapolis Lane—in order to remain close to their friends and Ridgewood Park Methodist Church:

> It was a bigger house. . . . It featured four bedrooms, a full den, a living room, a separate dining room, and three bathrooms. . . . Our kids were getting bigger. So, we needed a little more space. At the same time . . . we wanted to stay near the church. After the relocation, we spent nine very happy years in our new home at 6341 Annapolis.

The restraint they showed in selecting their new residence was meant neither as a criticism of American consumer culture nor as a rebuke of the fundamental assumptions of their consuming peers. In fact, Jess and Betty Jo's perspective supported the conclusion that stewardship of God's material and financial blessings did not demand austerity, but rather encouraged the use of those blessings by those who had worked for them, as well as in the service of others.

With that, the Hays began to enhance their new environment by utilizing what, in the past, might have been considered unnecessary extravagances. To begin with, they engaged the services of an interior designer and replaced most of their previous furniture, bringing an end to the days on Fisher Road when Betty Jo, to save money, simply would have spruced up the old chairs by reupholstering them. They also had professional landscaping done to transform the exterior of their new home.

Around this time the Hays joined Lakewood Country Club, adding yet another

156

dimension to their rapidly-changing world. Susan Pittman Wilson, one of Debby's best friends and a next door neighbor on Fisher Road, remembers those country club days with great fondness, especially "hanging out at the club swimming pool during the summer. They had an outdoor grill where we'd order cheeseburgers, drinks, and ice cream bars. My sister JoEllen, Debby, Patty, and I didn't go out to eat much back then, so ordering lunch from the grill was sort of a big deal."

And although the move upward did not diminish old friendships, former neighbor Jerry Pittman said there was no getting around the fact that Betty Jo and Jess had made an extraordinary ascent. "Everyone kind of started out the same economically in these smallish houses like the ones on Fisher Road, and then, boy, Jess is taking off with the law practice, and they moved to Annapolis." Betty Jo's cousin, David Albert, describes the advancement of Jess Hay's professional career during this period of time as a "very fast track, meteoric rise. Over the course of about seven years, their station in life had changed significantly, from hardworking, poor newlyweds to—made it."

As Hay's career gathered momentum, there arrived on the scene a person who not only would prove instrumental to his future business success, but also would play a key role in the life of the Hay family. Ramona Taylor—hired as a legal secretary by the Locke, Purnell law firm—was assigned to work for Jess Hay in January 1962. Viewed from forty-plus years hence, Hay recalls Ramona's arrival as "a great day":

> Ramona Taylor has been a vital part of my career and a close friend of our family for more than 45 years. As those years passed, she not only served my needs but also worked with Betty Jo, and even with our two daughters, on various projects, trips, events, etc. Of course, Ramona's daughter, Cheryl Watson, along with Sue Bishop, Carol Brabham, Anita Coyle, Gwen Ferrell, Donna Henderson, Lorraine Grant, Sylvia Ivy, Judy Justice, Heidi Kirkpatrick, Blanche Kline, Jeanne McDonald, Lori Moody, Loma Rayburn, Rebecca Rooney, Nita Swafford, Betty Watson, Joy Weldon, Cynthia Wiler, Valerie Woodward, Tricia Zimmerman, and numerous others have contributed much along the way.

> But from 1962 on, Ramona has been the coordinator and principal source of our administrative support. She also has been a wonderful and loyal friend to Betty Jo and me, and indeed our entire family. Our careers and public outreaches have been significantly enhanced by Ramona's presence and by her helping hand. The fact is that for decades, Ramona, in every material respect, has been a member of our family.

Within the first year of Taylor's employment at Locke, Purnell, reliance upon
her skills grew as Wallace Investments, Inc.—the former Wallace Properties—began to
founder. By mid-1963 the company's future was in jeopardy following a downturn in the
real estate market which had begun to impair profitability. Further complicating matters
was ineffective management. Still, Gene Locke and other major stockholders believed
the company could turn itself around with the right leadership, so they called on Jess Hay
to analyze the situation and recommend possible solutions.

During the next few months, and assisted by the gifted and diplomatic Taylor, as
well as by three very talented and concerned officers of Wallace Investments—M. D.
Wommack, Lanelle Latendresse, and John Sexton—Hay produced a suggested strategic
direction and specific tactics which, if implemented, he believed would get the company
back on course. His proposals, although not immediately adopted by the company's
management, did earn Hay increased credibility among the company's directors and also its
creditors. On September 27, 1965, as a result of his patience, diligence, effectiveness, and
leadership during that trying time, the board elected thirty-four-year-old Jess Hay president
and chief executive officer of the company, which by then had been renamed Lomas &
Nettleton Financial Corporation.

Though he could not know it at the time, Hay's departure from Locke, Purnell,
and indeed, from the practice of law altogether, represented a decisive turning point in the
life of his family. Soon, Hay said, he and Betty Jo would begin to experience the far-reaching effects brought on by this critical shift from corporate law to corporate management:

> Our vista was broadened and the entry into the securities and corporate field
> ultimately changed the course of our lives. . . . It led in 1965 to my departure from
> the practice of law and to my becoming the chief executive officer of a diversified
> financial services company. That move, in turn, had a positive and significant
> impact on our lives and in a variety of ways contributed to our joint efforts to serve
> various public causes, most of which related to children, social justice, politics,
> mental health, medical care and research, public education, higher education, and
> women's rights.

Lomas & Nettleton Financial Corporation grew and prospered under Hay's leadership, and because of his position as the chief executive of a major corporation, Betty Jo was able to gain greater visibility and a larger platform from which to conduct public outreach and build political support. With her daughters getting older and growing more independent, Betty Jo's involvement in civic affairs expanded considerably, invigorated by the dramatic social upheaval and turmoil that was to define the late 1960s.

PHOTOGRAPH ALBUM

3

JUNE 1955

through

SEPTEMBER 1965

Ridgewood Park United Methodist Church, Dallas, was the Hay family church from June 1955 to 1970.

Betty Jo, Jess, and Debby, 33 months, have a Galveston vacation. Summer 1955.

The Albert siblings: Carl, Earl, Kathryn, Noal (also known as Budge), and Homer. McAlester, Oklahoma, 1956.

Jess Hay's only sibling, Patsy Hay, was with Betty Jo in her last three months of pregnancy with her second daughter, who was named after Patsy. Circa 1956.

Debby and recently arrived Patricia Lynn Hay, share a sisterly moment in 1957. Lovingly called Patty, she was born October 26, 1956.

Patty attended by Ella Washington in the backyard of the Hay home on Fisher Road. Spring 1957.

In July 1957 the Hay family, on their way home from South Fork, Colorado, stopped in Mangum, Oklahoma to visit members of the Albert family. The photograph includes Kathy Albert, Nancy Albert, Betty Jo holding Patty, Doris Albert holding Polly Albert, and Debby. The cabin visited in Colorado was owned by Jo and Roy Guffey, parents of Jerry Pittman, who was next door neighbor of the Hays on Fisher Road.

Judy and Anne Albert, Betty Jo's cousins, at
their home in Wichita, Kansas. August 1958.

Mac and Ina McCormick, Ned and LeAnn Harris, Jess and Betty Jo, and Brownie Shytles
on an outing to Eagle Mountain Lake. August 1957. Photograph by R. W. Shytles.

Debby with Lewis and M.C. Sweet at the Hay home on
Fisher Road. Circa 1959.

Sallie Duncan (Aunt Sadie), Betty Jo's paternal great-aunt,
in the Peacock home on Milton. Circa 1959.

Nancy Ellen, Susan, Richard, Jr., and Paul Bush
in Dallas, ready to return with their parents to
Hong Kong and then back to Taiwan. Circa 1960.

The Hay family: Patty, Jess, Debby, and Betty Jo. 1960.

Enjoying a dinner outing in Dallas on the eve of the Bush's departure for Hong Kong. John and Martha Binion, Ned and LeAnn Harris,
Jess and Betty Jo, Dick and Mary Bush, and Harold and Juanita Smotherman. Circa 1960.

Ned and LeAnn Harris, Betty Jo and Jess were in Fort Worth
for the rodeo. Front row: Debby Hay, Bruce and Neil Harris,
and Patty Hay. Winter 1961.

Patty with Harold and Juanita Smotherman in
the living room of the Hay home on Annapolis
Lane. Christmas 1961.

The Hay residence from June 6, 1961 to June 6, 1970 was at 6341 Annapolis Lane, Dallas.

A family gathering in Oklahoma. Beginning at back, left to right: Earl and Doris Albert, Jess Hay, Duncan Peacock, Merle Williams, Budge Albert, Kathy Albert, Judy Albert, Betty Albert, Betty Jo Hay, Kathryn Peacock, Myrtle Williams, Carl and Mary Albert, Mary Frances Albert, Patty Hay, Polly Albert, Nancy Albert, Debby Hay, and David Albert. 1962.

Jess and Betty Jo step out at dance club. 1962.

On a vacation trip to Washington, D.C., staying with Mary and Carl Albert, there was an opportunity to meet President John Fitzgerald Kennedy. Betty Jo, Jess, and Debby Hay, David Albert, Carl Albert, and Patty Hay. Mike Mansfield, then Majority Leader of the U.S. Senate, in background. July 1963.

Patty, front row center, with a few of her good friends and classmates at
Dan D. Rogers Elementary School, Dallas. Circa 1963.

Debby, front row, third from left, with some of her closest friends at
Dan D. Rogers Elementary School, Dallas, Circa 1964.

Dick, Nancy, Mary, and Susan Bush in Dallas on leave from their mission assignment in Taiwan. Circa 1964.

Judy Albert and Ernest Hooter's wedding in Dallas. Kathryn Peacock, Jim Theakston, Anne Albert, Betty and
Budge Albert, Judy Albert, Ernest Hooter, Carl Albert, Debby Hay, Betty Jo, Patty Hay, and Jess.
The Reverend Wallace Chappell officiated. December 12, 1964.

Patty, 8 years, Betty Jo, and Debby, 12 years, at the Annapolis house, Dallas. Easter 1965.

Betty Jo, back row, with the cousins Bramblett: Patty, holding
Amy, and Richard. Front row: Richard, Jr., Nancy, Sandra,
and Linda, with Debby Hay on the end. Backyard of the
Hay home on Annapolis Lane. 1965.

At the Hay home on Annapolis Lane. Judy and Ernest Hooter, Myrtle Hay, Debby, Betty Jo, and Eileen Finley, the daughter of the next door neighbor. Circa 1965.

Mac and Ina McCormick, Jerry Pittman, Betty Jo, and Myrtle Hay at the Hay home on Annapolis Lane. Circa 1965.

Debby with Rebecca and Charles Sweet at their home in Dallas. Summer 1965.

CHAPTER
4

OCTOBER 1965
through
DECEMBER 1970

Betty Jo continued to focus her attention on family and friends during the last half of the sixties. Among the Hays' growing circle of friends were David Farr, hired in 1967 as the new youth minister at Ridgewood Park Methodist Church, and his wife, Sondra. "They took us in right away, and included us in social activities that went beyond the church and the youth program," said Sondra. In fact, the Farrs soon found themselves sharing after-church lunches with the Hay family, attending weekend parties—during which, David recalls they "had some scotches together"—and occasionally babysitting the Hay children when Betty Jo and Jess attended out-of-town business functions. "It was really fun for us," said Sondra, "because Debby and Patty were just terrific."

The amount of time they spent together enabled Sondra to get a first-hand look at Betty Jo's skill as a mother, and she remembers liking what she saw:

> She was there for her girls. . . . She was the room mother, in the PTA, all of that, but she was also there when they came home, and they would talk to her. A lot of girls don't talk to their mothers. She was close to them and very supportive. She was proud of her girls and very realistic about them. She didn't think they were perfect. . . . They had a nice family life, which made you want to be around them. We enjoyed our time with the four of them, just as much as we did . . . with Jess and Betty Jo.

As Debby and Patty grew older and became more involved in school and teen activities, the need for close supervision by Betty Jo diminished. For her part, Debby found satisfaction in academic excellence and also tested her leadership skill on the junior high and high school drill teams where she served as a lieutenant, sharing responsibilities for choreography and training.

But it was journalism that opened the most important door for Debby. Early on at Hillcrest High School, she discovered an interest in writing—as well as the various other aspects of student newspaper production—and by the time she was a senior, Debby, with her proven leadership and organizational abilities, was appointed co-editor of the *Hillcrest Hurricane*. The *Hurricane's* legendary student newspaper advisor, Judy Jeffress, guided Debby throughout those years and played a vital role in her academic development. Jeffress not only provided exceptional instruction, but she also left on Debby a lasting impression which influenced her decision to pursue what would become a successful career in advertising, public relations, and marketing. "She was a superb teacher," said Debby. "Even though I majored in journalism in college, I probably learned more from her in those three years than I did from my university experience. . . . What she taught me really created the foundation for everything that came after that."

Outside of school Debby nurtured some of her closest friendships in a group known as Tri-Hi-Y, comprised of about fifteen girls who met once a week for fun, and to organize community service projects. She also enjoyed friendships through Ridgewood Park's Methodist Youth Fellowship under the direction of David Farr, assisted by his wife, Sondra, who recalls Debby's seriousness of purpose as one of her most striking characteristics. "Debby was very driven. She studied really hard. . . . She was always studying and wanted to excel and achieve." Indeed, during her senior year at Hillcrest High School, Debby's classmates acknowledged her dedication and reliability in the 1971 yearbook by naming her "Most Dependable" of the class.

Patty, meanwhile, had a different personality and other priorities altogether. "Patty was just adorable," remembers Sondra. "She was cute and funny and a cutup. Smart as a whip, but she wasn't as dedicated to structured education, shall we say, as Debby was." Even so, Patty did follow in some of her sister's footsteps by joining the drill team and working on the school newspaper. One of her greatest passions—at least for a time—was a palomino called Nugget, who came to Patty as a Christmas gift in 1970. When he first arrived, Nugget was boarded at Caruth Stables, conveniently located near the Hays' home, but eventually he was moved to the more desirable Harris farm in Sanger, Texas. Thirty-six years later Patty still remembers the wonder of waking up on that Christmas morning to find a golden-colored horse tied to a tree in her front yard:

> I had wanted a horse for years. Finally one Christmas, "Santa" brought one! Ned
> and LeAnn gave their son, John, an Appaloosa the same Christmas. Daddy and Ned
> went to the stables—across from NorthPark—early Christmas morning and rode
> them to our houses. It was soooo much fun, though Mom said it was years before
> the yard recovered in the area where Daddy had tied Nugget to a tree!

As she moved through her teen years, the Hays' younger daughter thrived on very close—and what were destined to become lifelong—friendships, among whom were JoEllen Pittman, Pat Haines, Juliette Zarafonetis, Michelle McCormick, and several others. She also indulged her broad love for animals by adopting a steady stream of pets: dogs, cats, hamsters, guinea pigs, baby ducks, and an aquarium full of fish. Betty Jo, who felt no fondness for such creatures, nevertheless suffered their presence in order to gratify her daughter's enthusiasm—except when it came to addressing Patty's favorite feline, "Ginger," by her given name. That's where Betty Jo drew the line, preferring instead the alternate and much more colorful, "THAT DAMN CAT!"

Patty's sense of compassion was one of her strong suits and she felt it not only where animals were concerned, but for people, as well. Consider the example of eight-year-old Juliette Zarafonetis. In 1963, Juliette and her family moved into the neighborhood, and as do most young newcomers, she found herself in an unfamiliar school, ostracized by the other children. Of those children, only one—Patty Hay—chose not to exclude her, but instead reached out and welcomed her. As it turned out, Patty made a friend with that simple gesture and, at the same time, left an indelible mark on her second grade classmate. "Patty Hay was the type of person who always picked up stray dogs and cats, and she picked me up, too," Zarafonetis said nearly forty-five years later.

Not surprisingly, Juliette and Patty's friendship led to a friendship between their mothers, Georgette and Betty Jo, and through Georgette, Betty Jo came to know Helen Shropulos, Helen Trapalis, Helen Yampanis, and Angel Pappas, all part of a cluster of Greek families living within the neighborhood, and each of whom welcomed the Hays' generous display of kindness. Soon, these new friends also became eager supporters of Betty Jo's political candidates, and when needed would spend hours at the Hays' home preparing campaign mailings. In looking back, Juliette remembers the call her mother inevitably would get from Betty Jo when a political race was underway and it was time to stuff envelopes. "Betty Jo would call her up and ask her to mobilize the Greek women in the neighborhood," she said.

As for the role Betty Jo was playing in her daughters' lives during this time, much of it revolved around their friendships and the importance she placed on those relationships. To encourage and strengthen Debby and Patty's relationships with their friends, Betty Jo did what she could to create a warm and welcoming environment. Juliette recalls that effort with great clarity, especially "Patty's movie birthday parties," and, she added, "I remember they took us all to see *Funny Girl*. They took us bowling. They had Halloween parties. The Hays were very family-oriented."

And no more so than when it came to relatives, as Ruth Ellen Peacock can attest. In 1967, Ruth Ellen—Edgar and Ruth Peacock's daughter—moved to Dallas to attend dental hygiene school at Baylor College of Dentistry and immediately became the grateful recipient of Hay family hospitality. While Ruth Ellen's official residence was a dormitory on campus, Betty Jo made sure she had a key to their home and an open invitation to use it frequently, which she did. "Whenever I wanted to stay out later than my dorm stayed open I spent the night at their house. That was wonderful." And like many others, Ruth Ellen found herself at the Hays' home during political campaigns. "I would go over a lot and stay with Debby and Patty and fix dinner while Betty Jo and Jess were out for the evening. I spent a lot of time there."

Meanwhile, cousins Kathy, Nancy, and Polly Albert—the daughters of Betty Jo's Uncle Earl and Aunt Doris—continued to exchange summer visits with Debby and Patty, traveling as they did between Dallas and McAlester, Oklahoma. Eventually, in 1970 when Kathy and Nancy were older, Jess found summer jobs for them in Dallas, including a position for Nancy at Ned Harris's insurance company:

> It was so much fun. We had a great time. Sometimes Kathy and I would meet downtown for lunch. . . . Jess is so fabulous. We'd get home and then we'd wait for him to get home from work and we'd all sit together in the conversation pit and talk. He would ask us about our day. He was so involved in what we were doing and what happened that day. . . . We wouldn't have dinner until 9:00 or 9:30 because we were having such a great time talking. . . . It is a . . . sweet memory for me.

Kathryn and Duncan Peacock also were regular guests at the Hays' house, which allowed Betty Jo's daughters the privilege of knowing their grandparents just as she had known hers. "We saw them very frequently and they were always a major factor in our lives," said Debby Hay Spradley. "My grandmother was my role model in terms of a

businesswoman and someone that worked very hard. . . . She was a great lady and a
real loving . . . person to be around." Debby recalls her grandfather, Duncan, with equal
affection. "He was the sweetest man on the planet, the kindest, nicest person in the
world."

■

In the late 1960s, Kathryn and Duncan experienced a substantial transition in their
lives. Earlier in the decade—with an eye toward retirement—they had built a house at
Lake Eufaula, located on Albert family farmland eight miles north of McAlester. However,
when 1968 came around and Duncan had an opportunity to sell The Peanut Shoppe and
move to the lakefront house, Kathryn, who was only fifty-five, announced she had no desire
at that time to leave an immensely satisfying career as a partner in R. M. Noblitt's cotton
company. The couple ultimately compromised, fashioning an arrangement which each
found satisfactory. As a result, they sold their home in University Park, Kathryn moved
into Jess and Betty Jo's guest room, and Duncan—an avid outdoorsman who loved to fish
and work outside—took up residence in Oklahoma. Kathryn began working a Monday
through Thursday schedule at Noblitt which enabled her to commute to the lake house on
weekends. But Duncan soon discovered he wasn't particularly suited to a life of lazing
around, so he found himself a job as a rural mail carrier in the McAlester area. To further
challenge his prodigious work ethic, he strung together a regimen of additional activities,
describing for Kathryn in this 1969 letter some of the strenuous pleasures of country living:

> I came home today [from my rural postal delivery route] and tried to dig out the
> front ditch so it would drain. It drained pretty good but the ditch going down the
> hill will have to be opened up some also. I went down to the water tank and pulled
> all I could get of that growth off the water. It will grow back but I will keep the
> runners pulled out so it will not take over the tank. It was a big job.

In addition to resolving issues of the land, Duncan's pastoral lifestyle included
raising calves, which occasionally required the employment of rudimentary veterinary skills:

> We had a calf with the pink eye and warts over in the Duran pasture. So Earl
> [Albert] and I vaccinated him yesterday afternoon and wormed another one that has
> been dragging around lately. . . . Then after I got home, I mowed our front and

back yard. The Bermuda had gotten about 6-inches high.

Whether cattle ranching—albeit on a modest scale—or tending to the needs of his property, Duncan Peacock clearly had raised the bar on the nature of retirement, and when he began dabbling in winemaking, the bar went still higher. Drawing on the resourcefulness and determination he'd shown throughout his life, Duncan succeeded at planting a grape-producing vineyard, processing the fruit, and bottling the product under none other than the *Duncan Peacock* label, and in so doing distinguished himself as a retiree extraordinaire.

During this time, portions of the correspondence from Duncan to Kathryn reveal his deep love for her and his appreciation for what she meant to him and others:

> Apparently, you had a nice Mother's Day today. That is great and you deserved it too. You are one of the most devoted mothers and grandmothers that ever lived and you deserve all the attention and affection that is bestowed upon you at any time. . . . Remember, I think of you many times everyday and wish you were with me. From the bottom of my heart—Love, Duncan.

Betty Jo and the Hay family also held a special place in Duncan's heart which he expressed in this 1969 letter to Kathryn:

> I certainly did enjoy seeing Betty and Jess and the children today very, very much. They give me a lift every time I see them. Kinda like fresh air. I wouldn't trade having them and being close to them for anything in the world. They're certainly wonderful people. Of course you knew that already, but I wanted you to know that I had kinda noticed it too. Betty Jo was always the most wonderful little girl in the world to me.

Duncan's continued affection for Betty Jo played out in numerous ways, particularly through the generosity he displayed toward her daughters. When it came to the lake house, for instance, he purchased a motorboat with enough horsepower to pull his grandchildren, nieces, and nephews on water skis, a further statement of Duncan's passion for family, fishing, and the outdoors. "He bought a boat and named it *The Dan Dan,* which is what we called him," explained Patty. "The name came from Debby. She was trying to say granddad and it came out Dan Dan. They thought it was cute so it stuck, and it suited him. Everybody called him Dan Dan, all my friends, all Debby's friends."

While the late 1960s provided Betty Jo with many opportunities for family together-ness, it goes without saying those years also bore the imprint of serious bridge playing. Betty Jo's enthusiasm for the game, as well as for her close friendships, coalesced around a monthly bridge club which was formed in 1968 and met regularly throughout the balance of her life. Co-founders Peggy (Smith) Pittman and Shirley (McVey) Lassiter organized the group, and when they invited Betty Jo to join, she eagerly accepted, thereby becoming a founding member. In addition to Peggy, Shirley, and Betty Jo, the club's long-term mem-bers included Katherine Bauer, Claire Brainin, Pat Dippel, Bobbie Dixon, M. C. Guilloud, Margie Harmon, Bobbie Hopkins, Bobbie McCann, Charlene Miller, Jerry Pittman, and Joanne Turner. They fondly referred to themselves as *The Esteemed First Tuesday Bridge Club*—or simply as "the gang"—and absences from their monthly gatherings were rare.

The women played three-table duplicate bridge, described by Peggy Pittman as more competitive and challenging than the "party" bridge to which most of the women were accustomed. All the better for Betty Jo. She loved the high-intensity game and the friendships that propelled it. "It was a big part of our lives," Peggy said. "We all had kids in school, and we got to know each others' families, at least through conversations. We started meeting at 9:30 and we'd get through in time to be home by 3:00 because that's when the kids got out of school." Over time, the bond between these women intensified, growing especially tight in subsequent years when Betty Jo sponsored bridge club junkets to her vacation home in Acapulco, Mexico. On the rare occasion when a member was unable to attend, she normally would be replaced by one of the club's regular substitutes, either Patty Bramblett, Rand Sale, Pat Smiley, or Nancy Stalcup.

Yet beyond the bridge games, the easy days at the lake house, and caring for their two daughters, Jess and Betty Jo's political involvement remained ever in the wings, and would escalate in early 1968. It began in 1965 when President Lyndon Johnson rewarded Eugene Locke's friendship, dependability, talent, and loyalty with two ambassadorial appointments: first to Pakistan, then to South Vietnam. However, as prestigious as those assignments were, they didn't satisfy Locke's personal political aspirations, so in January 1968 he resigned from the Department of State and returned to Dallas to run for Texas governor. Given the close bond between Betty Jo and Jess Hay and Adele and Gene Locke, it was all but certain the Hays would play important roles within the campaign.

The first order of business was to make up for Locke's late start in the spring primary campaign. To that end, and with the goal of introducing himself to Texas voters, Locke wisely took the advice and counsel of Liener Temerlin—then a partner of Dallas-based

178

**Eugene Locke
should be Governor
of Texas.**

Words & Music

The Eugene Locke campaign for Governor of Texas in 1968 was serious, but it had lighter moments as well. The political jingle *Eugene Locke should be Governor of Texas* was an important element in a public relations initiative that resonated long after dust of the campaign settled. Reproduced are the cover and the sheet music of the campaign song.

Glenn Advertising Agency—who suggested Locke blanket the state with a catchy jingle that voters might take to. Temerlin's clever strategy got the desired result, and Locke, who entered the race as a relative unknown, soon began to enjoy considerable statewide attention. In fact, the jingle which launched his campaign was so catchy that, if asked today, people still can sing it: *Eugene Locke should be governor of Texas; the governor of Texas should be Eugene Locke.* Patty claims even the campaign workers of one of Locke's primary opponents, Preston Smith, were humming the song at their headquarters. "The significance of that radio jingle," said Hay, "was that it moved Gene's name recognition among Texans, in just three weeks, from less than two percent to over eighty-five percent."

It also fueled the energies of core campaign workers such as Betty Jo and Jess. Jess not only became campaign finance chairman, but he also wrote some speeches, and—along with Charles Purnell and Trammell Crow—served as one of Locke's personal advisors. Crow, in addition to being Locke's close friend and personal confidant, was by far the most generous financial contributor to the campaign. But finances and campaigning aside, the genuine, all-around effort made on behalf of Locke's candidacy brought about a deepened friendship between Margaret and Trammell Crow and the Hays, a relationship that would endure throughout the remainder of Betty Jo's life and beyond.

As the campaign progressed, Betty Jo put her expert organizational and speaking skills to use, recruiting volunteers and coordinating campaign tasks. Sondra Farr, who worked at the Dallas headquarters as an office manager, remembers the degree of enthusiasm and leadership Betty Jo brought to the job:

> Betty Jo was very involved. She made speeches at events and organized the women volunteers. . . . I remember going to teas and Betty Jo would get up and tell why she endorsed Eugene Locke. She was a terrific speaker. Very convincing. She had a personal relationship with Adele and Eugene Locke and that came through.

Gene Locke's quest for the governorship of Texas was the first big campaign in which the Hay children and their neighborhood friends were old enough to participate. As such, it made for an exceptional introduction into the world of politics, giving Patty's friend Michelle McCormick good reason to remember it distinctly. "One of the most exciting times in our childhood was when Betty Jo and Jess did the Eugene Locke campaign," McCormick said. At the all-important kickoff rally, Betty Jo enlisted the help of Debby and several of her ninth grade friends who were part of the school drill team, the Franklin Falconettes. They were to perform a high-kick drill routine to the tune of the

Eugene Locke campaign song. Said younger sister, Patty: "They called themselves the *Lockettes*. It was really cute."

Eleven-year-old Patty and her friends, meanwhile, unleashed their own brand of campaign enthusiasm on the customers at nearby shopping centers. "On Saturdays, my friends and I would make these goofy *Locke for Governor* posters which we drew ourselves and wore like sandwich signs at shopping centers," she laughed. "We'd go to Hillside Village and Medallion Center and ask people, 'May we put a bumper sticker on your car?' It seems hokey now when you think about it, but it was a lot of fun and quite effective at the time."

Unfortunately, the Locke campaign failed to energize Democratic Party regulars, who chose instead to go with the incumbent Lieutenant Governor and eventual primary winner, Preston Smith. In the end—catchy jingle and professional advertising notwith-standing—Locke finished fifth in a field of ten, slightly behind another gubernatorial candidate, Dolph Briscoe, who came in fourth. Briscoe's finish, however, was duly noted by Betty Jo and Jess who were impressed with him as a candidate, and with his campaign. A few years later, that powerful impression would lead to Jess and Betty Jo's heavy involve-ment in yet another campaign—one that would land Dolph Briscoe in the Texas Governor's Mansion and launch Betty Jo toward a dynamic career in volunteer service.

Dennis Barger continued to be a meaningful presence in Jess and Betty Jo's life. From the moment they first met him at the Ridgewood Park Methodist Church youth group, through the years that followed, their regard for this remarkable young man grew steadily. And it seemed Dennis affected others in much the same way. They simply found his charisma irresistible. "He stood out," said LeAnn (Harris) Solomon, recalling the times when, as a high school student, Dennis would baby-sit her children. "He was just one of those fine, handsome, talented young men who seemed to have it all together. He was very good with people. He had good people skills. . . . Jess and Betty Jo were crazy about him." Sondra Farr, who was close in age to Dennis, remembers he "was lots of fun and a very mature person who knew where he was going and what he wanted, a lot like Jess." But above all else, said David Farr, Dennis Barger was an easy person to love. "He was cool. . . . He was very bright and spirited. This was a guy who was always in high spirits. He was sort of an all-around American good guy, very personable. Dennis had an almost instant charm to him."

One who fell under the spell of that charm was Ruth Ellen Peacock, who met Dennis on a blind date in 1968. As it happened, Dennis recently had graduated from Dartmouth College in Hanover, New Hampshire, and had planned to attend law school, but first was required to fulfill his military obligation as a Marine fighter pilot. While still in flight school, he and a Marine buddy at one point traveled to Dallas on leave, and—as a matter of course—inquired of either his mother or Betty Jo about the availability of eligible young women for possible dates. When Ruth Ellen's name came up, Dennis placed the requisite call, and life as they knew it would never be the same. "He called and we chatted," Ruth Ellen remembers nearly forty years later. "Since I trusted Betty Jo, my roommate and I went out on a blind double-date. It was great. Dennis and I hit it off beautifully. It seems like he was in town on leave for a couple of weeks, and we saw each other almost every evening." By that time, Dennis and Ruth Ellen had fallen happily in love. What came next, she said, was a long-distance relationship punctuated by periodic visits when Dennis could take leave:

> We kept in touch. We were just bowled over with one another. I was twenty, and he was twenty-five. We knew a lot of the same people. Many of the people that I knew through Betty and Jess at Ridgewood Park had known Dennis forever. He would call every Sunday, and we would talk for about an hour. We also wrote letters and made cassette tapes and sent those back and forth. So our relationship developed quite naturally, and I felt like I knew him very well.

On the occasions when Dennis was able to make it home, he and Ruth Ellen often socialized with David and Sondra Farr. "They'd come over and we'd either make dinner or go out to dinner and a movie," said Sondra. "He was a terrific guy, and we were crazy about Ruth Ellen, too, so it was fun. They were very much in love."

Even so, an ominous and ever-present tension hung in the air during this time in Dennis and Ruth Ellen's relationship, namely, the raging war in Southeast Asia, which was at its peak in 1968. Dennis knew once he finished training as a fighter pilot he would be going to Vietnam, and as fate would have it, he received his orders to ship out in August of that year just as he and Ruth Ellen had begun discussing their engagement and marriage. Despite this disappointing turn of events, though, Sondra remembers everyone agreeing Ruth Ellen and Dennis were a beautiful match. "Betty Jo and Jess were thrilled because they loved both of them. Everybody was happy about it."

Dennis Barger, 1968, age 25. Before his death during the Vietnam War, Dennis—a Dartmouth College graduate and Marine fighter pilot—had hoped to marry Ruth Ellen Peacock, Betty Jo's cousin. From the time he was in the seventh grade, Dennis had been a special part of Jess and Betty Jo's life, whether through his involvement in the youth group at Ridgewood Park Methodist Church, or moments at the Hay home, where dinner time discussions often led to probing questions of destiny and faith.

Poised to face the harsh realities of the Vietnam War, Dennis was armed with his faith, which fortunately had seen him through years of struggling over what it meant to live a truly ethical life and other difficult moral questions. During those early years of his life—in addition to helpful discussions he'd had with Betty Jo and Jess—Dennis received the prudent counsel of Wally Chappell, who had served as his pastor in junior high and high school. Wally continued to guide Dennis during his college years at Dartmouth, and in a letter which would have a profound impact on Dennis, Wally explored the subject of faith. The letter became one of Dennis's most prized possessions, and as such, went with him to Vietnam.

Once there, Dennis was conflicted. It wasn't the carrying out of military orders he found so difficult, but rather the contradiction between his actions during combat and his own essential nature. Thus, as he flew bombing missions over Vietnam, his conscience required him to question the morality of what he was being asked to do. "Dennis was a peaceful, loving kid," said his sister, Erin Barger Orgeron. "He was not a fighter. He was too loving and too caring to be belligerent." Through it all, she said, Dennis stayed true to his principles and acted upon them when given the opportunity, like the time he spotted a group of Vietnamese children near his barracks:

> He informally adopted one little Vietnamese boy to make sure he had a safe place to sleep and food to eat. . . . It might have assuaged somewhat the way he felt about the bombs he was dropping every day, which weighed heavily on him. He had enormous questions about what was going on. . . . He began to feel the war was wrong. He saw so much atrocity. . . . Dennis did have grave doubts about the war, but he was very much a man of honor.

On November 11, 1968—three months after arriving in Vietnam—honor sent Dennis Barger to his death when enemy ground fire shot down the F-4 Phantom he was flying. Betty Jo got the news on a Saturday morning and called Jess, who was working at the office. Ramona Taylor took the call:

> I answered the phone and it was Betty Jo. She was sobbing and said she needed to speak to Jess. I ran down the hall and got him out of the conference room. . . . When he finished talking to her he stepped out of his office terribly upset. He told me Dennis Barger had been killed in Vietnam.

Patty was returning home from an overnight visit with a friend when she heard about Dennis. She remembers Betty Jo meeting her at the door, saying, "'Dennis has been killed,' and bursting into tears. . . . I went inside and could hear my Dad crying. It was the first time I ever saw my Dad cry."

On November 21, 1968, Jess Hay delivered a moving tribute to Dennis during a memorial service entitled, *Reflections On The Life Of Dennis Barger*. Among his memories, Hay included several that were wrenchingly personal:

> I remember the added sparkle in his eyes after he found "his girl," as he called Ruth, and how pleased I had been with his choice and what a great marriage I thought theirs was destined to be. . . . I remember also that I had invested great hope in Dennis; for I felt his prospects were without limit, and I thrilled vicariously in his evolving approach to life. In short, I remember that I loved Dennis as if he were my own son. . . .

In the eulogy, Hay imagined how Dennis might have responded to his own passing, and concluded he would have exhorted those remaining not to forsake their own continuing journeys. "He would challenge us to affirm the goodness of life . . . and encourage us to be alive, to pick up the pieces and proceed with *our* quest. . . ." Betty Jo and Jess responded by establishing the Phillip Dennis Barger Foundation in honor of their friend's life and memory, the contributions to which were used over the ensuing quarter century for the education of young men and women.

Following months of shock and mourning, Ruth Ellen Peacock gradually began to renew her interest in life and to reaffirm its possibilities. Over time, her strong faith led her to a deep and loving relationship with Terry Leever, a pharmacist at Baylor Medical Center, who would go on to attend medical school and become a physician specializing in radiology. Much to Jess and Betty Jo's delight, Terry and Ruth Ellen were married in February 1970, and within a week of the wedding the Hays received a letter from Ruth Peacock—Ruth Ellen's mother—acknowledging her high regard for two special people who had meant so much to her family:

> Dearest Betty and Jess,
>
> It would be difficult for a very eloquent person to express their thanks properly to you two—and for me it is impossible to tell you how much we truly thank you for

all you have done—not only at this time but for the two years Ruth Ellen has been in Dallas. . . .

In our "Mother and Daughter" talk before the wedding regarding marriage, Ruth Ellen and I both agreed that if she and Terry could pattern their marriage after yours it would be a perfect marriage. You and Jess have a very rare and wonderful thing that cannot be defined. Your love for each other reflects in all you do—and your children also reflect the closeness of your love for each other and for them.

Ruth Ellen's close ties to Betty Jo and Jess continued, and Terry was warmly welcomed into the family. "Betty Jo and Jess were very generous to us as a couple, and invited us to many social events," said Terry. "Ruth and I would also sit for them and their daughters when they traveled out of town. When they went to Democratic conventions, we'd stay at their house and keep an eye on the kids."

■

Spectacular success in the corporate world proceeded to transform the Hays' life during the late sixties. It not only opened the door to national prominence, but also led to expanded opportunity on all fronts, from community service, volunteer outreach, and politics, to international travel, personal affluence, and their relationships with family and friends.

Theirs was a classically American tale—proof that good fortune can indeed come from hard work, perseverance, courage, and a commitment to working constructively with others. Central to the Hays' success story, of course, was the turnaround Jess had orchestrated while at the helm of the troubled Lomas & Nettleton Financial Corporation (L&N). It was so impressive a story that the national financial press scrambled to tell it, and *Fortune* magazine did as much in its October 1968 issue by profiling Hay in a section entitled, *Businessman in the News:*

In dire straits three years ago, Lomas & Nettleton Financial Corp., a Dallas-based mortgage-banking and real estate company, asked Jess Hay, then 34, to take over as president. The young lawyer, who had a bookkeeper's job while working his way through SMU Law School (first in his class), quickly unloaded $26 million in low-yielding assets, cut overhead costs in half, and refinanced the company's debt.

From a $1,500,000 loss in its 1966 fiscal year, L&N posted a $945,000 profit this year. Now Hay, seeking new horizons, has bought the mortgage-servicing portfolios of the T. J. Bettes Companies, making L&N the biggest mortgage-banking firm in the world (servicing more than $2 billion in loans). Next target: expanding operations in the Southeast and Northwest.

Launched into the national spotlight by *Fortune* and other publications, Lomas & Nettleton began reaping the rewards of good press and high visibility. In early 1969, for example, First National Bank in Dallas proposed an attractive merger offer which had been designed by the bank's president, Dewey Presley, and which Lomas & Nettleton considered advantageous. While federal regulatory delays ultimately scotched the deal, the mere flirtation by a prominent bank was enough to raise L&N's profile and attract still more national attention. It also enhanced Hay's respect for Gene Bishop, First National Bank's executive vice president and chief lending officer, with whom Hay enjoyed a personal friendship. In fact, he, Betty Jo, and Gene had close ties dating back to the mid-1950s.

To be sure, in the late sixties it was not uncommon for Hay's business relationships to be influenced by social interaction, and with good reason: personal connections added depth to relationships which, in turn, brought trust and confidence to business transactions. But social success depended to a large degree on the efforts of the spouse, as wives were expected to support their husbands' careers by entertaining at dinners, organizing cocktail parties, opening their homes to weekend guests, and hosting corporate gatherings. Not surprisingly, Betty Jo met these critical obligations with grace, aplomb, and confidence. She was, in the words of Josiah Low, "the quintessential wife of a corporate executive." Low was an investment banker then with Merrill, Lynch, Pierce, Fenner & Smith and later with Donaldson, Lufkin & Jenrette, and one of the many senior corporate executives who valued his friendship with the Hays:

> Betty Jo understood that various relationships were important for her husband and as such she made an effort to know and understand the people Jess asked her to spend time with. I never felt that it was obligatory that she spend time with me. Quite the contrary, she always was a warm and naturally friendly person who was at ease and made her guests exceedingly comfortable.

Betty Jo's role at her husband's side assumed increasing importance in 1968 with the acquisition of the Bettes mortgage banking portfolio and, further in 1969, with the organization of Lomas & Nettleton Mortgage Investors (LNMI), an affiliated company designed to serve real estate developers by making short-term construction and development loans.

Hay answered the expansion at Lomas by adding a number of skilled supplemental managers charged with overseeing the company's growth, and in his search to fill those vital positions he needed to look no further than the friendships he and Betty Jo had forged. Therefore in 1969, Hay said he reached out to his trusted friend Gene Bishop, who joined the company as president:

> His expertise and incredibly sound judgment helped set the company on a productive course and establish effective systems relating to our much-expanded land development and construction lending activities. After the organization of LNMI, that became a huge part of our business. The policies and practices refined by Bishop, and executed by an unusually gifted direct lending staff then led by Ted Enloe, resulted in Lomas & Nettleton Mortgage Investors becoming one of the most successful short-term real estate lenders in the business throughout the 1970s and 1980s.

Where Ted Enloe was concerned, his quick intellect and aggressive style had appealed to Jess Hay from the beginning, starting in 1964, the year Enloe graduated with high honors from SMU law school and the same year Hay helped recruit him as an associate of the Locke, Purnell firm. What followed was an enduring friendship between the Hays and Enloes—Ted and Bess—and the hiring five years later of R. Ted Enloe III as executive vice president of Lomas. Enloe was, Hay said, an outstanding addition to the company's senior management team, just as he had been years earlier as a young recruit with Locke, Purnell:

> During the recruiting process, Betty Jo and I had taken Ted and Bess to dinner on several occasions, and both of us were impressed with the character and quality of the young couple. We frequently were together socially during the following 35 years or so. Ted and I became very good friends and colleagues during his first 18 months at Locke, Purnell when he worked primarily under my supervision. The resulting mutual respect led in 1969 to Ted's decision to leave the practice of law and accept the proffer of a position as executive vice president of Lomas.

Gene Bishop and Ted Enloe thus rounded out a superb team of Dallas-based corporate executives at Lomas, which then included Hay, Albert N. Rohnstedt, DeWitt T. Ray, Sr., John F. Sexton, Richard Bramblett, M. D. Wommack, H. H. (Buddy) Miller, Paul Low, Fred Morrison, David Kelly, Lanelle Latendresse, Gary White, Mike Karlak, Gary Kell, Dick Danley, Mike Walker, Daryl Anderson, and Warren Caldwell. In addition, there was a cadre of new talent derived through Lomas' acquisition of the T. J. Bettes Companies, including notably James M. Wooten, Everett Mattson, E. G. Bray, Hugh DeWitt, Dan Stoltje, Jim Ludman, William Barbish, Carl Geiser, Sid Kelley, Ray Ryan, and scores of others. Many key people were to be added in future years as the company continued to expand through internal growth and subsequent acquisitions.

These folks and their spouses—all of whom became close friends of the Hays—worked in concert with thousands of other Lomas officers and employees to shape a unique corporate culture that made Lomas an ideal environment for collegial endeavor, and enabled it to produce commendable corporate results over the years.

With Lomas gaining momentum, it didn't take long for the scope of Betty Jo's responsibilities to increase, as she and Jess began forming personal relationships with many commercial, savings, and investment bankers, insurance executives, real estate developers, and other business associates. In part, these relationships grew out of L&N's efforts to obtain from the capital markets the funding necessary to implement its expansive business strategies. They were crucial relationships, said Hay, and Betty Jo possessed the artful skill required to maintain them:

> It was fairly common at that time . . . for the chief executive officer and his wife to host functions . . . designed to build goodwill for the company among commercial bankers, investment bankers, mortgage investors, customers, and other constituencies of the enterprise. As our aspirations for expansion grew . . . Betty Jo served as hostess for scores or perhaps even hundreds of such events. It was fairly routine for us to entertain employees of the company or people who otherwise were involved in the company's affairs. . . . Betty Jo was very much a key player in that outreach, and she was, I think, exceptionally good at it.

She also had a knack for reinforcing the so-called "family" culture Hay was attempting to create within the company:

190

Betty Jo was never aloof or distant. She always was warm and friendly. Indeed, she considered each person, no matter what his or her role at Lomas, to be a very important part of the organization. . . . There was never a doubt in anybody's mind that Betty Jo cared about them and that she didn't consider herself above anyone. . . . That made a huge difference in terms of building a spirit of family and collegiality within the company.

During those years many people recognized the significant influence Betty Jo had on the culture at L&N and on the company's strong sense of team spirit. Among them was public relations and advertising executive Liener Temerlin who, only half-jokingly, described Betty Jo as "the mother of the company."

But even more important than her ability to entertain and nurture was Betty Jo's skill as a shrewd judge of people, and it was upon this talent her husband relied most of all. With Hay's boundless optimism and inclination to trust, he said it fell to Betty Jo to assess the deeper currents of character among the many people they met:

Betty Jo proved particularly adept at evaluating the underlying character of people involved from time to time in the affairs of Lomas. She had an uncanny ability to sense hypocrisy, phoniness, and outright evil in the nature of the few bad apples encountered during the period. She was equally skilled and graceful in affirming the best and the brightest who crossed our paths. She was my closest confidant, most reliable advisor, and concurrently my most honest critic and my most enthusiastic and loyal supporter.

David Farr said he believes Betty Jo's fierce allegiance to Jess was rooted in wisdom, which gave her the vision to see her husband's outright need for such loyalty. "Betty Jo was really clear about Jess's vulnerabilities, and she tried to protect him . . . from being exploited. . . . Betty Jo was a lot more savvy about how people manipulated Jess than Jess ever was. . . . She didn't like it when people tried to use Jess." Looking back, Hay said there is no doubt his wife's insight and honesty served him well. "Betty Jo was a lot more discerning people-wise than I am. She helped me winnow out some people who turned out to be pretty bad characters."

The lifestyle to which Betty Jo and her family had been accustomed would be altered significantly as a result of the dramatic growth of The Lomas Financial Group. It started with their home, and the realization that if Betty Jo and Jess were to accommodate the related increased social responsibilities that came with Hay's position as chairman and chief executive officer of one of the nation's leading mortgage firms, a new residence would be required. "It became clear that our role at Lomas was such that it was appropriate for us to think in terms of a little larger home where we might entertain people related to the company and to our civic interests as well," said Hay. "We also wanted a place that would be ideal for our daughters and their friends." And because Hay now enjoyed a level of compensation that provided substantial financial resources, cost presented little obstacle.

They selected a lot in an attractive new development known as Windsor Park, which featured a small lake as the focal point of its residential layout. It was a neighborhood conveniently located to downtown Dallas, close to the schools Debby and Patty were attending, and which soon would be the sight of what Hay describes as his family's dream home:

> In 1968, we purchased what we believed to be the best lake lot in Windsor Park. Located at 7236 Lupton Circle, the lot provided the broadest vista available of a small lake on which twelve houses, including ours, ultimately would be built. We designed the house with two things in mind: first, our daughters' use of the home for their pleasure and for sharing with their friends, and second, for our own enjoyment and use in hosting small and large gatherings of our friends and associates.

Construction at Lupton Circle began in late 1968 and was completed within eighteen months, thanks in large part to the work of architect Frank Meier, builder Beverly Harris—Ned Harris's sister-in-law—and interior designer Maxine Tadlock, all of whom successfully met the goals laid out by Betty Jo and Jess. Meier and Harris were known for designing and building high-end homes for senior corporate executives, including the likes of cosmetics queen Mary Kay Ash, whose home adjacent to the Hays' lot was finished in 1969. By coincidence, 1969 also marked the beginning of a Mary Kay tradition which would come to symbolize the culture of her corporation. That year, Ash awarded "Mountain Laurel" pink Cadillacs—the shade of her company's pink lipstick and eye shadow palettes—to her top five independent sales directors, a move that eventually brought her worldwide name recognition.

Meanwhile, Meier went to work designing the Hays' 8,400 square-foot home with the location's natural beauty at the forefront of his plan, followed closely by his determination to compensate for limited street parking. To tackle the parking question, he called for a wide circular drive off the street, which was to be partially covered with a large porte cochere. As for capitalizing on the beautiful site, the skillful Meier oriented most of the rooms in the home towards the scenic lake. "The floor space inside the house was designed for entertaining," Meier said. "It encouraged groups to flow through the house, view the lake, and access the back patio, swimming pool, and yard."

Never one to sit idly by, Betty Jo took the lead in the planning and decorating of her new home. "She was involved in every step of it, from the architectural designs to everything that went in the house," said daughter Debby Hay Spradley. "Of course, she had a great deal of help, mainly from a lady named Maxine Tadlock, but mother's hand-print is all over that house."

In addition to the primary objectives for the new house, Betty Jo insisted on functionality, particularly in those homemaking spheres where she knew she would be spending a great deal of time. The kitchen for example was, by design, not large. Instead, Betty Jo opted for the convenience of a manageable space that would better suit her petite size. "Mother was a fabulous cook, and she cooked most every night," said Debby. "But because of her size and commitment to functionality and related convenience, she did not want a huge, elaborate kitchen." Another critical area for Betty Jo was the utility room—located adjacent to the kitchen—which not only housed her laundry appliances, but as Debby explained, also "had a drop from the upstairs to the utility room for clothes, so Patty and I could drop our towels and clothes straight down into the room where the washer was. . . . Things like that made it an easier house to manage." No one understood or appreciated Betty Jo's idiosyncrasies better than Jess. "She knew exactly what she wanted in the utility room, including the sewing area," he said. "It's not the prettiest room in the house, by any means . . . but it is a functional room that she designed for her specific needs and uses."

As for the children's playroom, Betty Jo and Jess designed it in hopes of pleasing its primary users: their daughters. The end result—a playroom decorated in red, white, and blue celebration colors—was nothing short of the ultimate entertainment area for 1970s teens. "We specifically wanted a pool table," said Jess. "We wanted lots of room for teenagers to play, and it was an adjunct to the swimming pool, so they could swim and when they got tired of that they could dry off in the little bath area and then come inside and listen to their favorite music, play pool or card games or whatever."

Still, there was even more to the evolution of the Lupton Circle home, and it came from one Maxine Tadlock, an interior designer of singular attainments. In fact, it is Tadlock whom Jess Hay and others credit "for whatever pizazz the house has," by-products, no doubt, of the flair and energy only she could have brought to the project. "She was a fascinating woman, and the very definition of style and cool," said Patty Hay. "Maxine was bigger than life." As such, Tadlock not only was a force to be reckoned with, but according to others who knew her, exceedingly fun to be around. Sondra Farr remembers her as a striking personality, someone who came across as a "tough, old broad—in a good sense. She said what she thought. . . . Very outspoken."

A college graduate with a degree in engineering, Tadlock's credentials enabled her to go far beyond questions of mere style and into the more complex issues of home construction. "Not only did Maxine have the aesthetic sense to do wonderful design and creative interiors, but she also knew the structural aspects of building," said Debby Hay Spradley. "If she was getting flak from a builder or architect, she knew what could be done and she would fight those battles for you. She was an amazing decorator and a wonderful friend. I don't think any of us could say enough good things about her." To give the home a more spacious feel, Jess said the take-charge Tadlock didn't hesitate to recommend structural changes, as in the case of one upstairs room. "This ceiling is a foot or two higher than it would have been without Maxine," he explained. "In the primary living areas downstairs, instead of being ten feet, the ceilings range from twelve to sixteen feet in height, again due to Maxine's suggested enhancements."

In addition to being a firm believer in the hands-on approach to her business, Maxine Tadlock also had a reputation for perfectionism, and it wasn't unheard of for those two traits to collide now and then. Like the time she stopped by the house to check on a painting contractor and noticed the shade of color didn't quite meet her specifications. No matter her expensive suit, jewelry, and high heels, Patty remembers Tadlock assuming control of the paint can, and stirring, as the painter gradually added color at her direction. With Tadlock, attention to detail and accuracy were matters of the highest order, said Sondra Farr. "I remember Betty Jo telling me one time, 'Oh my gosh, this is the second or third time Maxine's redone such and such, because it just wasn't done right.' She made them do it over until it was right."

However, as one might expect, such verve and vigor could take its toll from time to time, and when that happened, Betty Jo—herself strong-willed—was just the person to meet the challenge. This was the case at those moments when Tadlock's creativity veered a tad off course and Betty Jo would take it upon herself to step in and get things back on track.

194

True gumption, remembers Sondra Farr, but more than anything, vintage Betty Jo. "Maxine would have this, that, or the other idea, and Betty Jo would just turn to her and say, 'Maxine, that will never work for my girls. We're not going to do that.' I remembered those conversations because not many people talked to Maxine like that. I certainly wouldn't have."

But those moments were surely the exception, according to Ruth Taylor, who worked for Baker Knapp & Tubbs in the Dallas Design Center, and remembers more than anything else her friend's unerring eye for quality. "Maxine was a unique person, and I've dealt with many Dallas designers. She had a special knack. She could walk inside an antique store and immediately pick out all the best pieces. She didn't settle for anything but the best and never looked at the price tag." Indeed, Maxine Tadlock was not for the faint of heart or cost-conscious client. On the contrary, said Debby, she was a "master at pushing you to do the maximum amount possible in terms of what you could afford."

But when it was all over, the spectacular results helped soothe the sticker shock as Tadlock brought to her projects a polished decorating style that blended European antiques, Asian accent pieces, and contemporary artwork to elegant effect. And most important, she left her clients satisfied. "The house was a great piece of work," said Hay. "If anything, its result was probably better than either one of us had anticipated."

■

The Hays moved into their fashionable new home at 7236 Lupton Circle on June 6, 1970, the day of Betty Jo's thirty-ninth birthday, and twenty years to the day after her first "pre-arranged date with Jess." A few weeks later, the house made its debut as a venue for entertaining when a flatbed trailer full of Ridgewood Park friends pulled up in front, surprising the Hays with a memorable housewarming blowout.

On that occasion, Ned and LeAnn Harris were two of the primary instigators. Ned was determined to settle a score from the previous year, and the housewarming presented the perfect opportunity. It seems ten months earlier, Jess and Betty Jo had surprised Ned with a fortieth birthday party at the upscale, private Dallas Club. "When we arrived, there must have been over a hundred people," said LeAnn (Harris) Solomon, thinking back to the lavish event. "They had a band and a buffet, and a huge birthday cake. There was also a sing song where they had the words to the songs blown up on a screen and you followed the bouncing ball—old-time songs like *Let Me Call You Sweetheart* and *Home on the Range*." Ned's birthday party was by all accounts a dazzling affair, and one which left little doubt as to the Hays' new position within the social hierarchy. Gone were the days of plain-Jane, backyard, baked beans and potato salad potluck dinners. These were times of increasingly elaborate events attended by an ever-growing network of friends.

Nevertheless, what made the birthday bash most meaningful to Ned Harris was not its glitter, but rather the deep and enduring bond of friendship it represented, and Harris expressed as much in a thank-you letter to Betty Jo and Jess:

> I have told you before and I'll keep telling you that I have received three great blessings. Being born into the Harris family with parents like Felix and Mama Felix, marrying that little Red Head [LeAnn], and having the friendship of Betty Jo and Jess Hay. These have made life so much richer. Never have I known a couple who attracted (as the two of you do) the love and respect, admiration, and loyalty of all who know you.

Evidence of that widely-held sentiment came in late June 1970, ten months after Harris's birthday party, as more than seventy friends descended—most via flatbed trailer—on Lupton Circle. Unbeknownst to Betty Jo and Jess, "the group" and other old friends from Ridgewood Park Methodist Church had planned a surprise christening of sorts, which included such festivities as a catered meal, the Levee Singers, and plenty of good-natured ribbing about the prosperous circumstances the Hay family now enjoyed. As would be expected, Jess bore the brunt of the teasing, first with a roast led by Ken Dippel and then with a song and dance number by Betty Jo's church and bridge pals. Dressed in matching white shirts and slacks, red vests, red satin top hats, and canes, the women performed an amusing version of *Hey Big Spender,* with appropriately revised lyrics directed at Jess.

At the end came the housewarming gift. A vessel, so to speak, intended as a means for their big spender friend to cruise his backyard lake. While a yacht might better have made the point, they instead presented a simple, small rowboat—and a heavily gold-braided admiral's hat—which couldn't have been more perfect, considering its source: lifetime friends and family who respected the hard work that had brought the Hays to this point in their lives. "It was a great evening," said Hay, "with a fabulous gathering of relatives and close friends which, to the best of my recollection, included Martha and John Binion, Benny and Gene Bishop, Sandra and Corky Bridgeman, Claudia and Irwin Carroll, Stell and Wally Chappell, Pat and Ken Dippel, Bess and Ted Enloe, Sondra and David Farr, Iva and Lindsay Fleck, Joy and Jim Goyen, Elaine and Eddie Haines, Margie and Wayne Harmon,

LeAnn and Ned Harris, Bobbie and Al Hopkins, Margaret and Doug Jenkins, Gwen and Al Krutilek, Edna and Bob Lancaster, Ina and Mac McCormick, Shirley and Lee McVey, Charlene and Buddy Miller, Jerry Pittman, Nancy and John Sexton, Brownie and Bob Shytles, Peggy and Ken Smith, Juanita and Harold Smotherman, Sue and Al Stockard, Alice and Rex Stultz, Ramona Taylor, Frances and Jimmy Thomas, DeWayne Wommack, Patsy, Don, and Roddy Harlow, Myrtle Hay, Kathryn and Duncan Peacock, Patty and Richard Bramblett, Kathy, Nancy and Polly Albert, and perhaps a dozen others."

The message behind the housewarming antics, of course, was clear and, if spoken, might have gone something like this: "You may have a fancy new house and more money than we may ever see, but, dammit, we love you and you better not get all hoity-toity and forget us." Betty Jo and Jess spent the rest of the summer proving they wouldn't. "Our first summer at the house," remembers Jess, "was spent principally entertaining our close friends and hosting weekly cookouts for our daughters, Betty Jo's cousins—Kathy, Nancy, and Polly Albert, who spent most of that summer as our guests—and many other friends and relatives."

For Patty and Debby, times were good, and the effort and energy expended by their parents did not go unnoticed or unappreciated. "There's no telling how many hot dogs and hamburgers Daddy cooked that summer," said Patty. "Just masses of humanity at this house all the time. Our house was like the country club. Everybody came here instead of the country club. It was great fun." No question about it, added Debby, one would be hard-pressed to forget those 1970 weekends and the special touch her parents gave to the all-American backyard barbecue. "We served three thousand hamburgers that summer, if we served one. . . . Mom and Dad did the cookout routine every weekend and some week nights," said Debby. "There was a lot of activity. I think they were enjoying the new house. They had spent a lot of time working on it, and now they were enjoying it."

In all of its splendor, though, the Lupton Circle dream home clearly had the potential to overwhelm. And that's precisely the effect it might have had on Betty Jo's bridge friend, Peggy (Smith) Pittman, if not for Jess and Betty Jo's down-to-earth ways, which simply wouldn't allow it. "They were the warmest, most generous people and made you feel so comfortable in that house," Pittman said. By end of summer it was evident that what Betty Jo and Jess were showcasing at their new home wasn't wealth or possessions—it was community. David Farr regarded the home as "a gathering place for people" and a venue for what he described as Jess and Betty Jo's "vital need to facilitate community for people they cared about."

And though they cared about many, none were considered higher priority than their two daughters. Specifically, Betty Jo promoted Debby and Patty's enjoyment of the new house by welcoming their friends and hosting numerous social events. The night of Debby's high school prom in 1971, for example, Betty Jo arranged a festive backyard dinner party. "The dinner was outside with tables set up around the pool," remembers Susan (Pittman) Wilson. "Of course, all the girls were in long formals with their hair perfectly coiffed. I know the party included all the Tri-Hi-Y girls and their dates, other close friends, and a lot of the parents who were close friends of Jess and Betty Jo."

Patty was treated to her fair share of Lupton Circle entertainment too, particularly as she neared the end of her senior year of high school in 1974. That year, in addition to throwing a party for members of the school drill team and band, Betty Jo put together a magnificent gathering at the conclusion of Patty's senior year at Hillcrest. Michelle McCormick was there and recounts it as a "huge party for Patty and all of us. . . . The boys wore suits and the girls wore long dresses and heels. Betty Jo had it catered, and the food was wonderful. There was a trampoline in the backyard, and we were jumping on the trampoline and our dresses were fluttering above our heads, and people were pushing each other into the lake. We had so much fun."

But beyond the fun—and with the benefit of nearly thirty-five years hindsight—McCormick realizes those days of parties and high-spirited energy, as much as being about the good times, actually and more significantly were a symbol of her deep connection to Patty, Debby, Betty Jo, and Jess, and to a very special home on Lupton Circle. "We came of age in that house. . . . Their home was always open. In other words, their friends were their family. I felt like I was one of their kids."

■

Amid the swirl of activities associated with the corporate world and building a home, Betty Jo and Jess were determined never to lose sight of the relationship that mattered most—their own—and they devoted both time and energy to maintaining that critical bond. For one thing, they periodically scheduled weekends of togetherness at the Peacock's lake house in Oklahoma, before it became Duncan and Kathryn's primary residence. They also managed to get away at least once a year for longer renewing retreats, either to the Hana Ranch on Maui, Hawaii or to Little Dix Bay on Virgin Gorda in the British Virgin Islands. And finally, there existed between Betty Jo and Jess a habit of regular written communication which not only fortified their relationship, but also placed it in a category unfamiliar to many married couples. Betty Jo had a fondness for cards, and consistently sought those with heartfelt inscriptions she knew would be personally meaningful to Jess. Jess, on the other hand, preferred handwritten letters as they allowed him the freedom to express to Betty Jo his innermost thoughts, feelings, and gratitude. This example from February 4, 1969 illustrates the prose-poetry style Jess favored, as well as his intense feelings for Betty Jo:

Your love,
> *intense and constant,*

Your presence,
> *redeeming and reassuring,*

Your understanding,
> *perceptive and deep,*

Your being,
> *beautiful and tender:*

> - *these have been the splendid sources*
>   *of sustaining grace for me*
> - *and I thank God for them.*

And if, from time to time, I seem to expect too much, know that it truly is because I love too much and have been too fulfilled, enriched, and rewarded by the full dimension of your love.

> *So, with a heart*
> > *nurtured by memories of yesterday,*
> > *warmed by the fullness of today,*
> > *and excited at the prospect of tomorrow,*

> - *I give thanks for another day of loving*
> - *And for a life shared with you.*

> *All my love, all my life*

Jess

At about this same time—in the late 1960s—Betty Jo and Jess took part in a Ridgewood Park Methodist Church study group which led to an affirmation of their personal philosophy of marriage and provided a means of clearly expressing the way they viewed and appreciated their relationship. The principal text for the seminar was *The Prophet*, written in 1923 by Kahlil Gibran, a Lebanese mystical poet and novelist who celebrated the quest for self-fulfillment, individual freedom, and the brotherhood of man. During the 1960s, the book became especially popular within the American counterculture and New Age movements. Gibran's spiritual perceptions and poetic style appealed to Betty Jo and Jess, thus inspiring them, as a couple, to study his work.

They found his insights into love and marriage meshed well with their own deeply-held convictions, particularly regarding the concept of unity. From the beginning, they had rejected the traditional "unity candle" marriage model—which symbolized two individuals becoming one—and instead acknowledged the notion of individual autonomy as an essential component of their marriage. Said Hay:

> We recognized that marriage is . . . a form of unity between two people who remain two people, but who are linked in a very decisive and committed way. They continue to function as individual human beings, each supported by the other, which results in each member of the pairing being stronger than either would have been standing alone. Part of that insight came from our reading together *The Prophet* by Kahlil Gibran. That book presented a clear statement of what was already our view of marriage.

The following excerpt on the subject of marriage illustrates the power of the book's spiritual thought and the beauty of its language:

> *And what of marriage . . . ?*
> *And he answered saying:*
> *You were born together and together you shall be forevermore.*
> *You shall be together when the white wings of death scatter your days.*
> *Aye, you shall be together even in the silent memory of God.*
> *But let there be spaces in your togetherness,*
> *And let the winds of the heavens dance between you,*
> *Love one another but make not a bond of love:*
> *Let it rather be a moving sea between the shores of your souls.*

Fill each other's cup but drink not from one cup.
Give one another of your bread but eat not from the same loaf.
Sing and dance together and be joyous, but let each one of you be alone,
Even as the strings of a lute are alone though they quiver with the same music.
Give your hearts, but not into each other's keeping.
For only the hand of Life can contain your hearts.
And stand together, yet not too near together:
For the pillars of the temple stand apart,
And the oak tree and the cypress grow not in each other's shadow.

Drawing upon the wisdom of Gibran, the Hays crystallized their formula for a loving, mutually-supportive marriage and gave voice to it through the mantra: "Unity between two people who remain two people." This became the basis for what Hay called "a partnership driven by profound love, trust, respect, and constant availability to be supportive of one another no matter what."

And so, buoyed by the strength of her partnership with Jess, and motivated by a strong religious faith that called upon her to meet human need, Betty Jo would spend the next quarter century expanding her commitment to public service. Her passion and energy would be poured into the defense of children, advocacy for those afflicted with mental illness, education, rights for women, and political support for candidates and policies advancing those causes.

The 1970s had arrived, marking the beginning of a new journey for Betty Jo, one which Wally Chappell later would describe as "self-giving on a grand scale."

PHOTOGRAPH ALBUM
4

OCTOBER 1965

through

DECEMBER 1970

202

Jess, Betty Jo, and Carl Albert at a dinner honoring Carl Albert in Dallas, benefiting the National Jewish Medical and Research Center, Denver, Colorado. Circa 1965.

Ned Harris, Irwin and Claudia Carroll, Wallace and Stell Chappell, Raymond and Patsy Nasher, and LeAnn Harris at the Carl Albert dinner in Dallas. Circa 1965.

Betty Jo, Eugene and Adele Locke, and Jess enjoying lunch at the Dallas Country Club. Circa 1967.

Eugene M. Locke at or about the date of the conclusion of his service as Deputy Ambassador to Viet Nam. December 1967.

Betty Jo relaxed and feet up in her easy chair. Fall 1966.

"Lovers." Betty Jo and Jess in Colorado. 1968.

Jess and Betty Jo dressed for the Neiman-Marcus Italian Fortnight Ball. Fall 1968.

On a trip to Puerto Rico at Thanksgiving in 1968, the Hays stayed at the Dorado Beach Resort. From left: J.D. Francis, Betty Jo, Martha Francis, Jess, Charlie Beebe, Ruth and Al Rohnstedt, and Elizabeth Francis.

Betty Jo and Jess awaiting dinner service at the Persian Room of the Plaza Hotel in New York. May 2, 1970.

Patty, Betty Jo, Debby, and Jess celebrate Debby's 16th birthday surprise party at the Teenage Room, Dallas Country Club. December 8, 1968.

Betty Jo, who is a bit surprised, and Jess, welcome guests to their housewarming. Don Roddy Harlow, Jess's nephew, is in the background. July 1970.

Betty Jo and Jess greet the first day in their new home at 7236 Lupton Circle. June 6, 1970.

The Hay family church, attended from time to time after 1970 and regularly after 1994, was Highland Park United Methodist Church, Dallas. They joined as members on the first Sunday of January 2000.
Photograph by James A. Ledbetter.

CHAPTER
5

JANUARY 1971
through
NOVEMBER 1985

Betty Jo's decision to expand her commitment to public service did not arrive in a nice, neat package. It was, instead, thrust upon her in response to what contemporary American writer Gail Sheehy has since called "the predictable crises of adult life." In her research, Sheehy observed the difficulties experienced by people as they passed from one phase of life to another, and surely the life changes Betty Jo went through during the early 1970s were a reflection of that troublesome, sometimes painful struggle which—Sheehy concluded— inevitably accompanies human growth.

Particularly painful was the realization that her role as a mother was changing, but considering the earnest investment Betty Jo had made in motherhood, this was inevitable. Indeed, she felt a tangible sense of loss as her daughters matured and no longer needed close nurturing. It began when Debby left home to enter Southern Methodist University in the fall of 1971 and though SMU was only two miles from Lupton Circle, the Hays' exceedingly independent oldest daughter chose to live on campus. Betty Jo felt her absence. On top of that was the prospect of additional loss as Patty's 1974 graduation from high school neared. With the nest beginning to empty, Betty Jo was forced to confront the end of what had been her primary role and sphere of responsibility.

And so, disconnecting from the past but not yet connected to the future, Betty Jo entered a period of introspection during which she pondered this new phase of her life in search of where she truly wanted to go. Sondra Farr recalls conversations she had with Betty Jo as these impending changes loomed. "I remember when the girls were getting older and not needing her as much, she was wondering what she was going to do because

208

her focus had been on the girls. She said, 'I've got to find something to do. I don't know what I'm going to do when they don't need me as much.'"

Reflecting on that phase of her mother's life, Debby Hay Spradley remembers it as a turning point. "When Mom saw Patty and me on the verge of leaving home she was still a very young woman of thirty-nine. That's incredibly young to have your kids already gone or about to depart. She was a very energetic, productive woman. So, faced with the fact her kids were leaving, she had to do something. She wasn't just going to sit around."

But just what she was going to do remained uncertain, and with that uncertainty came anxiety. David Farr encountered the distress firsthand one night when Betty Jo surprised him with a phone call requesting his counsel. While Farr's background in pastoral counseling and his close personal friendship with the Hays made him a frequent confidant for most members of the family, Betty Jo usually was not among them. "Patty would come over and talk to me about her issues," Farr said. "Debby would talk to me about her issues. Jess always talked to me about what he was struggling with, but Betty Jo rarely did that." Farr continued:

> When she came over she was tearful and sad. Some of her tears were flowing from her frustration. . . . Betty Jo was one of those people who was an achiever. . . . I think one way to look at it is she had run out of achievement. She'd had her kids. She'd done the church thing. She had done a lot of activities at which she excelled, and I think she had run out of things to do. She'd experienced the empty nest to some extent, or could see it coming. . . . As well as I can remember, she was trying to figure out how she could achieve apart from her life-role as a mother.

As she struggled to find a new beginning Betty Jo did not reject her past. Rather, she took from the past those resources she needed and put them to use in her journey toward the future. At the top of the list were strong religious convictions which provided a degree of continuity as her search for "something to do" intensified. She was helped, according to Farr, by "the provocative and prophetic preaching" of Reverend Wally Chappell's ministry at Ridgewood Park Methodist Church, which Farr said grounded both Betty Jo and Jess in a social action theology that they integrated into their political philosophy and civic outreach.

Church study group presentations written by Betty Jo in the mid-sixties give an indication of the direction her life eventually would take. For example, in one fourteen-page lesson titled, *Faith Means Witness,* Betty Jo asks, "What does living within the

Kingdom of God mean to men and women . . . who want 'to do' something that will give purpose to their lives?" The answer, she concluded, was found in loving action:

> The ministry of "doing" has always been recognized by Christians as a sign that the Kingdom of God is present in the world. . . . We can see, then, signs of God's kingdom in the lives of people. Jesus said that his disciples were to be salt, light, and seed. All these words suggest action, work, and results. The Christian must witness to the reality of the Kingdom of God by what he does. . . . So we ask ourselves is the Kingdom of God present in our lives or are we too self-centered to care for our fellow man?

Betty Jo held firm to the conviction that a purposeful, Christian life, above all else, must involve selfless service, and be centered around a ministry of "doing." With that core belief at the heart of what would be one of her most important life transitions, Betty Jo now could move forward knowing the foundation for a future of meaningful outreach to others was in place.

Consequently, she not only embraced the Christian duty to comfort the afflicted, but answered a similar calling to afflict the comfortable, when necessary. In a lesson entitled, *Sarah,* the gritty Betty Jo spoke out against the lack of caring too often evident in the privileged middle-class suburban lifestyle to which she and her friends had grown accustomed:

> Here we sit in our fine air conditioned church—we return to our fine air conditioned homes—we are an isolated and insulated suburban society here in Ridgewood Park, and we know little of the world of want and the depth of its needs and problems. We aren't really open to the Gospel and its promise of a new life because most of us like our life as it is. We are too comfortable. . . . We fortunately don't have to fight for our very physical survival and for the bare necessities, as many of the world do.

> What do we know of war, poverty, crowded conditions, loneliness, hopelessness, and discrimination? What do we know of sacrifice—for God—or anything else? . . . We don't go about the mission of the church because we are too self centered. We give very little of our funds away and give virtually nothing of ourselves away.

> We, in our pious attitudes, tend to reject the new, the lonely, the alcoholic, the ex-con, the black, the brown, the different, the down-and-out, and so on. Sure, we say we ought to do this or that—we hear the Word proclaimed but we don't live it out in our daily lives. . . . Instead of living exclusively for ourselves, we need to reach out and extend a loving hand to the needy among us.

It was a passionate, brutally honest religious critique, one that affirmed Betty Jo's solid understanding of right and wrong. Indeed, according to contemporary theologian Dennis Bratcher, such upright conviction would have earned her a place among the so-called "prophetic voices" of the time:

> A prophetic voice is one who calls God's people to return to their calling as His people. . . . A prophetic voice is one that will not settle for the status quo. . . . A truly prophetic voice is a radical voice, a liberal voice that calls for change, even if that change is a return to a vital tradition long obscured by false piety and self-righteousness. A prophetic voice will not gloss over injustice or oppression, will not be silent in the face of bigotry or prejudice or false pride.

Although indecision about what to do with "the rest of her life" didn't fully resolve itself for another two years, Betty Jo began in 1971 to concentrate her attention on political activism guided by personal ethical values. That was the year moral outrage over political corruption inspired Betty Jo to raise her "prophetic voice" and take action against status quo politics in Texas. The event that triggered her ire became known as the Sharpstown Stock Fraud Scandal, and it centered on charges that state officials had made profitable quick-turnover bank-financed stock purchases in return for the passage of legislation desired by Houston financier and businessman Frank W. Sharp. By the time the scandal died down a year later, considerable and widespread political carnage lay in its wake. An excerpt from the *Handbook of Texas Online* totted up the butcher's bill:

> The incumbent governor was labeled an unindicted co-conspirator in a bribery case and lost his bid for reelection; the incumbent speaker of the House of Representatives and two associates were convicted felons; a popular three-term attorney general lost his job; an aggressive lieutenant governor's career was shattered;

and half of the legislature was either intimidated out or voted out of office.

As news of the scandal began to break, anger ignited Betty Jo's activist spirit, plunging her into the political fray that was shaping up. She honed in on the race for Texas governor, just as she and Jess had done in 1968 when they supported Eugene Locke's bid. Tragically, several years after the 1968 election, and much to the Hays' deeply-felt sorrow, Locke developed a brain tumor that would end his life in May 1972 following nine-and-a-half months of illness. "During those dark days," said Adele (Locke) Seybold, "Betty Jo and Jess's friendship and support . . . truly brought me through that sad period." And though Gene now was gone, Betty Jo and Jess would remain close to Adele and her family for the duration of their lives.

Meanwhile, the 1972 gubernatorial campaign was promising to be a far different race from that of 1968. Whereas much of the Hays' passionate support for Locke was based on years of close, personal friendship, they were motivated this time by a desire for reform. And on that front, Betty Jo took the lead. "Betty Jo wanted to get involved in the 1972 governor's campaign because she was upset about Sharpstown," Jess remembers. "I told her, 'Whatever you want to do I'll support you, but I'm not going to just be against somebody. You've got to find somebody to be for.'"

Betty Jo found Dolph Briscoe—South Texas rancher, businessman, and banker. She, along with friends Charles Purnell and Jim Sale, concluded Briscoe not only was a man of integrity, but also a candidate who shared their thirst for reform. A conservative Democrat noted for compassion, Briscoe offered discontented voters an anti-incumbent option under a "throw the rascals out" banner. For Betty Jo, it was the combination of Briscoe's platform and personal qualities which led her to support him early on, said Hay:

> Dolph is probably as decent a human being as you can find and he stood in sharp contrast to the perception that there was a lot of corruption among Texas old guard politicians. . . . He also was a tremendously loyal family man to his wife and his children. All of those things were very appealing to Betty Jo. He had a moderate tone in his background of public service . . . progressive in the sense he cared about people. . . . Betty Jo got on board before I did. . . . There is no question that, in this instance and numerous others, she was the leader between the two of us.

Briscoe's moderate political temperament attracted Betty Jo and Jess. "Typically," said Hay, "Betty Jo and I had a commitment in common to a centrist Democratic Party."

In fact, they believed that only by supporting moderately progressive politicians and legislation would it be possible to successfully implement their core values in the drive toward a more socially just society. It was, at its base, a practical approach, and one which fell in line with their theory that the way to political accomplishment was through reasonable negotiation and compromise. "Betty Jo was a pragmatist," said Bernard Rapoport, a life-long Democrat who, along with his wife Audre, formed a political alliance and personal friendship with Betty Jo and Jess. "That was her strength," Rapoport said. "She always wanted to deal with what's possible, without compromising her values."

Well before the Briscoe campaign, the Hays' stake in the political center had led them to support Lloyd Bentsen in his 1970 victory over Ralph Yarborough, the liberal incumbent United States senator from Texas. Again, said Hay, political moderation guided their actions:

> If you were pragmatically dedicated to the actual achievement of constructive objectives then you worked for someone like Lloyd Bentsen instead of Ralph Yarborough, who may have proclaimed some stuff you might cheer, but who would be less likely to achieve desirable change. We were for Bentsen in 1970, because to us he represented the moderate wing of the Democratic Party. . . . We viewed him as a natural heir to the policies and directions of Lyndon Johnson, Sam Rayburn, and their allies at the center of the Democratic Party.

Within a few years of the election, Betty Jo and Jess had developed a lasting friendship with Bentsen and his wife, B. A., and from that relationship came a bond of mutual respect between the senator and Betty Jo which would have a significant impact on her future advocacy work at the national level.

As for political moderation and pragmatism, Betty Jo knew both to be long-standing trademarks of the Albert family. Her uncle, Carl Albert, had built a spectacular career in the United States House of Representatives by bringing such approaches to the problems and affairs of Congress. In 1962, shortly after Albert became house majority leader, reporter Paul Duke profiled the congressman in the *Wall Street Journal*. Many of the traits noted by Duke bore a strong resemblance to characteristics held by Betty Jo and Jess, the most prominent being Albert's willingness "to compromise and forge middle grounds":

> As a believer in the art of the possible, he subscribes fully to the doctrine that it is better to move modestly by compromise than to founder on rigidly-held principle.

> In many ways Mr. Albert is cut from the same cloth as . . . Sam Rayburn. He, like the late speaker, is a restrained liberal but party loyalist; he too, shuns the dogmatic for the pragmatic; prefers reason and persuasion to the brickbat . . .

Betty Jo felt an enormous sense of pride at the political accomplishments of her uncle, dating back to January 1947 when, as a fifteen-year-old girl, she witnessed his first oath of office as a United States congressman. Nothing, however, compared to the drama of the moment, nearly twenty-five years later, when he was elected Speaker of the U.S. House of Representatives. The entire Hay family—teenage daughters included—was present in 1971 to watch Carl Albert formally accept his new position as the most important member of Congress. That year also marked the occasion of Jess's fortieth birthday, giving the family an opportunity to tie two significant events into one first-class celebration. It took place at the elegant Madison Hotel, a luxurious address five blocks from the White House known for catering to an elite clientele among whom frequently were diplomats and heads of state.

Meanwhile, as second in line of succession to the President of the United States, Carl Albert had reached the highest echelon of political power. The prestige of his position not only intensified Betty Jo's already strong interest in state and national Democratic politics, but also served to enhance the political profile of Betty Jo and Jess as a couple.

However, not even the Hays' growing clout could improve the chances of Dolph Briscoe winning the 1972 race for Texas governor. In fact, most political analysts put the likelihood of that happening at somewhere between slim and none. The unequivocal frontrunner was Lieutenant Governor Ben Barnes, whose charisma, political skill, and financial backing from the Texas political establishment made him a shoo-in. What's more, he also happened to be a protégé of former President Lyndon Johnson, who had declared that one day Barnes would be the President of the United States.

Even so, it would take a concerted effort at "door-to-door" fund-raising in Dallas for Briscoe to get the picture he didn't have much chance of winning. To test the waters, he and his Dallas County campaign chairman, Roy Coffee, arranged to meet with some of Dallas' top business leaders, starting with Ben Carpenter, a personal friend and fellow rancher. As Coffee remembers it, the Carpenter meeting was the good news-bad news sort:

> After the niceties, Dolph said, "Ben, I'm going to run for governor." And Ben said, "Dolph, I don't think you're going to win it, but I supported you in 1968 and I'm going to support you now." Carpenter gave him a check for $25,000. I almost fell over because that was a lot of money, then.

214

Subsequent meetings, however, produced fewer dollars, provided little hope, and in effect confirmed Ben Barnes' dominating lead. "We went to twenty or thirty of those guys," said Coffee, "and most of them said the same thing, 'Dolph, we like you, love your wife, but we're supporting Ben Barnes.'" It was a sobering moment, not unlike John Adams might have experienced as the second President of the United States when he proclaimed, "Facts are stubborn things." Indeed they were, and after considering the stark facts of his gubernatorial campaign, Dolph Briscoe concluded he would not carry Dallas. So he set a more realistic goal and instructed Coffee to try to keep his loss in Dallas from exceeding 10,000 votes.

The campaign continued, but in Dallas, aside from the financial support of Ben Carpenter, encouragement from the George Cullum family (relatives of Briscoe's ranching partner and close friend, Red Nunley), and the political know-how of Roy Coffee, the only bright spots appeared to be Betty Jo, Charles Purnell, and Jim Sale, each of whom was determined to fight the uphill battle. To that end, Betty Jo hosted a reception for Briscoe at her home in August 1971, an event that attracted 75 to 100 guests—mostly personal friends—including many from Ridgewood Park Methodist Church, as well as former Gene Locke supporters and campaign volunteers. When the time came, Betty Jo introduced Briscoe, who proceeded to speak convincingly about his credentials and reasons for running, and although difficult to convey, the candidate placed considerable emphasis on integrity and honesty in government. The Lupton Circle reception hit the mark, as it gave Briscoe something he sorely needed: a core group of enthusiastic supporters. "I was extremely fortunate that Betty Jo was interested in my campaign," he said, looking back nearly forty years later. "She put on a reception in her home . . . that included many of the younger crowd and a few of the leaders in Dallas. . . . Jess was there, but this was her idea."

Jess was there in full support of Briscoe if for no other reason than the successful recruiting effort undertaken by Betty Jo during her planning of the reception. "I became an enthusiastic supporter of Dolph Briscoe in response to her advocacy, Charles Purnell's urging, and to a lesser extent, that of Jim Sale," said Hay. "The three of them were committed to Briscoe before I was, and they got me involved."

With Jess now focused on getting Briscoe elected, he and Betty Jo devised a plan of action which, according to the former governor, proved instrumental to the upturn in his campaign. Working as a team, the Hays put together a pivotal dinner event for Briscoe set for January 1972 at the Fairmont Hotel in Dallas. It was a strategy they knew well, said Hay:

Betty Jo and I co-chaired the event. It was not a fund-raiser. Rather, it was an occasion designed to introduce Dolph Briscoe to the Dallas community. Our objective was to have eight-hundred people in attendance. The tickets were $22.50 each. That was payment for a complete dinner. You couldn't get chicken soup and salad for that cost today. Anyway, we got couples to agree to be responsible for a table of ten, and they typically sold their tables to their friends. It's a system we've used innumerable times. We used it some in the Locke campaign, but this was the first time we really demonstrated its potential. My memory is that we had eighty such host couples, which resulted in a structure designed to deliver eight-hundred people. It actually delivered 750, which was terrific.

Achieving such a challenging goal required just the type of skill Betty Jo had utilized countless times before, and thus, she assumed responsibility for much of the event's planning. The precision with which she executed the strategy remains a vivid memory for Janis Coffee— the wife of campaign manager Roy Coffee—who worked closely with Betty Jo on Briscoe's behalf:

> I do remember Betty Jo would organize mail-outs at her house. . . . She had a big room, and she had all the material laid out and everything organized the way she wanted us to do it. She had a plan. It wasn't just, "Oh, come in and do whatever you think you need to do." She was a very capable person. She was very articulate and had great leadership ability.

And like any great leader, Betty Jo was persuasive, said Janis Coffee, in large part because she was "very charming and very direct. She spoke her mind and wouldn't beat around the bush. . . . I thought she had a very strong personality, strong character."

She also had Jess, and while the two of them were very much individuals, Janis remembers that on issues of common cause Betty Jo and Jess could unite with the greatest of ease. "I had the feeling they were a really strong team and that they worked on a lot of things side by side . . . that they were in this campaign together and she was going to do as much as she could to make it happen."

No question about it, said Roy Coffee, the Betty Jo mystique was a thing of beauty:

> First of all, Betty Jo was as cute as she could be. She was kind of a June Allyson type . . . really pretty, really ebullient, outgoing, well met, had a great smile.

216

Betty Jo had great organizational ability. . . . In other words, she was a pretty gal, always well dressed and on and on and on, but she also was very talented. . . . The team of Jess and Betty Jo was a strong, strong team. . . . I know that Dolph Briscoe recognized that real quick.

Coffee had it right. Briscoe clearly was struck by the vitality of the Hays' relationship and, particularly by their desire to work in partnership. "They had an extremely strong personal connection," said the former Texas governor. "It was obvious that they were very happy with each other, very much in love, and they wanted to be partners in everything they did. . . . They were an unbeatable team."

But it was more than just coordinated effort and determination that gave Betty Jo and Jess an edge in producing a positive outcome for Dolph Briscoe. As chairman and chief executive officer of Lomas & Nettleton Financial Corporation—the nation's premier mortgage banking company—Jess Hay, by this time, had become a certified member of Dallas' business elite and, in the process, according to a 1972 *Dallas Morning News* story, had achieved a degree of financial independence. As a result, Roy Coffee credits Hay's connections to the rich and powerful for the success of the January event at the Fairmont:

When Betty Jo and Jess came on board, they had the big party, and they got all the big people in Dallas lined up. . . . This is what Jess and Betty Jo were really good at. . . . They were involved in sending out the kind of personal letters to major movers and shakers in Dallas that would get people to a political party. . . . The beauty of Betty Jo and Jess was that their position in the business strata of Dallas was right at the top, and they were able to attract prominent people.

Between 700 and 800 people attended the event, and Hay remembers them as "wildly enthusiastic." He and his fellow campaign watchers dubbed it the "January miracle" and were convinced it altered the course of the 1972 governor's race. "It was a dynamite deal," said Hay. "It just electrified Dallas and put the other candidates on the defensive. From that point forward, Dolph was in ascendency . . . and Ben Barnes was in decline."

For Briscoe himself, the Fairmont dinner event was the break he'd been waiting for. "It was extremely important," he said. "I'll put it this way, it turned out to be absolutely vital because it gave the campaign a start in Dallas that it otherwise would not have had. I needed help very badly. I was trying to start a campaign in Dallas where I did not know very many people and to get a start through such respected individuals was invaluable."

Putting into action his status as a nationally-known, highly-regarded business leader, Hay convinced a number of prominent people to attend the dinner, thereby paving the way to the credibility Briscoe's campaign had been lacking. From among the top tier of Dallas' corporate ladder, Hay persuaded the likes of John Stemmons and Trammell Crow not only to attend, but ultimately to contribute financially to the campaign, a remarkable accomplishment given the overwhelming support Barnes had received from the Dallas establishment.

Briscoe's January boon led to the formation of what most campaign strategists consider to be the backbone of any viable political operation: a small coterie of close political and personal associates, of which Betty Jo and Jess soon became a part. "Dolph immediately gravitated toward Jess and Betty Jo," said Roy Coffee, a Briscoe confidant, and later, a member of the governor's staff. "Dolph didn't waste any time pulling them into the inner circle. In other words, he really ingratiated himself to them and they to him. There was no doubt Dolph knew they had major, major connections in Dallas."

And along with those connections came money. Following the "January miracle," Betty Jo and Jess chose to apply their talent where it would be most effective—toward raising funds for a campaign that was beginning to gather momentum. Jess understood all too well that political success depended on financial resources, and he now possessed the status and professional standing to attract the level of support needed to fund a winning campaign. Said friend and confidant David Farr about Jess:

> He was very highly regarded in the business communities nationally and especially in Texas. People trusted his judgment.

> In terms of politics, Jess became clearer and clearer on what politics was all about. He ceased to be a political operative and started being a fund-raiser. . . . He realized that money was an indispensable component of political outreach to, and effective communication with, an increasingly complex population. . . .

Jess agrees with David's observation that, by 1972, money had become a vital part of political endeavor in America, but, at the same time, he has a quarrel with the implied and commonly held notion that it is necessary to divide the process into two distinct parts: fund-raising on one hand, and political or organizational effort on the other. And while the vast majority of twenty-first century political consultants or "gurus" continue to see a need for this sharp division, Hay remains firm in his age-old belief that "the best fund-raising involves a political component aimed at motivating the participants to spread the word in support of their candidate or cause, thereby encouraging others to join in the effort." He offers the following scenario in support of his opinion, and an explanation of how it evolved:

> One million dollars raised at an open and public gathering of one to two thousand folks, is worth more in the long run to any campaign than a million dollars generated in the seclusion of a closed assembly of forty people, each of whom contributes $25,000. This conviction initially was based on intuition, but it subsequently was reinforced through thoughtful discussions in early 1977 with President Jimmy Carter, Frank Moore, Hamilton Jordan, and other Carter advisors which led to a determined effort to open Democratic Party fund-raising to public view, and to broaden, dramatically, the number of people participating in that dimension of the Party's political outreach.

From the beginning, Betty Jo and Jess had taken this "inclusive" approach in their political fund-raising activities, and working on Dolph Briscoe's 1972 gubernatorial campaign would prove no exception. Their involvement in the effort became official after the January Fairmont Hotel triumph when Calvin Guest, Briscoe's campaign chairman, asked Jess to serve as the campaign's finance chairman. This allowed Betty Jo and Jess to make their next move: a large fund-raising rally in March at the Dallas Apparel Mart which attracted more than 1,700 people, brought in hundreds of thousands of dollars in contributions, and generated remarkable momentum for the campaign. Typically speaking, participants left the Apparel Mart determined to do all they could to help elect Dolph Briscoe governor, affirming both the political and the financial value of the event.

However, as with any hard-fought political battle, the ebbs and flows of fortune often derive from multiple sources. In Briscoe's case, part of the upswing certainly was due to an effective, positive campaign and the enthusiasm of his backers, but there was no way around the fact that Briscoe was catching fire because Barnes was flaming out. The unraveling began in February and March of 1972 as the Speaker of the Texas House of Representatives and two of his associates—entangled in the web of the Sharpstown scandal—went on trial in the case, generating intense media attention. The crescendo came on March 15, 1972, as the three were convicted of conspiracy to accept a bribe. Along with the guilty verdict came a dramatic shift in the direction of the governor's race and a burst in momentum for those candidates riding the reform wave. And though Lieutenant Governor Ben Barnes was not personally involved in the affair, he was connected to it in the arena of public opinion, if for no other reason, simply because at the time he was the state's second-ranking official and as such was the presiding officer of the Texas Senate. As tangential and unfair as this linkage may have been, the taint nonetheless was enough to torpedo his race for governor.

This significant turn of events quickly made Briscoe a more attractive candidate. He offered voters a socially sensitive and fiscally responsible alternative laced with the credible promise of reform, which, by this time, normally conservative Dallas was ready to embrace. When the votes were counted on the night of the Democratic primary, Briscoe had carried Dallas County, beating Barnes by 15,000 votes. "As far as I was concerned," said Roy Coffee who had been asked to stay within 10,000 votes of Barnes, "that was a 25,000 vote swing. It was a tremendous victory."

But it was not a decisive statewide win. Instead, Briscoe found himself in a runoff with Frances "Sissy" Farenthold, a liberal candidate who had capitalized on reform and other progressive issues. The Hays responded by continuing to whip up support in Dallas and throughout the state as the campaign slogged through the primary, the runoff, and eventually, on to the general election. Danny Pounds, a close aide to Dolph Briscoe during the campaign, recalls the intensity of Jess and Betty Jo's commitment and the close relationship that had developed between the Briscoes and the Hays:

> Jess and Betty Jo were key supporters in the Dallas community and were instrumental in the fund-raising effort, not only in Dallas but statewide, and they worked very diligently with Dolph and Janey any time there was a major fund-raiser going on. Betty Jo was very strong in helping coordinate these events in concert with Ramona Taylor. These were high-profile deals, and they raised a lot of money for that time. It took a lot of coordination to get them done right.

> Dolph's an interesting person. If somebody steps up to the plate and he asks them for their help and they follow through, he's committed to them; he believes in them. It's a very close relationship. . . . I traveled with Dolph and Janey everywhere in his private airplane so the people I knew were close to the Briscoes, and Jess and Betty Jo were the closest of anybody. . . . They were fun to be with. They would hang around after an event and we'd get together and have a cocktail late in the evening. . . . It was a very casual, close-knit group.

As their friendship grew, so did Briscoe's confidence that he had found in Betty Jo and Jess an astute, truthful pair of advisors on whom he could wholeheartedly depend. "Jess was not only a major fund-raiser, he was an ear for Dolph to bounce things off of and get input from," said Pounds. "Jess was a very successful businessman; his input was very important on a lot of issues and Dolph relied on his input."

"We were very close," said Briscoe, "Janey and I and Jess and Betty Jo. . . . I was always very interested in Betty Jo's ideas and her thoughts about what should be done. It was a good situation where I could try out various ideas on them and get an honest reaction. . . . They would tell it like they saw it."

Briscoe went on to defeat Farenthold in the runoff, securing the Democratic nomination for governor and ultimately the office itself, following a narrow victory over his Republican opponent in the November 1972 general election. Meanwhile, he nominated Jess Hay as one of two Texas members of the Democratic National Committee. And while the role wasn't one Hay had sought, it did enable him to represent Briscoe and the state of Texas on a national level, and, most important, to advance his moderate Democratic Party views on a larger, more influential stage.

Less than a month after the appointment, the Hay family was swept up by the political whirlwind of the 1972 Democratic National Convention in Miami Beach, Florida. Jess went as a delegate, while Betty Jo obtained floor credentials and worked closely with the Texas and Oklahoma delegations. Their objective, working with Bob Strauss, John White, George Bristol, Gordon Wynne, Jr., Bernie Rapoport, and a number of other friends, was to secure the Democratic presidential nomination for Washington Senator Henry "Scoop" Jackson, and in pursuit of that goal, Hay said he and Betty Jo "participated with great enthusiasm." Although Jackson lost the 1972 bid to South Dakota Senator George McGovern, the Hays nevertheless were reinvigorated by their experience and subsequently returned to Dallas, as Jess put it, "strongly committed to the Democratic Party." As for daughter Patty Hay's convention visit, it became an item in the Hillcrest High School student newspaper under the headline, "HHS Jr., daughter of delegate, experiences Demo convention," and contained the following excerpt:

> Patty spent the first two days in the visitors' gallery observing the activities on the floor. She and the rest of her family were allowed to sit on the floor level with the actual delegates the last two nights. During the convention, Patty came in contact with several politicians including Lloyd Bentsen, Hubert H. Humphrey, Dolph Briscoe, and Carl Albert. Albert, Patty's great-uncle, is the Speaker of the House of Representatives.

The 1972 Democratic National Convention was the first of seven in which Betty Jo and Jess would take part. Another "first" came four days after the hoopla and hullabaloo in Miami had ended, and the Hay family embarked on a three-week European vacation. Like Grand Tourists of centuries past, they traveled in aristocratic fashion, taking in the ancient culture and high society of the European continent. "Once my parents had the financial resources to experience that kind of travel," said Debby Hay Spradley, "they both wanted to add that to the broadened range of our family activities. My dad likes nice things."

It was their first exposure to Old World refinement and they spared no expense at expanding their cultural horizons during what would be an unforgettable family adventure. The itinerary leaned heavily toward England, and while in London for five days, The Dorchester—an exclusive Mayfair hotel overlooking Hyde Park—more than accommodated their stay. "It was the ultimate in luxury," recalls Patty Hay. "I remember thinking I've never been in such a comfortable bed with such comfortable pillows. The hotel had elegant high teas in the afternoon in the lobby. It was very posh."

Private tour guides, in the custom of eighteenth century "tutors," not only maximized the efficiency of exploring Europe's must-see cultural highlights, but they also provided a fascinating means by which the Hay family could increase its knowledge of the world. In London, the tour guide was known simply as Mrs. Dean— teacher of history, passionate royalist—and a woman who left a lasting impression on Patty Hay. "Mrs. Dean brought history alive for us. She captured the spirit of England." Mrs. Dean also was a staunch supporter of the British monarchy, said Patty, and she had a gift for relating "incredibly colorful stories. It didn't seem educational, but it was. She was lots of fun and had that wonderful British wit."

Across the English Channel, the Hays discovered the tourist treasures of Paris and Madrid. "It was our first exposure to that dimension of international culture," said Debby. "It was an exciting experience."

Jess Hay couldn't have put it better. "We had a great time," he said of that 1972 European holiday, "and our family's taste for foreign travel was whetted."

■

222

Betty Jo's personal journey also took on a broadened perspective in 1972. As she began to delve into new interests, the path toward a more meaningful life became clear, and not surprisingly it had evolved out of her growing commitment to political activism. Following a period of concentrated involvement in state and national politics, Betty Jo's attention now was drawn to the issues of the day, particularly to those involving inequality. Soon she would find herself advocating on behalf of the marginalized—speaking out for people within previously ignored segments of society who had begun to demand fair treatment after years of neglect and discrimination. Indeed, the early seventies witnessed the emergence of many such groups, a majority of whom had been stirred by the upheaval of the civil rights movement and antiwar protests of the 1960s. By 1972 their concerns had made it to the Democratic Party Platform:

> It is time now to rethink and reorder the institutions of this country so that every-one—women, blacks, Spanish-speaking, Puerto Ricans, Indians, the young, and the old—can participate in the decision-making process inherent in the democratic heritage to which we aspire.

The march toward equality thus encompassed a wide variety of groups demanding full participation in government and the democratic experience, and gaining the support of the Democratic Party in the process. Those singled out for special mention in the 1972 platform included: "Rights of Children, Rights of Women, Rights of Youth, Rights of Poor People, Rights of American Indians, Rights of the Physically Disabled, Rights of the Mentally Retarded, Rights of the Elderly, Rights of Veterans, and Rights of Consumers." Few stones were left unturned. There even was a category opposing homogeneity in favor of diversity—referred to in the platform as "The Right to be Different."

But one of the most persistent voices came from women. In 1966, twenty-eight professional women, including Betty Friedan, founded NOW, the National Organization for Women, a group determined "to take action to bring American women into full participation in the mainstream of American society now," according to its credo. Three years later in 1969, NOW sponsored a weeklong event at the White House, entitled "Freedom for Women Week," which kicked off on Mother's Day and featured demonstrators pointedly demanding "Rights, *NOT* Roses!" In 1970, NOW marked the milestone fiftieth anniversary of the nineteenth amendment to the U.S. Constitution—which gave women the right to vote—by organizing "Women's Strike for Equality," and proceeded to watch with pride as activities took place across forty states in more than ninety American cities and towns. To further salute the anniversary of their long-overdue right to vote, fifty thousand women marched along Fifth Avenue in New York City. Then, in 1972, *Ms. Magazine* hit newsstands. Founded by journalist Gloria Steinem, along with several female comrades, this bold, new national publication not only gave voice to the feminist cause, but it lent credence to feminist journalism, and made available to the masses the feminist worldview. More than anything else, though, *Ms.* reporters translated "a movement into a magazine," said founding editor Letty Cottin Pogrebin, and in so doing, took their place among the primary architects of contemporary feminism.

Organized activity on behalf of women's rights and issues reached a high point in the early 1970s. Betty Jo personally witnessed one of its historic, watershed moments in Miami when Congresswoman Shirley Chisholm of New York took the podium at the 1972 Democratic Convention as the first African-American woman, indeed, the first African-American candidate, for President of the United States. Chisholm championed the causes of the poor, the young, minorities, gays, women, and other marginalized Americans. "I ran for the presidency despite hopeless odds," she said, "to demonstrate sheer will and refusal to accept the status quo." And although Betty Jo likely shared few of Chisholm's more extreme liberal political views, there was at least one—the presidential hopeful's uncompromising belief in the right of minorities to full engagement in American life—which would have struck a sympathetic nerve. Likewise, Betty Jo would have been in full accord with Chisholm's strongly-held conviction that the country belongs to those who dare to claim their place in it. At the close of the convention, though, Chisholm would come up short in her quest to win the Democratic nomination, but not before leaving her mark on history and on those fellow Democrats—Betty Jo included—who witnessed her moment in the spotlight during the summer of '72.

Meanwhile, as the burgeoning women's movement was enjoying significant support among liberal bastions on the East and West coasts, the response to contemporary feminism in Dallas and around the state of Texas was slow and largely hostile during the early 1970s. "The women's movement was just beginning to hit Dallas about that time," remembers Debby Hay Spradley, "and my mother was beginning to be aware of it. Women's issues were very prominent. It was something that was beginning to evolve for her, but she probably would not have taken a radical approach to any of the women's issues." Rand (Sale) James, a friend and political ally, agrees Betty Jo was in tune to the movement of the times, but not intent on pursuing all items on its agenda. "I would say she was more for equality, not necessarily feminism. If somebody was qualified, she didn't want the woman to lose out because she was a woman. She wanted the best person."

The day came in 1972 when Betty Jo decided to engage the women's movement, and she did so by joining the board of the YWCA of Metropolitan Dallas at the request of Molly Stewart, a friend from SMU, and board member herself. "I knew she was pretty sharp and if she volunteered for something she did what she said," explained Stewart of her decision to nominate Betty Jo for the position. "She was also interested in women's issues." It wouldn't take long for Betty Jo to find that the YWCA of Dallas—with its thrust on social action—was a perfect match for her, and that her arrival was well-timed. By 1972, an upsurge in demand for action generated by the women's movement had set it on a course of change. Thus began a breathing of new life into the century-old YWCA, and eventually, liberation from its long-held image as a stodgy institution. Yet, even in the face of reform, the organization managed to stay within the bounds of mainstream moderation, demonstrating that it could pursue progressive programming and shift to a more activist mission of empowering women, while still retaining its reputation as a non-threatening, establishment organization. That is to say the YWCA of Dallas was "out there," but not edgy.

The appeal was mutual. Betty Jo had found a place to hang her hat, and the YWCA board secured for itself a super fund-raiser with powerful political connections. "I probably proposed her name to the nominating committee," said Stewart. "By 1972, Betty Jo was beginning to be known in Dallas for volunteering and also through politics." Almost immediately after joining the board, Betty Jo applied her skills and resources to a major capital fund drive which led to the construction of a new downtown YWCA building on Ross Avenue, an accomplishment of great importance to Betty Jo.

Equally important to her were the individual accomplishments of women who were beginning to break down the barriers to advancement. Molly Stewart remembers the day when a gleeful Betty Jo arrived at a YWCA board meeting and took a seat next to her. "I asked, 'What's going on? What is it?' She whispered to me that Locke, Purnell, Jess's former law firm, had just hired its first female lawyer, a young woman named Harriet Miers. Betty Jo was really excited about that." It didn't take long for Betty Jo to meet with Miers, develop a friendship, and subsequently persuade her to join the YWCA board. From that point forward, Betty Jo would follow Miers' distinguished and barrier-breaking career with pride, from her early days as a partner and then the managing partner of her law firm, to her service on the Dallas City Council, to her presidency of both the Dallas and Texas Bar Associations. Miers would go on to serve for six years as a key staff member for

President George W. Bush, after which she returned to Dallas to resume partnership in her old firm. And though she and Betty Jo may have sported different political stripes, they paid little attention to that fact and the two remained friends throughout the last thirty-three years of Betty Jo's life.

In 1976, the YWCA board asked Betty Jo to chair its annual dinner, slated that year to honor Johnnie Marie Grimes, a long-time driving force behind the organization. As the occasion coincided with the nation's bicentennial celebration, Betty Jo had all the more reason to plan a high visibility event, a sneak preview of which she gave Stewart during a casual conversation they had at the time. "I remember sitting in somebody's backyard and talking to her about it," Stewart said. "She thought it should be a really big deal and suggested inviting Lady Bird Johnson. . . . She knew how to get in touch with her." Although the former First Lady was unable to attend, Betty Jo had a top-notch backup. Janey Briscoe, First Lady of Texas, agreed to give the keynote address, and shortly after receiving the invitation, arrived in Dallas, husband in tow. The event was publicized in a Dallas newspaper and contained a portion of Betty Jo's introductory remarks during which she threw a one-line zinger at Texas Governor Dolph Briscoe. The story read, in part:

> Betty Jo Hay, who chaired the dinner, warned the governor: "I have seen Janey sit
> in rapt attention through every word of your speeches, and I'm going to keep my
> eye on you to see that you honor her in the same way."

The reference, of course, was to the widespread perception that the governor's stump speeches, like those of all political candidates as they move from town to town during a campaign season, were invariably quite repetitive. Sitting "in rapt attention," therefore, would have required the acting skills of a truly devoted wife. It was classic Betty Jo. With disarming candor, she had lightened things up, put yet another group at ease, then proceeded with the business of advancing the agenda of a worthy cause.

Four years later, in 1980, the YWCA of Metropolitan Dallas would honor Betty Jo and six other women for the contributions they had made to the organization and to their community. A plaque bearing their names and the inscription "YW Women—Our Greatest Resource," would stand as a visible reminder of the significant roles they played at a crucial time in the organization's history. Not long afterward, a new YWCA facility designed to meet the contemporary needs of women opened in Dallas. Known as the Women's Resource Center, it offered "Displaced Homemaker Services, Employment Services, an Alcohol Intervention Program, School-age Mother's Program, and Therapeutic Counseling," each reflecting the mission of an organization intent on removing the barriers to self-sufficiency. "The YWCA is a life-changing organization dedicated to improving women's lives," its mission statement read. "We know that enriching and empowering the lives of women builds better families, better communities and a brighter future for all."

To further polish its public image, the YWCA took the important step of updating its slogan. *"It's not the same old place anymore,"* the organization now proclaimed, leaving little doubt that times were indeed changing. A Dallas newspaper underscored that theme in its coverage of the resource center's opening:

> The new resource center at the YWCA's central branch . . . is an eye-opener for those who still view the organization as a place where doting do-gooders teach young girls to knit, swim, and tread the narrow path to salvation.

Women who remained unconvinced as to whether the YWCA actually had gotten into the swing of the seventies needed only to check the revised list of class offerings to see otherwise. For the first time, belly dancing was being taught, and Betty Jo—a dance enthusiast all her life—signed up for the cutting-edge class, thus adding a Middle Eastern art form to her mostly Western repertoire. It was "the thing to do for exercise," she told Molly Stewart. "It does wonders for you." Soon, Betty Jo's friends were blazing the belly dancing trail with her, among them Georgette Zarafonetis, who years earlier had pitched in to help with campaign mailings during their years on Annapolis Lane. "Betty Jo called my mother and told her that a few of her friends were going to take belly dancing at the Y, and invited her to join them," said daughter Juliette Zarafonetis Balabanian, Patty's good friend. "Of course, my mother jumped at the opportunity to do something fun with Betty Jo."

In 1972, Betty Jo's expanding interest in meritorious causes led her to a matter of growing public concern which would dominate the future of her service career. That year she accepted an invitation from E. V. "Bud" Hyde, president of the Mental Health Association of Dallas, to become Dallas area chairperson for the Galaxy Ball, the annual fund-raising event for the Mental Health Association in Texas, which was to be held in El Paso. Though it was unfamiliar territory for Betty Jo, Jess said it didn't take long for her to grasp the overwhelming need for mental health services, and to see that what little was available, was shamefully under funded:

She was always very open to new possibilities, but she was very discriminating. She didn't take on things that she didn't really want to give 100 percent to. . . . Once she heard what the mission of mental health was and got into some of the needs, particularly as they related to children, it became a driving passion of hers. . . . She was comfortable taking on the Galaxy Ball and did a bang-up job.

Prior to the Galaxy Ball fund-raising event, Betty Jo took advantage of a newspaper interview to make substantive public comments about the seriousness of mental illness and what she perceived as the issue's growing and unmet needs. Even at this initial stage of her association with the mental health movement, it was evident from the story that her interest was far more than perfunctory:

As I've been working on this year's Galaxy Ball, I've been amazed how little people know about mental illness. . . . It's very important that people know what a serious health problem mental illness is, that one person in every ten during his or her lifetime will have some form of mental illness requiring professional help.

In the same news story, Betty Jo expressed dismay at the considerable lack of state resources being allocated for mental health services, not to mention the sheer lack of interest, both of which she found troubling, especially when it came to children:

Betty Jo is deeply concerned at the lack of children's residential mental health facilities in this state. "It's disturbing," she said, "that the only such public facility is a ten-bed unit recently opened at Terrell State Hospital."

The solution, she concluded in the story, would have to be two-fold—increased funding and a commitment to action:

Betty Jo believes it takes money to get things done and knows money will help make the public aware of the problems of mental illness and the need for a more enlightened mental health policy in this state.

"We must care about mental health programs and mental illness problems, we must keep on working for understanding. Each of us, as we work together, can make a difference," the Galaxy Ball chairman said.

The Galaxy Ball leader took her own advice about "working for understanding" and making a difference on mental health issues when she accepted an invitation to join the board of the Mental Health Association of Dallas (MHA Dallas) in early 1973.

That same year, Betty Jo's distress over mental health issues rose to a new level when a crisis focused public attention on child abuse in Dallas. It had been reported in the media that suspected child abuse cases arriving for treatment at Parkland Hospital's emergency room were not being adequately investigated to determine the sources of the abuse, leaving many children to return in six months time needing medical attention for injuries similar to those previously treated. In response to what clearly appeared to be child abuse, the Mental Health Association of Dallas stepped in and rallied a multi-disciplinary team of social, health, and law enforcement agencies to tackle the problem in a conference setting. The initiative was taken by executive director of MHA Dallas, Katherine Reed, and MHA Dallas president Oswin Chrisman, a Dallas County District Judge whose responsibilities included the Dallas County mental illness docket. Reed not only was an attorney, but also a dynamic, determined advocate for the mentally ill whose network of sources included emergency room nurses at Parkland Hospital who provided her with vital information needed to initiate action.

As for Judge Chrisman, he distinctly remembers his growing concern during the early 1970s, particularly one week before the conference when he said "a little boy who previously had been treated at Parkland's emergency room . . . soon returned to the emergency room, and this time he had been scalded in boiling water. . . . I think he died." While the tragedy shocked the community—child abuse, after all, was an issue long shrouded in silence—it also galvanized many into action.

The conference team began by generating a report in September 1973 that contained recommendations on how to strengthen community capabilities in the areas of prevention and treatment. MHA Dallas followed up by establishing a permanent interdisciplinary Child Abuse Committee aimed at providing "an efficient and effective community network of services for the prevention and treatment of child abuse and neglect." At the state level, the committee succeeded at proposing and lobbying for legislation that not only mandated physicians to report suspected cases of child abuse, but elevated non-reporting to a criminal offense.

Impressed by the high caliber of leadership within the Dallas organization and by its willingness to take meaningful action, Betty Jo made a decision to devote the lion's share of her volunteer time and energy to the Mental Health Association (now called Mental Health America). An excerpt from a speech she gave in 1978 outlined the purpose of the nonprofit advocacy organization and her reasons for supporting it:

> The Mental Health Association is a volunteer organization. Its function is to promote citizen interest and activity, to bring about prevention of mental illness, promotion of mental health, and improved services for the mentally ill. Our job is to determine what needs to be done and then stimulate and arouse public concern. We also feel it is our responsibility to keep our elected officials aware of mental health issues and needs on a local, state, and national level. We have no vested interest except to be an advocate for the consumer in need of mental health services.

In 1974, she went a step further in her commitment to trumpet the cause of mental health by joining the state board of the Mental Health Association, known as MHA Texas. "She saw it as a cause that had never had enough prominence or enough people really interested," said Governor Briscoe. "It had been neglected. . . . She saw the need."

It was an easy need to neglect, Betty Jo discovered, because mental illness not only was an immensely complex disease with no simple solution, but it also had been plagued for decades, indeed even for centuries, by misconceptions and related lack of caring. As she educated herself on the subject, Betty Jo learned that strongly-held negative stereotypes about the mentally ill too often turned those who suffered from it into social outcasts, and that many of them encountered the added burden of rejection in their struggle to overcome psychological disorders. She found that widespread lack of knowledge about the disease had led to the mistaken belief that individuals with mental illness were weak in character or inevitably dangerous. Overcoming these misconceptions became of paramount importance to Betty Jo, and a vital part of the MHA's advocacy work. And although raising money would continue to be the Galaxy Ball's primary purpose, Katherine Reed and Betty Jo determined that in Dallas, at least, the time had come for the event to serve as a vehicle for conquering the fear and shame associated with mental illness. With Betty Jo now firmly behind the cause of mental health, supporting it soon became less of a social stigma.

Before long, women who previously would have sidestepped the issue began to find value in it as a volunteer opportunity that merited their participation. Using her credibility and influence, Betty Jo was able to draw the interest of elite society women known for supplying the horsepower behind Dallas charities. "Betty Jo was kind of a heavy-hitter," said Chrisman. "When she got involved, things really started happening. . . .We suddenly got community support." Dr. Peggy Wildman, former MHA Dallas vice president, and self-described "worker bee" within the cause, characterized Betty Jo as a "money bee" who persuaded "the monied people in Dallas" to sign on to the mental health cause.

In 1973, the Galaxy Ball celebrated its tenth anniversary and Dallas was selected to host the event. This time, Betty Jo demonstrated her ability to make things happen from behind-the-scenes on the advisory committee. Yet even in that capacity, remembers Oswin Chrisman, she held sway, enticing some of Dallas' most influential figures to serve within the volunteer ranks in planning the statewide event. Among them were two socially prominent Dallas women: Jane Murchison, who acted as honorary ball chairman, and Geri Neill, the ball's general chairman. To snag the biggest attraction, though, Betty Jo turned to the political establishment, securing the "Honorable and Mrs. John Connally" as honorary anniversary chairmen. "Betty Jo got the Connallys lined up," said Chrisman. "She was the kind of leader who didn't particularly want to be front and center . . . but she knew who to call on, who to get for this and that." Following the event, Betty Jo and fellow MHA Dallas board member Paul Raigorodsky were presented "super" volunteer awards for their contribution to the Galaxy Ball's success.

And while it certainly was good to be "super," Betty Jo instead preferred the term "professional" to describe the work she was doing. Indeed, professionalism had been the hallmark of every endeavor that ever mattered to her, whether debate, homemaking, church volunteering, political campaigning, or advocating for the mentally ill, children, women, and education. Each was undertaken with painstaking care and attention to detail. In fact, she occasionally touched on the subject of professionalism, oftentimes during speeches before audiences of women, as in this 1985 presentation to a Mental Health Association audience:

> I believe each of us must be truly professional. Professional in the sense that you have taken the time and applied the energy necessary to master the special knowledge needed to fulfill your particular responsibilities. Professional in the sense that you accept responsibility for your work, and you are committed to the highest possible standards in the performance of your jobs. Professional in the sense that you take pride in what you do, and you take satisfaction in performing up to your own demanding standards.

Betty Jo's was an exacting standard, to be sure, and she proved capable of living up to it time and again throughout her life. Her fund-raising efforts for the 1973 Galaxy Ball furnish a prime example of her usual work ethic, evident in a document she prepared for a MHA fundraising workshop, in which she noted: *"1973—Galaxy Ball—I raised approximately $50,000 from sending personal letters to 60 friends asking for $1,000 each."*

A simple-sounding task on the surface, yet as the devil invariably is in the details, there was far more to it—but then details were Betty Jo's specialty. Other workshop notes from the document show the degree of professionalism she brought to each of her fund-raising commitments:

1. Raise money for only one organization a year.
2. Set a dollar amount as your goal.
3. Always include something about that organization in your conversations with friends and be enthusiastic about what you are doing in that organization.
4. Solicit contributions from people you know.
5. Tell them some of the things the organization does.
6. Ask for a designated amount.
7. If solicitation is done by mail, enclose a self addressed return envelope.
8. Use your own personal stationery and make it a personal letter.
9. Challenge other board members.

At the top of the page, above her typewritten notes, Betty Jo added the postscript, *"No magic,"* in long hand, an indication, perhaps, of the thought process she may have used when deciding how to approach a particular endeavor. That is to say, while Betty Jo's professional success clearly was derived from hard work—and, to her credit, had resulted in a formula which could be replicated by other volunteers—there was no denying the star power, indeed, the magic, of "Team Betty Jo and Jess Hay." Together they exuded a remarkable aura of unseen might to which Betty Jo turned when necessary. In time, this merger of power, resources, and high-level political connections would cast an even more enchanting and alluring spell, making continued success possible, and above all, positively impacting the lives of people.

As Betty Jo worked on the Galaxy Ball in 1973, Jess continued to build his reputation as a political money magnet. That year, he—along with Trammell Crow and John Stemmons—co-hosted a pre-inaugural ball at the Fairmont Hotel in honor of Governor-elect Dolph Briscoe. According to news accounts at the time, the event was seen as a major flexing of the state's Democratic Party muscle. One newspaper reported, "An array of state and local Democratic leaders, as well as a few sometime Republican supporters were among the some 800 guests, as were city and county dignitaries."

Hay's arrival as a player on the national political scene was further solidified in 1973 when a small, but select group of guests attended a fund-raising dinner at his home. Touted as a low-key affair, the event nevertheless attracted plenty of news coverage:

> Financial heavyweights in the Dallas Democratic camp have pledged $130,000 to the 1974 party cause at a "quiet dinner" here attended by House Speaker Carl Albert and U.S. Sens. Lloyd Bentsen and Henry "Scoop" Jackson. . . . The Monday night dinner was attended by 85 men and women from the local business and professional community at the North Dallas home of Democratic National Committeeman Jess Hay.

Bentsen followed up the dinner with a handwritten note of thanks, which alludes to the initial feeling of closeness he and his wife, B. A., felt for Betty Jo and Jess:

> Dear Jess: You are a superb and effective organizer, a fine fund-raiser, and Betty Jo is a warm, gracious hostess—and you, too, of course. . . . B. A. and I will long cherish the memory of a beautiful evening with good friends.

A subsequent visit to the Hay home in October 1973 prompted another note from Bentsen, this one emphasizing the couples' personal and political compatibility, and acknowledging their growing friendship:

> B. A. and I enjoyed very much the opportunity to spend the weekend in your home. . . . I believe what I enjoyed most was having an opportunity to visit with the two of you the next morning at some length. It's great to see the two of you having such a mutuality of interests, and in this day and time to see other happy couples.

As it turned out, the "quiet dinner" on Lupton Circle was a prelude to an even bigger event later in the month, this time in Washington, D.C. where a national fund-raising dinner generated more than $1 million. Under the headline, "Jess Hay Plays Big Role in Democrats' Rebound," *Dallas Morning News* columnist Carolyn Barta wrote, "That ought to give local pols some muscle in national party affairs." The story went on to read:

Much of the success of the event from the Dallas end can be attributed directly to Democratic National Committeeman Jess Hay, chairman of the board of Lomas & Nettleton. . . .

Already, Hay is proving his salt as a money-getter, and is highly regarded by Democratic National Chairman Robert Strauss. . . . "If we can just keep Jess Hay working, we've got it made," said Strauss.

Meanwhile, Hay scored another victory on October 30, 1973 following an appreciation dinner and fund-raiser for Governor Briscoe, who used the gala occasion in Austin to announce his intention to run for reelection. The event was an impressive political happening, even by Texas standards, noted *The Dallas Morning News:*

It was . . . the biggest political event of its kind in Texas history—with more than 9,000 lunch-pails distributed to guests who filled Austin's municipal auditorium to standing room only. . . .

It seems certain that Briscoe's bash will prove to be the year's single biggest political money raising event in the state. . . . Jess Hay, the Dallas investment man who had been a great help in Briscoe's political career, estimated ticket sales around the state may net a total of more than $750,000. . . . Hay, who is a Democratic national committeeman, can be credited with putting together one of the most impressive productions in history for the Briscoes' "appreciation night."

To get the job done, Hay used his discerning eye for talent and hired his longtime friends J. Liener Temerlin and Stan Richards—topnotch Dallas public relations professionals—to handle the creative heavy lifting required by such a major undertaking. Temerlin and Richards proved their capabilities by putting together a fast-paced, entertaining production that included a crowd-pleasing sound and light multimedia show. Over the years, Hay would continue to rely on this talented twosome and their agencies to cleverly communicate many of his most important political, as well as business, messages and ideas.

Hay, himself, possessed a flair for the spoken word, which might have explained the conspicuously large number of Dallas celebrants attending the Briscoe appreciation dinner in Austin. Determined to make a good out-of-town showing, Hay delivered a powerful message on the importance of a strong turnout and apparently was heard loud and clear.

CLAP, CLAP.

We're going to make "The Face of Texas" the biggest event yet in Texas political history.

But to make it happen, *your* part is indispensable!

As a member of the Participation Committee, it is absolutely imperative that you uphold your commitment to sell tickets, to attend the gala in person and to assure the attendance of just as many other people as possible.

Applaud
Governor Dolph Briscoe
on Appreciation Night
on October Thirtieth at
The Municipal Auditorium
in Austin, Texas.
Hurrah!

Thanks to the efforts of some 500 members of a participation committee of Briscoe supporters, thousands of people gathered on October 30, 1973, at the Municipal Auditorium in Austin—which was packed beyond capacity—to express appreciation to Janey and Dolph Briscoe for their distinguished service as First Lady and Governor of the State of Texas, and to applaud Dolph's announcement at the event that he intended to seek reelection in 1974.

"Dallas had the largest delegation of any single area at the event," he told a newspaper reporter. "The crowd included more than 750 Dallasites—including about 500 who made the trip in two chartered jetliners and three chartered buses."

And on the heels of this latest success, came a personal thank-you letter from Janey Briscoe to Betty Jo:

> You and Jess have got to be the greatest! Dolph and I feel very blessed and humble to share your friendship. Not only are we proud of you for the fine, Christian couple you are but we respect you each for your intelligence, ability, and accomplishments. We're very lucky to be your friends.
>
> The dinner you just put on for Dolph was simply—as the kids say—
> "super fantastic!"

■

236

The Hay family raised its hometown visibility another notch when Debby Hay accepted an invitation from the exclusive Idlewild Club to participate in its 1973-1974 debutante season. Before the invitation arrived, however, Debby said she had given little thought to the high society affair. "Mom and Dad asked me if I wanted to do it. I didn't know anything about it; I had never been to a deb party. I think it was more of a family decision. It was nothing I was longing to do." Still, making a formal debut into Dallas society sounded like fun, Debby said, not to mention "it provided an opportunity for all of us to meet a lot of nice people that we might never have met." As part of the process, she was interviewed for a newspaper story entitled "Meet the debs," during which society editor Janet DeSanders took note of Debby's earnestness when it came to the topic of travel:

> "I love New York," she beams, and you would gather that this chic, fashionable young lady would shop from sunup to sundown but no—"I hate to waste my time in the stores all day," she said, "I'd rather be at the Metropolitan Museum or seeing the shows!"

The debutante season included four bustling months of brunches, lunches, teas, and balls. "It was an enjoyable time for Betty Jo and me," recalls Jess. "We probably attended a total of fourteen formal balls and some forty to fifty parties of various types. . . . As you might expect, we thought Debby was the belle of every ball." To further mark the occasion, several of the Hays' close friends, including Adele (Locke) Seybold, hosted parties in Debby's honor. "Betty Jo agreed to let me give the seated dinner before Debby's debut dance and it turned out to be an elegant evening," Adele said. "I had been very close to the Hays' children, Debby and Patty, for many years. . . . So, I had a seated dinner at the Dallas Petroleum Club. It was Debby's twenty-first birthday. . . . I considered it a privilege and a joy to be involved with the Hay family all through the years."

The next year, Debby continued her studies at SMU and developed a relationship with Charles Werner—Chuck, to those who knew him. Chuck had graduated from SMU in 1974 with a business degree. "Chuck was great," said sister, Patty Hay. "He was very laid-back, funny, fit in with everyone, a really good guy." "Chuck was a fine young man," echoed Ramona Taylor. "He was smart and funny."

By the time Debby graduated from SMU in the spring of 1975 with a degree in journalism, Chuck already had asked Betty Jo and Jess for permission to marry their daughter, and plans got underway for the couple's union later that summer. On August 2, 1975, they were married at Highland Park United Methodist Church, and afterwards, they shared in festivities at the Fairmont Hotel's Regency Ballroom.

■

Three years later, Debby announced she was pregnant, prompting immediate celebration by Betty Jo and Jess, surpassed only by the much-heralded arrival of Jessica Kathryn Werner on June 30, 1978. "When Jessica was born, it was a huge event in terms of its significance to Betty Jo and me," said Jess. "It regenerated both of us and gave us a renewed sense of purpose and all those things that go with being a grandparent."

As would be expected, they were doting grandparents, and wore that richly-deserved mantle with great pride. When a babysitter was required, for example, not only did Debby never need to hire one, but Betty Jo, Jess, and Patty fought over whose turn it was to take care of Jessica for an afternoon or an evening. And on that subject, one classic babysitting tale has taken its rightful place among the annals of Hay family lore. It occurred on a weekday when Patty was unavailable to help with Jessica, and Betty Jo had a mental health association meeting she couldn't miss. That left Jess, who considered the predicament more of an opportunity than a crisis. Ever true to his belief that family came first, Jess Hay— most certainly one of the country's busiest corporate executives at the time—solved the dilemma by having Jessica brought to Lomas & Nettleton's executive offices where he proceeded to watch over her while going about the day's business. And although Jessica would have no memory of her grandfather's gesture of kindness, she would come to know it well through a photograph snapped by a quick-thinking secretary wise enough to recognize its significance. The image captured Jess presiding over a meeting of senior executives as Jessica slept peacefully on a blanket beside his chair. "He would bring her to the office, and we would all care for her," Ramona Taylor affectionately remembers. "Jessica was always so happy, social, and cuddly. She was a delightful baby."

In addition to those occasional childcare adventures at the office, Jess took pleasure in stopping by Debby's house to see Jessica nearly every day on his way to work. "He didn't stay long," said Taylor. "He just wanted to stop in and get a hug. He's always been very, very involved in Jessica's life." Jess was even known to make a visit at the end of a workday, or—remembers Jane Garner, the English nanny who eventually would join the Hay family in caring for Jessica—to stop by the house on his way to the airport if he was going on a business trip, "to say goodbye to her before he went out of town."

Jessica had the love and attention of her grandmother, as well, and it was displayed in all manner of ways. One way in particular has remained with Ramona Taylor for these many years because, she said, it was so uniquely Betty Jo:

> Betty Jo was an accomplished seamstress. I can remember her sewing darling two-piece outfits for Jessica when she was a toddler. She had a good time buying fabrics, finding patterns, and sewing. Jessica always looked adorable. She was always perfectly dressed whatever the occasion—playing, going to church, or out to dinner.

Such was the advantage of being a stylish, young grandmother with a discriminating eye for fashion, and talent with a needle and thread. "My parents took to grandparenting like ducks to water," said Patty. "They were both very young grandparents. They were in their forties. They were playing with her and swimming with her. Everything you would do with your own children, my parents would do with Jessica." And so it was that Betty Jo and Jess—vibrant forty-somethings and thrilled to be grandparents—were among the regulars at Pennywhistle Park, an indoor amusement park for small children and one of the most popular play destinations of its day. They spent many an enjoyable afternoon with Jessica at that venerable Dallas institution, a place Taylor remembers as if yesterday. "The park had a carousel and other little rides, games and prizes, ice cream and cotton candy. It was all inside, air-conditioned in the summer and heated in the winter. You could put them on the rides and stand right there and watch them. It was very safe and a fun place to take the little ones."

And that was just one activity. In addition, Jess taught Jessica how to fish and ride horses—and pampered her in every other conceivable way, the ponies being a good example. "Jessica loved ponies," explained Patty. "So, my dad bought her two miniature horses that she named Bandit and White Cloud." Two horses, explained Jess, because "Betty Jo and I always thought in terms of not only reaching out to our own kids and grandkids, but facilitating their sharing whatever they had with friends. That was sort of the idea which led to our purchase of the second horse." On that note, and much to Jessica's delight, the two horses soon arrived unannounced at her home. "Of course Jessica loved them, and they were very gentle," said Hay.

Unfortunately, it didn't take long for Bandit and White Cloud to wear out their collective welcome at Jessica's house, which point occurred about a week after their arrival when they made the decision to take a stroll through the neighborhood without permission. Luckily, the ever-vigilant Jane Garner made the discovery, "one day looking out the window and suddenly seeing these two horses going down Desco Drive. So, we had to run outside and catch them. They were smart little horses and probably unbolted the backyard gate," Garner said, giving proper credit to the escapees for their ingenuity. "After that, we decided they would go and live up at Ned Harris's farm."

Meanwhile, Jessica's affability made her a much-loved family favorite whose company was highly sought. She spent a good deal of time with her great grandparents, growing as she did to appreciate the value of family just as Betty Jo and Jess and their own children had. With Kathryn still working in Dallas several days a week, she and Duncan were able to develop an uncommonly close bond with their great-granddaughter, said Patty:

> Granny and Dan Dan were very, very important in Jessica's life. And once she was old enough, she would go to Oklahoma and spend a week or more with Granny every summer. She and Dan Dan would work in his garden. . . . Jessica stayed close to them and called Granny every week even after she was in college.

Theirs was a strikingly similar relationship to that which Betty Jo had nurtured some thirty-five years earlier with her grandfather, Ernest, during her many stays at the Bug Tussle family farm in Oklahoma. "It was a very, very close-knit family," Jane Garner was coming to learn, "all the generations."

Jessica's stature confirmed that children held prominent positions within the Hay family hierarchy and were to be included in most family activities. Indeed, throughout their years of raising two daughters, Betty Jo and Jess had leaned so strongly toward the concept of inclusion that when Debby and Patty became parents themselves, they knew no other way. "Our children have always gone pretty much everywhere with us," said Patty, "and that was super-true of Jessica. Later when we had Rachel and Jess—it didn't matter, nice restaurants, big trips—we brought them along. That was part of it."

After Jessica was born, Debby left her full time job with Dallas Market Center (DMC) to care for Jessica. For the next two years, Debby continued to work part time during markets at the DMC in the public relations department headed by Debby's good friend and mentor, Delores Lehr. While she worked markets, Debby was fortunate that Tu kept Jessica for her. "Mother allowed me to continue my career during those two years, knowing that Jessica was well taken care of. I will forever be grateful to her for the time and energy she dedicated to Jessica's early development."

In 1980, Debby and Chuck divorced. Finding herself a single mom with a daughter to provide for, Debby forged ahead with her career and returned to work full time at the Dallas Market Center. Debby remained at the DMC until 1983 when she left to form

The Hay Agency, Inc., a small public relations and advertising firm in downtown Dallas. Her entrepreneurial initiative resulted in a work schedule affording Debby more flexibility in fulfilling her primary role: being a nurturing and loving mother to Jessica. On the other hand, ownership also brought with it the burden of greater responsibility which, when added to Debby's status as a single parent, made it clear that some assistance in caring for Jessica would be required.

Based on their knowledge of and interest in the broader childcare issue of the day, Betty Jo and Jess suggested a live-in nanny for Jessica, preferably from England, which at the time was turning out the best-trained and most experienced childcare providers around. That's when Margaret and Trammell Crow stepped in and enthusiastically recommended Knightsbridge Nannies in London, which proved instrumental to the cause. Acting on the tip, Debby and Ramona Taylor set out for the United Kingdom to conduct a series of interviews in London, whereupon they met Jane Garner and pronounced her their hands-down favorite, straightaway. Fully licensed by the National Nursery Examination Board, Garner's credentials also included teacher training and early childhood education. "Jane was a very polished lady," said Jess. "She was literate, well-mannered, a good teacher, and deeply caring. In short, she was an ideal nanny—one that Betty Jo and I considered comparable to Mary Poppins of Disney fame."

Garner was equally impressed by the Hay family. Looking back over their years of association, Garner remembers being drawn into a sense of closeness by the family's warmth and sincerity. "Debby and Mr. and Mrs. Hay absolutely went out of their way to make sure I was included as part of the family."

Where Chuck was concerned, the friendship he had built with the Hays, although somewhat strained immediately following the divorce, managed to remain intact, as did his relationship with Jessica. "Chuck adored Jessica," said Taylor, "and she him." Said Jane Garner: "Jessica adored her dad and he loved to go and do fun things with her. He loved to take her shopping and to Scarborough Faire."

Meanwhile, Betty Jo's own devotion and attention to Jessica, on top of her many civic responsibilities, had become such, that she, like Debby, now required additional outside assistance. So, at the same time Jane Garner was hired in the early 1980s, Betty Jo retained the services of Repina (Re) Ruru, whose job it was to keep Lupton Circle up and running. A native New Zealand Maori of Polynesian decent, Re Ruru had worked in England before coming to Dallas in 1983. "Mom was busy with Jessica and she had the mental health stuff going on," remembers Patty. "Re was the first of what I would call a house manager. . . . That house is not easy. It requires a lot of work to keep it going, so they needed someone with management skills." Re eventually would leave the post, making way for Marie Powis from England, who performed similar duties, but had the added advantage of being a versatile, exceptional professional chef. Within no time, Marie had mastered the art of "East Texas" cuisine, which earned her plenty of accolades in the Hay household, where—as she quickly found out—chicken-fried steak trumped chateaubriand any day.

■

Betty Jo's first formal commitment to the cause of education began a decade earlier in 1973 when Governor Dolph Briscoe became aware of her dual interest in education and public service, and appointed her to the Coordinating Board, Texas College and University System. "To me, it was a very simple decision," Briscoe recalled. "The Coordinating Board was relatively new and there was a need for members on that board who were dedicated to improving our institutions of higher learning." But not just any members, he explained:

> It came out during the campaign that one of her main interests was education. I thought at the time it was the perfect appointment, and it turned out to be such. . . . Here's a woman who . . . recognized the vital need for Texas to have an excellent system of higher education. She also brought the point of view of a woman.

The lone woman, to be exact. Of the eighteen appointed board members seventeen were men, and at the start of Betty Jo's tenure, some of them responded to her presence with the sort of cloying condescension and exaggerated courtesy that passed for gallantry among the unenlightened male population of Texas at the time. Wally Chappell remembers those days well, and revels in relating the 1973 tale of Betty Jo's legendary first brush with that manly assemblage:

> When she was appointed to the Coordinating Board . . . she was the only woman on the board, which according to Texas custom . . . was part of the Good Ol' Boy network. . . . They were a bit astonished to find a small, attractive, well-dressed lady in their midst . . . and proceeded to do their "bidness" as if she wasn't present. . . . After the meeting, Betty Jo swung into preparation: briefings by the staff and other carefully selected individuals; digesting stacks of reports; study of budgets, charts, and documents; preparing lists of questions; and learning the buttons to push.

THE COORDINATING BOARD · TEXAS COLLEGE AND UNIVERSITY SYSTEM

Resolution to

BETTY JO HAY

Mrs. Jess Hay, affectionately known to her colleagues on the Coordinating Board as Betty Jo, was a member of the Board from September 1973 until her term expired in August 1979. In addition to her Coordinating Board activities, she has been an active civic leader in both Dallas and statewide activities with particular emphasis in the areas of mental health and child abuse. Her membership on the Council on Postsecondary Accreditation in which she invested great time and energy was a particularly important adjunct to her membership on the Coordinating Board.

Mrs. Hay, during her six-year term, became a serious student of the challenges facing higher education in Texas and the United States. She developed a broad background of knowledge which enabled her to make decisions that were developed in-depth and carefully balanced in appreciation of conflicting priorities. Never doctrinaire in her views, she weighed the merits of each topic and proposal carefully. Her position was always noted carefully by her fellow Board members, as they knew it had been arrived at in a careful manner.

Mrs. Hay was appointed to the Committee on Program Development in November of 1973 and the Committee on Financial Planning in January of 1974, serving on both committees until the end of her term. She was named Chairman of the Committee on Financial Planning in January of 1976. In this role she exercised strong leadership in the Board's financial affairs. She was also appointed to the ad hoc committee to respond to SR 209, a restudy of higher education in Texas, in November 1974 and to the ad hoc committee on revision of Policy Paper 1 in January 1976.

Betty Jo Hay, through her service on the Coordinating Board, demonstrated that she is an effective and dedicated public servant.

THEREFORE, BE IT RESOLVED, by the Coordinating Board, Texas College and University System, that the Board expresses to Mrs. Jess Hay, its deep appreciation for her service on the Board and the great contribution she made to its deliberations. She will be remembered as a warm friend by her colleagues on the Board.

BE IT FURTHER RESOLVED, that a copy of this resolution be spread upon the minutes of the Board and that a copy be sent to Mrs. Hay.

DONE AT AUSTIN, TEXAS, THIS 25TH DAY OF JANUARY 1980

BERYL BUCKLEY MILBURN, *Chairman*

CHARLES BUTT

HAL DAUGHERTY, JR.

NEWTON GRESHAM

GWENDOLYN C. MORRISON

L. F. PETERSON

HERBERT G. SCHIFF

R. PAUL TEAGUE, SR.

M. HARVEY WEIL

TOM B. RHODES, *Vice Chairman*

HARLAN CROW

MARSHALL FORMBY

R. F. JUEDEMAN

ROBERT H. PARK

MARIO E. RAMIREZ, M.D.

RALPH SPENCE

WAYNE E. THOMAS

SAM D. YOUNG, JR.

Betty Jo was a respected member of the Coordinating Board, Texas College and University System from 1973-1979. On January 25, 1980, in recognition of the six years she had spent serving the needs of Texas college students, the board issued this resolution in her honor.

The Council on Postsecondary Accreditation

Acknowledges With Deep Appreciation
The Services of Board Member

Betty Jo Hay
1976-1979

Chairman

President

For three years during the late 1970s, Betty Jo was a member of the Council on Postsecondary Accreditation, a non-governmental body responsible for promoting and ensuring a basic level of quality within America's institutions of higher education.

When the board met the NEXT time, the Ol' Boys sat up and took notice—this attractive, petite lady knew her stuff, and was never thereafter treated condescendingly as an outsider.

With Texas colleges and universities at a critical juncture in the 1970s, Betty Jo's instinctive need to learn as much as possible about how they got to that point proved crucial to her effectiveness on the Coordinating Board. And there was a lot to learn. Here, after all, was a board charged with overseeing a vast system of colleges and universities comprised of nearly one hundred institutions with more than 650,000 students. Its legally defined purpose was to achieve excellence in college education "through the efficient and effective utilization and concentration of all available resources and the elimination of costly duplication in program offerings, faculties, and physical plants." For nearly ten years the board had been responding to the influx of "baby boomer" students by approving aggressive growth and expansion plans to meet the demands of a growing population. But by the time Betty Jo took her seat on the board, the numbers had peaked and the urgent need for additional facilities and programs had abated, at least for a time.

The upward momentum continued, however, fueled by ambitious college presidents, aggressive boards of regents, civic boosterism, and business and real estate promoters. To counter the system's runaway expansion, leaders of the Coordinating Board proposed moving toward a change in policy. Governor Briscoe liked the idea and in 1975 signaled his intention to apply the brakes to the creeping excesses of higher education by appointing Harry Provence chairman of the Coordinating Board. As editor-in-chief of the *Waco Tribune-Herald,* the scrappy Provence had earned himself a reputation for "taking on the mighty and powerful to help out the beleaguered citizen," a watchdog sentiment shared by board member Betty Jo Hay, who, along with Provence, most assuredly subscribed to the populist adage: "You have to get the hogs out of the creek before the water will clear up."

In 1976, Briscoe's policies of restraint took another step forward with the hiring of Dr. Kenneth Ashworth as Commissioner of Higher Education, the top staff position. Once on board, Ashworth said he sensed that change was in the offing. "From my very first meeting," Ashworth recalls, "Harry Provence, Harvey Weil, Betty Jo, and some of the other leaders of the board stood behind my recommendations to slow down the approval of doctoral programs . . . and to question the need for some of the new buildings being brought to the board for approval." And while this tightening of the purse strings surely wrinkled a few brows, college presidents inevitably realized there was no fighting a board bent on fidelity to its mandated responsibilities, and making no apologies about it. In fact, at a reception following a particularly heated exchange over pet building projects—which pitted board members against several university administrators—one of Betty Jo's board allies was heard to say: "We didn't just tell those presidents 'No,' we told them, *'Hell no!'"*

But college presidents were the least of the board's worries. The machinations of real estate developers often were the cause of greater concern and therefore required considerable scrutiny, which, according to Dr. Kern Wildenthal, Betty Jo was more than happy to oblige. During one of his first Coordinating Board meetings representing The University of Texas Southwestern Medical Center at Dallas, Wildenthal recalls coming to the swift conclusion that Betty Jo Hay didn't take kindly to political wheeling and dealing:

> The first time I saw her in action was at the Coordinating Board when one of the universities wanted to accept a land gift with the condition the university build all its future buildings on that land, and the land was in an area that was near another university. . . . Betty Jo realized what was happening and said . . . this is a real estate deal, and not for the benefit of college students or higher education. She made a persuasive case, and the proposal was voted down. She stood up to some very powerful political forces . . . and prevailed. I said to myself at the time, "This woman understands the issues, she can articulate her position, she's strong, and she gets her way."

For all her self-assuredness though, there did arise in 1976 one moment of uncertainty during Betty Jo's six-year term on the board when Harry Provence appointed her chairman of the finance committee, an area in which she had no previous experience. Betty Jo was willing to accept the position, but, even so, the prospect of entering wholly unfamiliar territory didn't fail to give her pause. Years later in reflecting on his decision, Provence would tell Jess and Betty Jo that at the time, he "thought it would be good for her and good for the board to have a new perspective." And with that, Betty Jo Hay—the single female appointee on a board responsible for overseeing the future of Texas colleges and universties—prepared to break another barrier, this time as leader of a prominent committee of that board. And who better to understand the historic significance of such a step than college-age women, to whom Betty Jo spoke in 1976 at Texas Woman's University in Denton:

> My work on the Coordinating Board . . . is the most challenging activity I have at present. I was appointed by the governor and I deeply appreciate the confidence he

expressed in me by appointing me to that board. At first, I was a bit apprehensive about being the only woman and about the task at hand. But through diligent effort and study, I now feel very comfortable in that role. . . . The chairman has just appointed me to chair the Financial Planning Committee of the board, and I know this will present a new challenge.

The Financial Planning Committee did indeed present a challenge, but confronting it only strengthened Betty Jo's confidence in her ability to successfully handle other difficult tasks, and there were plenty to go around. For example, dealing with the inappropriate conduct of a new board member. When that thorny issue came up, Ashworth recalls being struck by Betty Jo's seeming level of comfort with the uncomfortable, and by the finesse with which she managed the sticky situation:

> One night at dinner I saw her take one of our new board members aside. They chatted for awhile and then I heard her say, "I hate to point this out, but you know we have all noticed that when (your alma mater) has something come before the board you always leap at the chance to move approval before anybody else can do it. If we notice it, so do all those people in the audience. I don't want anybody to think you are just on this board to look after (your alma mater). Let me see if I can help you. Tomorrow when that new building comes up, why don't you let me move approval—and, besides, that way I can get you to owe me one. Okay?" That member never moved approval of another proposal from his school.

For Betty Jo, the outcome was a multiple victory—her colleague had corrected a personally embarrassing faux pas, the board had avoided a public relations black eye, and she had gained a new friend and future political leverage.

Kenneth Ashworth, meanwhile, enjoying the benefits of professional association with Betty Jo, couldn't help but reflect on her *modus operandi,* or contemplate the driving forces behind her actions. In so doing, he turned to the ancient Greeks, whom he suspected might have explained the fullness of Betty Jo's life in terms of how they defined human happiness. Among their philosophies, Ashworth points out, the Greeks believed that "The exercise of one's talents and powers in ways requiring excellence—in a life affording them scope"—inevitably would lead to a life of happiness. "Betty Jo lived such a life," Ashworth concluded, "and her time on the Coordinating Board permitted her to be a teacher, a policy maker, a leader, and, if required, even a disciplinarian."

Betty Jo's time on the state education board also reinforced her firm belief in the importance of individual civic responsibility and the profound impact it could have on effecting positive change within society. To that end, she spoke passionately about the need for community involvement in a 1978 speech at The University of Texas at Dallas:

> As citizens, parents, and grandparents we should be concerned with quality education, and we should do what is necessary to ensure quality education for ourselves, our children, and those yet to go to school. Of course, as taxpayers, we have a right to expect, and indeed, to insist on good judgment being brought to bear on expenditure of our tax money. But I also believe we, as citizens, can achieve desirable results and concurrently force cost effective judgments to be made if we learn the facts, demand answers, and—most of all—if we insist on quality education at all levels.

By 1976, Betty Jo's volunteer commitments had crystallized around several dominant themes—politics, education, children, mental health, and equality for women. These subsequently became the bedrock issues upon which she concentrated her service efforts and through which she moved steadily toward fulfillment. "I have found many outlets for my energies, talents, and time," she said in a 1976 speech. "Through my work in the political process, with the YWCA, the Mental Health Association of Dallas and of Texas, and other organizations, I stay busy and feel that I am making a contribution to society."

By this time in her life, and certainly by any measure, Betty Jo clearly was making a significant contribution to society, and she was just getting started. Her prominent role on the Coordinating Board gave way during the 1970s and 1980s to even greater involvement in the cause of education. With signature enthusiasm, she began bringing educational issues to the forefront by expressing her views emphatically, publicly, and often. She not only delivered the commencement addresses at Texas Eastern University and The University of Texas Southwestern Medical Center at Dallas, but she also was keynote speaker for the Texas Art Therapy Association at The University of Texas at Arlington and at Texas Woman's University in Denton.

Her most significant contributions to education, however, were made through direct action, reflected in a long list of volunteer appointments:

- Council on Postsecondary Accreditation
- National Task Force on Accreditation and the Public Interest

Fourth Annual
Commencement

TEXAS EASTERN UNIVERSITY
TYLER, TEXAS

Saturday, May Fourteenth
Nineteen Hundred and Seventy-Seven
Two O'clock in the Afternoon
Harvey Hall

Betty Jo addresses the Texas Eastern University Class of 1977 during its graduation ceremony in Tyler on May 14.

Betty Jo's interest in the cause of education took off in the 1970s and quickly led to a sharp focus on the quality of programs offered by Texas colleges and universities. In May of 1977 she was invited to deliver the commencement address at Texas Eastern University in Tyler, a school later renamed The University of Texas at Tyler.

- Southern Association, Commission on Colleges
- Statewide Task Force on Quality Education at the Baccalaureate Level
- National Task Force on Proliferation and Specialization of Accrediting Agencies
- Association of Higher Education for North Texas
- Board of Trustees, Baylor College of Dentistry
- Advisory Board, The School of Social Work, The University of Texas at Arlington

In 1977, Jess joined Betty Jo in furthering the Texas education effort when—after some initial hesitation—he agreed to serve on The University of Texas System Board of Regents at the request of Governor Dolph Briscoe. Jess's reluctance stemmed from his status as an alumnus of SMU, and though flattered by the governor's offer, he said at first he questioned the wisdom of such a move. "Out of the blue, Governor Briscoe told me he was going to appoint me to the UT Board of Regents," Hay said. "I discouraged it. . . . I told him it was a mistake politically and he shouldn't do it. There had never been a non-alum appointed to the board of regents in its entire history."

Briscoe recalls the conversation with great clarity, particularly Hay's plain-spoken response to the idea. "It was the most foolish thing I could do," he remembers Hay saying, and furthermore:

> He said, "Here I am from SMU and this appointment is the most important and most sought after appointment a governor can make." I said, "That's exactly right. I view it as the most important appointment a governor can make because it will determine the future of our educational institutions in Texas for many years to come, and in my opinion you're the best person that can get it done, and I don't know anyone else that could do it better."

Just the same, Hay knew full well the likely consequences of Briscoe's unorthodox appointment, the most obvious being its potential to draw the ire of the UT faithful. Briscoe, too, was aware of the political fallout, but unconcerned:

> In my opinion it was more important to think about the future of a great institution and take whatever might come. In some quarters there was great consternation. But as time went by, everybody connected with the university recognized that Jess was absolutely dedicated to UT. . . . Jess had the ability to bring people together and he had the vision to see what the UT system could be in the years ahead. . . . It turned out to be a great appointment.

Moreover, remembers Dr. Kern Wildenthal, Jess had the backing of Betty Jo, and not only welcomed her active participation, but appreciated the wealth of expertise she brought to educational issues. "When Jess was on the board of regents, Betty Jo was really helpful and involved," Wildenthal said. "She was right there with Jess as a very effective team member."

The Hay team proved its political effectiveness in 1976 by endorsing the presidential bid of Democrat Jimmy Carter, but not before giving their full support to Senator—and friend—Lloyd Bentsen, who also was making a run for Democratic nomination that year. Betty Jo and Jess had backed Bentsen from the start, but when his campaign failed to gain traction and he dropped out of the race, they changed course, joining numerous other Texas Democratic Party leaders in urging fellow Texans to cast a symbolic vote for Bentsen, the state's favorite son, in the March primary. Their intent was to give Texas and its two principal leaders—Governor Briscoe and Senator Bentsen—a stronger voice at the 1976 Democratic National Convention, but the plan fell short. In the end, Jimmy Carter won a decisive victory in the Texas primary, and proceeded thereafter to capture the party's nomination and, finally, the presidency.

As for Bentsen, following his spring withdrawal from the presidential race, he steamed ahead with his campaign for the U.S. Senate, easily winning reelection in 1976. At the same time, Bentsen maintained his close friendship with the Hays. But their regard for each other didn't detract from Jess and Betty Jo's admiration of former one-term Georgia governor Jimmy Carter and the traits he possessed. A peanut farmer by trade, Carter was an outsider and a moderate Democrat. He emphasized honesty, integrity, character, and fiscal responsibility, all of which appealed to the Hays and to an electorate exhausted by years of divisive conflict over the war in Vietnam and President Richard Nixon's Watergate scandal.

Under the circumstances, said former Carter speech writer Hendrik Hertzberg, looking back at his time in the administration, it wasn't hard to see what attracted voters to the soft-spoken, straight-laced Jimmy Carter. "'I will not lie to you,'" Hertzberg remembers Carter declaring, "and he meant it. The fact that he was unknown was part of his appeal. And he brought simple verities to the campaign trail: a promise not to lie to the American people, a promise to be good, a promise to love."

When the campaign trail brought Carter and his so-called "Peanut Brigade" to Dallas, Betty Jo and Jess greeted the candidate with a successful fund-raiser which helped

WHY BENTSEN DELEGATES?

Many Democrats have been asking themselves recently why they should support Senator Lloyd Bentsen's favorite son candidacy in the Texas Presidential Primary. Why support a candidate locally who has withdrawn from the race nationally?

The answer is simple: Lloyd Bentsen may have withdrawn from the Presidential race, but he has not surrendered his principles or his determination to fight for a Democratic ticket that we in Texas can be proud of, and can support next November.

We Texas Democrats have two choices.

We can go to the National Convention in New York next July splintered into a dozen factions, speaking with a hundred voices -- and accomplish nothing.

Or, we can go to New York united behind the leadership of Governor Dolph Briscoe and Senator Bentsen, and truly play a major role in selecting our nominee as befits a large and great State.

In the considered judgment of most of our elected State officials, we are heading toward a wide-open National Convention, where our standard bearer will be chosen by negotiation and compromise. Whether Texas has a role to play in that process depends on the delegates we select in our own primary next May 1.

By selecting Bentsen delegates, we will give the responsible political leaders of our State -- particularly Governor Briscoe and Senator Bentsen -- a mandate to lead in New York as well.

As the Bentsen nominees in the 16th Senatorial District, we solicit your support to that end.

Betty Jo Hay
Mrs. Jess (Betty Jo) Hay

Mike Dodge
Mike Dodge

Barefoot Sanders
Barefoot Sanders

In hopes of being selected as Bentsen delegates at the May 1, 1976 Texas presidential primary (and having a subsequent say at the Democratic National Convention in July) Betty Jo, Mike Dodge, and Barefoot Sanders drafted this manifesto asking Texas Democrats to support their nomination. Though Bentsen already had dropped out of the 1976 presidential race, this document makes clear there remained good reason to support him as the state's favorite son.

252

Vote for Betty Jo Hay, Mike Dodge and Barefoot Sanders

THE BENTSEN NOMINEES IN THE MAY 1 PRIMARY.

Follow Governor Briscoe's lead. Make Texas' voice heard at the 1976 Democratic National Convention.

The convention this year promises to be one in which the party's presidential nominee will be chosen by negotiation and compromise.

Such being the case, we Texas Democrats have two choices.

We can go to the National Convention in New York next July splintered into a dozen factions, speaking with a hundred voices—and accomplish nothing.

Or, we can go to New York united behind the leadership of Governor Briscoe and Senator Lloyd Bentsen, and truly play a major role in selecting our nominee as befits a large and great state.

Support the Bentsen delegates.

Political Advertisement
Paid for by the "Bentsen in the 16th" Committee

Vote for the Bentsen Delegate Nominees in the May 1 Primary

Betty Jo Hay Mike Dodge Barefoot Sanders

At a recent planning session in Austin, Governor & Mrs. Briscoe, Betty Jo Hay, Mike Dodge, Barefoot Sanders and Senator Bentsen.

Follow Governor Briscoe's lead. Make Texas' voice heard at the 1976 Democratic National Convention. Support the Bentsen delegates.

Political Advertisement.
Paid for by the "Bentsen in the 16th" Committee

Another appeal by the Bentsen nominees of the 16th Senatorial District. Unfortunately, their attempt to strengthen the hand of Texas Democrats at the party's national convention was thwarted by Georgia Governor Jimmy Carter, who handily won the Texas primary on his way to capturing the presidency. Betty Jo, Jess, Bentsen, and Briscoe later lined up behind and enthusiastically supported Carter.

Flanked by the state's two leading political figures—Governor Dolph Briscoe on the left with First Lady of Texas Janey Briscoe, and U. S. Senator Lloyd Bentsen at right— Betty Jo and fellow Bentsen delegate nominees Mike Dodge and Barefoot Sanders were featured in a 1976 poster promoting the need for a unified Texas front at the Democratic National Convention in New York City.

fuel his triumphant run in the Pennsylvania primary. Then, following his nomination at the 1976 Democratic National Convention at Madison Square Garden in New York City, the Hays made a genuine commitment to the Carter campaign, with Jess agreeing to serve as state finance chairman, and Betty Jo co-chairing the Dallas County effort. It was a year they wouldn't forget, Jess said:

> Betty Jo . . . joined me in various efforts aimed at securing Carter's election as president, with a particular focus on carrying the State of Texas. I . . . became Carter's Texas finance chairman, and in 1977, at Carter's suggestion, I was named national finance chairman of the Democratic Party. Betty Jo, Debby, Patty, Ramona Taylor, Maxine Tadlock, Kate and Jack Wheeler, Rand and Jim Sale, Sally and Charles Purnell, and hundreds of our friends from Dallas and other Texas cities joined at the Driskill Hotel in Austin to celebrate Carter's victory on the first Tuesday of November 1976. His success in Texas was particularly gratifying.

Hay's appointment as permanent finance chairman of the Democratic National Committee no doubt resulted from the favorable outcome he delivered during the campaign, and reflected the value Carter now placed on his continuing involvement. It was an appointment that didn't go unnoticed by the news media, as this newspaper account attests:

> Hay, who was credited with being one of Carter's most effective fund-raisers with big business interests wary of the upstart Georgian, has been serving as temporary finance chairman. He was reportedly the choice of the Carter team for the permanent post.

In February 1977, Carter firmed up his relationship with Betty Jo and Jess by extending them an invitation to his administration's first state dinner honoring President and Mrs. Jose Lopez Portillo of Mexico. More than simply political payoff, Carter's gesture was one of friendship, for, as with Dolph and Janey Briscoe, Lloyd and B. A. Bentsen, and Diana and Bill Hobby, Jimmy and Rosalynn Carter also had made a heartfelt connection with the Hays and wanted to show it. Soon, Betty Jo and Rosalynn discovered they had much in common, not only on the issues of public service and mental health, but also where marriage and partnership were concerned. Many years later in 1989, while introducing Rosalynn Carter at a speaking engagement, Betty Jo would refer to those qualities which had attracted her attention from the beginning, and with which she, herself, was intimately familiar:

When Rosalynn campaigned for her husband in 1976, the former first lady was doing something she knew and loved . . . working as her husband's closest political partner, understanding, and addressing important public issues.

But the hallmark of Rosalynn Carter was not simply her voice, but her unerring ability to match words with action. Her work in mental health . . . begun at home in Georgia . . . continued at the federal level. She was instrumental in the development and passage of the Mental Health Systems Act. . . .

The values instilled in the girl from Plains, Georgia . . . the commitments to church and community . . . to family . . . have been and remain present in the work of Rosalynn Carter.

And because Betty Jo was raised with the very same values and shared Rosalynn's passion for and interest in mental health issues, there was a fondness and respect they had for one another that would see them through nearly thirty years of friendship.

Yet even with friendships of that caliber, as well as relationships with other celebrated figures, Betty Jo—true to her humble roots—never gave in to pretentiousness or pomposity, when to do otherwise might have been expected. On the contrary, said Jess. "Betty Jo was as far removed from arrogance as you could possibly be. She viewed every individual who crossed her path—regardless of station, race, or gender—as a peer worthy of respect and, if in need, fully deserving of a helping hand." There was a warmth about Betty Jo that attracted people from every level of the social and economic spectrum, an undeniable openness that defined her personal relationships, and left those she encountered with a feeling of acceptance, indeed, of self-worth.

The same held true for strangers, and though Betty Jo knew few of them, there were those, from time to time, who had the pleasure of one of her most endearing qualities: sheer thoughtfulness. Paula Slaughter is a good example. Paula's chance meeting with Betty Jo—and the event of a lifetime that followed—occurred in 1977 on a flight from Dallas to Washington, D.C., where Betty Jo had planned to join Jess for a luncheon at the White House. As it happened, Paula, a Ph.D. graduate student at Texas Woman's University in Denton, was on her way to the capital to deliver a presentation at the U.S. Department of Education on the subject of "gifted education." During the flight, the two quickly discovered their mutual interest in education and children, and when Paula mentioned her six-year-old daughter's desire for Jimmy Carter's autograph, Betty Jo replied that she, in fact, could accommodate the request. To Paula's disbelief, Betty Jo then invited her to the afternoon luncheon, which she accepted of course, though with no expectation beyond an obscure out-of-the-way seat at a table in the back of the room. Instead, just hours later, Paula Slaughter found herself seated at VIP table number three, next to the Hays and, most astonishingly—near President Carter, all courtesy of Betty Jo Hay, and for no other reason than pure thoughtfulness.

Friends had similar experiences. Sondra Farr recalls one occasion in the early 1970s when the Hays were taking a flight to El Paso aboard Lomas & Nettleton's corporate jet. "I remember they were going to El Paso, and my sister happened to live there," Sondra said. "So, Betty Jo called and said, 'Do you and Jess and Laura [Sondra's children] want to fly to El Paso and see your sister? We've got some extra seats.' They were going to be there a couple of nights. So I said, 'Sure.'"

This was followed by an extra touch of kindness that involved, of all things, the in-flight meal. As had been her practice over the years when she and Jess traveled by private plane, Betty Jo would order catered box meals, although she rarely requested dessert. On this occasion, however, taking the children into consideration, she chose to add chocolate-chip cookies to the menu, which decision went over big—and not just with the children, Sondra said. "I remember we had box lunches on the plane," she said. "Apparently, Betty Jo didn't include cookies unless there were kids aboard, and my son, Jess, was all excited precisely because, in this case, the meals came with cookies. As I recall, Jess Hay also was very pleased about that."

Thoughtful though it was, the display of hospitality on the airplane paled in comparison to the full extent of Betty Jo's ability to entertain, as evidenced in 1980 when Jimmy Carter brought his reelection campaign to Dallas. That was the year the Hays held a fund-raising reception at their home on Lupton Circle as a symbol of their commitment to helping Carter secure a second term, said Hay:

> We hosted a major event for him at our home in . . . July 1980 at which approximately $800,000 was raised for the Democratic Party. As was usually the case, Betty Jo was a meticulous hostess and the entire event stands as a lasting tribute to her charm and grace in that capacity.

The reception went off like clockwork, all according to Betty Jo's exacting standards and attention to detail. Even the unexpected light summer rain that fell on the Hays' back patio during President Carter's brief outdoor remarks failed to dampen the celebratory mood.

Carter will visit Dallas area today

Carter campaign comes to Dallas

July 1980

President Carter will bring his campaign for re-election to Dallas July 21 and participate in two local fund-raising events.

Carter is expected to arrive in mid-afternoon and to attend a reception sponsored by the Dallas County Democratic Party at Union Station from 4:30 p.m. to 6 p.m.

Later that night, the president will attend a Democratic National Committee fund-raiser at the home of Dallas businessman and longtime Democratic contributor Jess Hay. Carter is expected to return to the White House the same night.

Prior to his Dallas visit, Carter is scheduled to attend another Democratic National Committee fund-raising event in Henderson, Ky.

In his bid for reelection in 1980, President Jimmy Carter relied on Betty Jo and Jess to generate support, particularly in Texas and neighboring states. Their involvement provided Dallas reporters with an ongoing national news story, which included this preview of Carter's summertime visit and his stop at Lupton Circle.

DALLAS TIMES HERALD, Monday, July 2¹ 1980 · · · · · A—5

— Staff photo by Rebecca Skelton

Betty Jo Hay will greet President at her home today

On July 21, 1980, *The Dallas Times Herald* carried a front page news story about President Carter's Dallas appearance, the bulk of which was devoted to the fund-raiser held at Jess and Betty Jo's Lupton Circle home that evening. When it was over, some $800,000 had been added to the coffers of the Democratic National Committee on Carter's behalf, and Betty Jo had secured for herself a place among the best in the business at hosting high profile dignitaries.

The only hitch came from an unfortunate incident involving Carter's brother, Billy, who threw a troublesome wrench into the campaign over allegations that he not only had become a registered agent for Muammar Gaddafi's regime in Libya, but also had received a $220,000 "loan" for oil sales he supposedly was to facilitate for the country. In response, the national news media dubbed the scandal, "Billygate," prompting a flurry of negative publicity, and angering President Carter's Dallas hostess, who spoke her mind honestly and directly when the local media descended on Lupton Circle for interviews. "It confirms what I've always thought about Billy," Betty Jo told a reporter, ". . . that he's not very bright and he has used his position as "brother" to make money. I am certain the president would like to wring his neck, and he ought to put a gag around him. But you know . . . you can't control what your brothers and sisters do." Yet, for all her candidness, Betty Jo's response was anything but full throttle, because if it had been, she might well have described the brother's actions as "stupid," and very likely wanted to. Instead—in an attempt to make the best of a bad situation—Betty Jo wisely opted for the more diplomatic, "not very bright," in her comments for public consumption, and moved on.

Looking back, it is doubtful that Billy Carter's missteps had any materially negative impact on the outcome of his brother's reelection campaign, but either way, Jimmy Carter came up on the losing end of that November 1980 contest, leaving the former governor of California, Ronald Reagan, to take his place. And, so, with Carter's time in the White House drawing to a close, he and Rosalynn made a sincere effort at showing their appreciation to friends and supporters, which, for the Hays meant a Christmas invitation to the Carter's home in December 1980, and a trip well worth remembering, said Jess:

> One . . . highlight of our political involvement occurred in December 1980, when we took Jessica, who was two-and-a-half at the time, Debby, and Patty to Washington, D.C., for a visit with the Carters at the White House. President and Mrs. Carter were extravagant in their hospitality and joined in a fairly extensive visit with us in the Oval Office and in the private quarters of the White House.

> Jessica played with a couple of the Carter grandchildren, creating some anxiety in Debby as she worried about Jessica's possibly damaging one of the numerous artifacts in the living quarters of the White House. At President Carter's invitation we also attended the White House Christmas reception for families of the diplomatic delegations in Washington.

JIMMY CARTER
January 27, 1983

To Betty Jo and Jess Hay

I will always remember the warm hospitality you extended to me during my visit to Dallas. Your help is important to me and has already greatly benefited the Carter Library and the Carter Center of Emory University. Thank you for your many efforts on my behalf.

With best wishes,

Sincerely,

Jimmy

Mr. and Mrs. Jess Hay
7236 Lupton Circle
Dallas, Texas 75225

We hope you had a great cruise —

Though Jimmy Carter failed to win a second term in 1980, the disappointing outcome did not affect the relationship he and former First Lady Rosalynn had forged with Betty Jo and Jess. In fact, the Hays continued to support Carter's endeavors, prompting a letter of gratitude from the former president in 1983.

Debby's concern for the well-being of White House *objets d'art* most certainly was shared by Betty Jo, considering she'd recently been selected to serve on the White House Preservation Fund committee which First Lady Rosalynn Carter had helped to create in 1979. It was a committee whose mission was old hat to Betty Jo—seeking donors to fund an endowment earmarked for the purchase of new acquisitions and the refurbishing of White House state rooms—and, as always, she answered the call. In recognition of her contributions to the enhancement of that fund, Betty Jo received a note of thanks on January 6, 1981, from the first lady. "You have helped significantly to carry out the committee's goal of raising funds to acquire important historic works of art and American antique furniture for the permanent collection of the president's house," Rosalynn Carter wrote.

Christmas away from home was a rare occurrence for the Hays. Because the holiday held such special significance as a family event, they felt strongly it was meant to be celebrated at home, and in reflecting on their long life as a couple, Jess said that's exactly what they did nearly every one of the years they were together:

> We spent some thirty-three Christmas Days at our home on Lupton Circle with family, always including Betty Jo's parents and frequently my mother; my aunts, Nora Roddy Bramblett and Jessie Roddy Dees; my cousins, Patty and Richard Bramblett; and Betty Jo's aunt and uncle, Ruth and Edgar Peacock and their daughter, Ruth Ellen; to open gifts, dine, and simply celebrate and enjoy our togetherness.

Betty Jo's cousin, David Albert—the son of Carl Albert—had the good fortune of attending many of those Lupton Circle holiday celebrations and remembers them fondly as the best of times:

> While I was in high school and college I spent lots of time at Lupton Circle. . . . I went to Harvard . . . and I would fly from Boston to Dallas at Christmastime.
> . . . Betty Jo and Jess threw big New Year's parties at their house on Lupton Circle. There were just huge congregations of folks with lots of young people—tons of people, and it was tons of fun.

"It was my observation," said J. Paul Lane, who married Betty Jo's cousin Nancy Albert, "that family was an integral part of their lives. . . . Betty Jo grew up in a home that considered family . . . the number one priority."

Naturally, there were occasional exceptions to the Lupton Circle Christmas tradition, and one such holiday in 1983 found the Hays in Brazil, aboard the cruise ship *Stella Solaris*—but they were not alone. It so happened that what started as a couples' cruise quickly mushroomed into a multi-family trip that eventually included—in addition to Betty Jo and Jess—Bill and Sally Brice, their four children, and Bill's mother, Jess's mother Myrtle Hay, Kathryn and Duncan Peacock, Patty, Debby, her friend Webb Spradley, Jessica, her nanny Jane Garner, and Albert N. Rohnstedt—eighteen people all told. Off they went, aboard the *Stella Solaris,* across the equator and down the Amazon River on a journey deep inside Brazil, celebrating Christmas Day and New Year's Eve along the way. "We brought a little bitty Christmas tree with us," said Jess, "and had a modest celebration on Christmas morning in Betty Jo's and my room."

The natural wonders they encountered, some during a short hike into the Amazon rain forest, were heightened by a feeling of community that made their experiences all the more pleasurable, Jess explained, recalling those long-ago, much-cherished moments. "It was fun being together on the ship," he said. "Betty Jo and I were grateful for the opportunity to spend eighteen relaxing days with our parents. It was the first such trip for her mother and father and for my mother, and it was a joy to see them having so much fun." But perhaps Jane Garner summed up that 1983 Christmas best of all when she said, "The Hays wanted to create memories for the family. Rather than simply giving gifts, the family cruise provided a way to create a wonderful memory by including all the generations, and I think they achieved that."

Family memories were a Hay specialty no matter what the season, and football was as good as any, especially if it involved Texas and Oklahoma. Even better was if it happened to be Texas/OU weekend during the State Fair of Texas, in which case the festivities routinely started on Friday evening with the arrival of the McAlester, Oklahoma crowd, as well as a few other guests, who always could count on Betty Jo to have a pot of taco soup simmering on the stove. This was one of her signature recipes, said daughter Patty, and a tradition for large, informal gatherings. "It was easy to make and people could eat it whenever they wanted to," she said. "It had pinto, navy, and ranch-style beans, taco seasoning, and ground beef. You served it with Fritos and cheese. It was one of Mom's easy, toss-together recipes, and everyone liked it." Patty even remembers taco soup doing its part to soothe the tensions of campaign workers stationed at various times over the years in the Hays' home, watching late-night election returns and anxiously awaiting the results of another cliff-hanger.

There were birthdays to be celebrated, too—and then *there were birthdays*—Jess's fiftieth in 1981 being one of them, perhaps even the best. If nothing else, it certainly went down in Hay family history as one of the most elaborate. Produced and directed by Betty Jo, with able assistance from Ted Enloe and John Sexton (president and executive vice president, respectively, of Lomas Financial Corporation), Robert Hardesty (a vice chancellor of The University of Texas System), and advertising guru, Stan Richards, it was the kind of grandiose affair for which the Hays were becoming well-known. To set the tone, Betty Jo christened the event "Fifty Years in Politics," which was an exaggeration, of course, but not by much, given the fact that Jess had supported his first political candidate—Texas Attorney

Betty Jo outdid herself in planning a surprise party to mark Jess's fiftieth birthday in January 1981, starting with this clever invitation. When folded, it read, "Let's hear it for Jess Hay," but once opened, the word, "Hurray," appeared. There would be much more to come.

The donkey, symbol of the Democratic party, and on this occasion, centerpiece of the surprise fiftieth birthday party for lifelong Democrat Jess Hay, courtesy of party-planner extraordinaire, Betty Jo Hay. The party was held at the Dallas Country Club and firmed up what most people already knew about its hostess: that she was a precision planner who left no detail unattended, was quick with a joke, and above all, knew how to have fun.

As a spoof on Jess's long time love affair with politics, Betty Jo chose the perfect birthday party theme—"50 Years in Politics"— and then relied on her cutting wit to play it out. The outcome featured party favors such as this one-of-a-kind Jess Hay campaign button, which is bound to be a collector's item today.

264

General Gerald Mann—at the ripe old age of nine. That would make Mann, a former SMU classmate of Jess's father, George Hay, the first politician ever to receive the backing of Jess Hay, a curious fact in its own right.

Forty-one years later, who possibly could have known that politics still would be a major contributor to shaping the life of Jess Hay, the man, or that he would have married a woman with the wherewithal to frame his entire fiftieth birthday celebration around the one outside interest he most enjoyed. But such was life with Betty Jo, shindig planner extraordinaire, and such was the shindig at the Dallas Country Club ballroom on January 20, 1981—extraordinary, indeed. "The program included music by two of our favorite groups, Mal Fitch's Orchestra and the Levee Singers," Hay said. "The theme was politics, of course, and Pat Paulsen, who, at the time, was a perennial satirical candidate for President of the United States, was delightful as the star of the show. . . . All of it was in the nature of a roast, and that made it even more fun. It was a delightful party."

Several years later, in 1985, the Hays left their distinctive mark on one of the most important events in the life of Kathryn and Duncan Peacock—their fiftieth wedding anniversary—a milestone Jess could recall in great detail a generation after the fact:

> To commemorate the occasion, Betty Jo and I arranged a surprise dinner-dance in their honor at the country club in McAlester, Oklahoma. . . . Approximately fifty of the Peacocks' friends from Dallas and some 100 from McAlester attended. It was a fun evening, at which Betty Jo and I both expressed our deep affection for Kathryn and Duncan and our great appreciation to each of them for all they had contributed to our lives. At the conclusion of a very brief program, Betty Jo presented to the Peacocks and two friends of their choosing, passage on a seventeen-day cruise to Brazil and back. . . . Betty Jo's aunt and uncle, Doris and Earl Albert, were selected by the Peacocks to accompany them.

Unfortunately, the cruise didn't sit well with Earl, and once at sea, he experienced the same problem that had plagued him years earlier during World War II when he shipped out to New Guinea from San Francisco. "I was just out of it for the first ten days, vomiting and carrying on just terrible," said Earl, remembering back to 1942. Seasickness was the culprit once again when he attempted Kathryn and Duncan's golden anniversary cruise, and by the time they made it to port in Brazil, Earl vowed the only way they'd get him back on the ship would be "in chains." That not being an option, he and Doris took an airplane back to the United States.

Shhhhhhh. . . . . . .Surprise

Dinner Party

Honoring

Kathryn and Duncan Peacock

on the occasion of their

Fiftieth Wedding Anniversary

McAlester Country Club

Saturday, September 21, 1985

7:00 P.M.

No Gifts, Please

*We are happy you are planning to attend
and look forward to seeing you.*

On September 21, 1985, in honor of her parents' fiftieth wedding anniversary, Betty Jo, along with Jess, surprised Kathryn and Duncan Peacock with a splendid celebration at the McAlester, Oklahoma Country Club. Betty Jo loaded a bus with Dallas well-wishers and headed north across the Red River where friends and relatives celebrated the lives of two people who had come a long way since their union in 1935, and given a great deal in the process.

Betty Jo and Jess, meanwhile, continued their practice of taking, in Hay's words, "private retreats to rekindle our keen and somewhat unusual sense of togetherness." They remained partial to Little Dix Bay on Virgin Gorda in the British Virgin Islands, as well as to the Hawaiian Islands, and though trips to Hawaii included de rigueur stays at the large luxury hotels on Waikiki beach and Diamond Head, their finest moments were spent on the undeveloped side of Maui Island at Hana Ranch and the Hotel Hana Maui. Described as the "ultimate escapist resort" this romantic getaway combined what Betty Jo and Jess considered the two foremost features of a perfect vacation: elegance and absolute seclusion. Nestled among a lush tropical landscape, the hotel and its luxurious plantation-style bunga-lows provided easy access to a beach once described by writer James Michener as "the most perfect crescent beach in the Pacific." It also offered the most authentic Hawaiian cultural experience. Stealing away in this manner provided Betty Jo and Jess with the time they needed to rejuvenate the soulful bond at the heart of the one relationship that mattered most of all—their own.

In 1981, Jess was appointed to the board of directors of the Exxon Corporation [the future Exxon Mobil], which, among other significant features, led to more opportunities for travel abroad. As part of its program of continuing education for board members and senior executives, Exxon arranged biennial trips to its various international operations, and consistently included spouses in the trips as a symbol of what Hay called a company culture intent on promoting a sense of corporate responsibility to the family:

> Spouses of the officers and directors were a vital part of the trips. Invariably, they enjoyed many educational experiences related to the culture of the particular region. Each trip offered an incredible opportunity to meet and relate to the key people in a given area, whether it was Hong Kong, Malaysia, Japan, Singapore, Australia, Belgium, France, Italy, Germany, Egypt, Dubai, Abu Daubi, Qutar, or Saudi Arabia. It was a great, broadening experience. . . . We were able to see parts of the world and get acquainted with people and cultures from around the world that never would have been possible without that kind of sponsorship.

Indeed, high level access was to be expected from a powerful multinational global giant such as Exxon, and the corporation did not disappoint, providing Betty Jo and Jess with their first taste of such in 1981, on a trip which included Malaysia as one of its primary destinations. Among the fluster of cultural briefings and tours, the Hays and other Exxon officials spent a splendid—and not to be forgotten—evening at a private dinner party in the state home of the Malaysian prime minister. Meeting the leaders of foreign countries was a regular feature of the Exxon trips, said Hay, and an education unto itself. "It's amazing how much commonality there really is among people once you start talking as human beings rather than as Americans or Malays," he said. "There are similarities, but there also are some differences, and understanding those cultural differences is a key to commercial . . . and diplomatic success in those countries."

Still, while spouses regularly were included in the undertakings of the board, they rarely found themselves at the center of the corporate spotlight—except on one memorable occasion when Betty Jo acquired that distinction while participating in a major corporate ceremonial function. As was Exxon's practice, the honor of christening its new ocean tankers rotated among women directors and the spouses of male board members. In the summer of 1982, when—as the spouse of a board member—Betty Jo's opportunity came up, Jess was unable to attend the ceremonies with her because of a pressing business commitment. In response, Exxon officials invited Betty Jo to bring along a guest in Jess's

The Honourable
Prime Minister Dato' Hussein Onn
and Datin Suhailah

requests the pleasure of the company of

.........Mr. & Mrs. Jess T. Hay..

....to...........Dinner Reception...................

at....Sri Taman, Jalan Perdana, Kuala Lumpur...................

on....Friday, June 19, 1981...........198...., at.....7:45 p.m....................

R.S.V.P.:
Personal Secretary to Prime Minister,
Prime Minister's Office,
Kuala Lumpur.
Tel. No. 203722.

Dress: Optional
           Formal

Long Sleeve
Batek

By the summer of 1981, Jess had taken a seat on the board of directors of what was then the Exxon Corporation, opening the door to extensive overseas travel. Because spouse involvement was encouraged by Exxon, Betty Jo almost always accompanied Jess, and in fact, made the first trip to Malaysia which brought this dinner invitation from the prime minister requesting their presence at his home in the capital city of Kuala Lumpur.

absence, and she chose none other than Charlene Miller, her close friend and member of "the group" from Ridgewood Park Methodist Church.

The christening took place in Taiwan, at the dock of the ship's manufacturer, China Shipbuilding Corporation. While there, and throughout the afternoon, Betty Jo and Charlene found themselves being treated to the kind of red-carpet protocol enjoyed by corporate titans and heads of state. To be sure, Charlene remembers the ceremony as an unforgettable spectacle that began with a limousine ride from their hotel to the shipbuilding company:

China Shipbuilding had a wonderful VIP room where they presented us with orchid corsages. Then they took us to this covered stadium-seated stand with a stage not far from where this huge ship, the *Esso Spain,* was moored. All the principal officials from China Shipbuilding and many of Exxon's regional representatives were there. They gave speeches, and Betty Jo gave a beautiful, beautiful presentation speech. They had this thing rigged up where she pulled a cord from the stage which triggered the actual christening of the ship, and then there were horns blowing and the band started playing. It was a gala event.

It was indeed. The official program called for "Music, release birds, streamers, fire cracker display, etc.," to be followed by a "tour of the vessel and an onboard tea party," and finally, a luncheon reception in the company's formal dining room. During lunch, the spotlight on Betty Jo intensified when China Shipbuilding presented her with a sumptuous, multi-tiered birthday cake, and though technically it wasn't her birthday—that came ten days later on June 6, 1982—company officials felt comfortable stretching the point in honor of their guest. When the luncheon came to an end, everyone in attendance received christening mementos, which, for Betty Jo and Charlene, included handsome coral necklaces.

And that was just the beginning. In addition to Taiwan, Betty Jo and Charlene also visited Japan and Hong Kong. "Everywhere we went, it was like the president had arrived," remembers Charlene. "Exxon people would greet us, pick us up, take us to dinner, and show us all the sights. It was very memorable."

During the course of Jess Hay's twenty-year service as an Exxon director, he and Betty Jo participated in eleven board trips spanning five continents. "All of these were magnificent," Hay would say later. "They were educational, and they were enjoyable. Betty Jo loved them." And the more they traveled, the more they wanted to see, so Betty Jo and Jess often tacked on a personal travel itinerary to the beginning or end of their corporate excursions, trips which frequently included family and friends.

The high priority they placed on family-oriented vacations played a major role in Jess and Betty Jo's 1980s decision to purchase one-half ownership in an Acapulco, Mexico vacation home. Up until that time, they had spent their vacations like most other contented families—in resort hotels or rented homes. But by the early 1980s Acapulco was becoming a favorite destination, and Betty Jo and Jess, along with their friends Sally and Bill Brice, decided the time had come to stop renting, so they agreed to share the cost of a vacation home. While the search for a suitable property required some persistence and several trips over a two-year period, in 1984 they finally found what they were looking for in the exclusive Las Brisas neighborhood. "Villa Vista Hermosa," as it was known, clung to the side of a mountain above the city, and as its name implied, the "vista hermosa,"—beautiful view—of Acapulco Bay, as seen from the rooms, outdoor pool, and patio was nothing short of spectacular.

But it would take more than simply a beautiful view for Villa Vista Hermosa to become the success that it was. A smooth operation required a top-notch staff, and above all, a "first-class cook," which the Hays were fortunate to find in Cecilia Sandoval, a retired chef known to possess the finest culinary skill in Acapulco. "She said she would come out of retirement and manage our house and serve as our cook if we would hire her son, René Romero Sandoval, as her management assistant," Hay said. "As it turns out, we got both the best cook in Acapulco and, from our perspective, probably the best house manager in René." Soon, Cecilia was creating the kitchen magic of the reputation that had preceded her. "Anything you could conjure up . . . she could cook, ranging from Mexican dishes to beef tenderloin to fish dishes. She was a wide-ranging, versatile cook." By 1985—with support from the multi-talented team of Cecilia and Rene Sandoval—Betty Jo and Jess were at last able to enjoy Villa Vista Hermosa in all of its splendor, not only as a much-needed refuge from their heavily scheduled lives, but as a relaxing sanctuary to share with family and friends.

■

In the late 1970s, the Hays found themselves part of a most intriguing group of friends, all of whom shared their ardent interest in civic and political affairs, and each of whom brought to the group a uniquely fascinating background. In addition to Betty Jo and Jess, the group included Diana and Bill Hobby, Kay and Ray Hutchison, Vicki and Ron Kessler, Stella and Charles Mullins, and Kate and Jack Wheeler.

Bill Hobby, at the time, was president and executive editor of *The Houston Post* and, as it turned out, became the longest-serving lieutenant governor in Texas history, holding the job from 1973 to 1991—eighteen years in all. His wife, Diana, a prominent and highly regarded literary critic and civic leader in the state, was for many years associated with Rice University in Houston. Kay and Ray Hutchison each served in the Texas Legislature during the 1970s. Kay went on to become state treasurer before her election to the United States Senate in 1993, while Ray continued to be one of the state's leading public finance lawyers. The Kesslers, also active public citizens, focused their attention on issues related to quality education, social services, and economic development. At the time of the group's forma-tion, Stella Mullins worked as a professional staff member at the Dallas Mental Health Association and was Betty Jo's closest friend and ally within the organization. Her husband, Dr. Charles Mullins, was a practicing cardiologist then, as well as a tenured professor at The University of Texas Health Science Center at Dallas. He later became president and chief executive officer of Parkland Hospital in Dallas, followed by twenty years as executive vice chancellor for health affairs of The University of Texas System. The Wheelers were educators. Kate taught in the Highland Park Independent School District, where she later served as a consultant to those responsible for administering academic programs for the district's most talented and gifted students. Jack was vice president for administration at The University of Texas Health Science Center at Dallas. He subsequently became an advisor to and advocate for all of the state's public hospitals—including Parkland Hospital in Dallas. Together, it was an engaging assembly of talented and accomplished women and men with enough credentials to last a lifetime, and all of them remain friends today.

As for political party affiliation, all were loyal Democrats, except the Hutchisons, who remained leading Texas Republicans, though in a group of this stature party allegiance hardly mattered. Instead, these were people who could rise above partisanship, said Hay, "and more often than not, find common ground on issues related to education, mental health, and the importance of fiscal accountability in the administration of our public affairs. But transcending those faint traces of shared convictions, the cohesion of the group is based primarily on the warmth of its members, who simply enjoy being friends." Said Jack Wheeler: "All of us have an interest in politics, but I don't remember our spending an inordinate amount of time talking about politics. We talked about kids and what was going on in Texas and what was happening in Dallas, Austin, and Houston."

And two or three times a year this singular group of friends would head to the small North Texas town of Ponder for an evening of fun at the tried-and-true Ranchman's Café. Ranchman's was about the only thing that wasn't a ranch in a town surrounded by them, a place described by Jack Wheeler as "a little jewel off by itself that time did not disturb." In fact, time had disturbed very little about the cafe since Wheeler and Charles Mullins first discovered it when they were students at North Texas State College [now the University of North Texas] in Denton. Opened in 1948 by Grace "Pete" Jackson, the Ranchman's Café had one dining room and no restrooms—except the outhouse in back—and it remained that way for thirty years until Jackson decided it was time to add another dining room and, probably more important, indoor restrooms. But the Ranchman's Café wasn't about show, it was about that perfect blend of food and authentic Texana—big, juicy steaks enjoyed from a 1950s vantage point. "It's just a cowboy place," said Hay, and from the looks of the gravel parking lot, the screen door, Formica-topped tables, and branding irons affixed to the walls, it surely was that.

Yet those were the very qualities that had attracted the Hays and their friends to the venerable Ranchman's Café in the first place and which brought them back so often they began referring to themselves as the "Ponder group." Hay remembers when they first showed up, "Pete" was there to greet them, "dressed in jeans, a checkered shirt, and boots. It was a fun place to let your hair down. . . . We'd usually bring wine and liquor. As Betty Jo once observed, the place was a lot more fun when I was drinking. . . . The restaurant featured hand-cut steaks and huge quantities of whatever they served." And size being what it is to Texans, Ranchman's upheld the standard by offering 16-oz. top sirloin and rib eye steaks and a hearty 24-oz. Porterhouse T-bone, all but guaranteeing no one went away hungry. And that's the way it would happen for the next quarter century or more—the "Ponder group," the Ranchman's Café, a little drink, and lots of good beef.

■

As Betty Jo stepped up her efforts on mental health issues she assumed a greater role within the Mental Health Association (MHA), gaining momentum in 1978 from her service on the national board's Childhood and Adolescent Committee, a committee she would chair in 1980 and 1981. One of her earliest advocacy endeavors as a committee member was on behalf of abused children. In a written report presented to the group, Betty Jo exhorted her colleagues to more aggressively seek ways of dealing with what she called "the major cause of death among children under two years of age," and on this front—the committee would come to realize—there was no putting her off. Betty Jo was a no-non-sense advocate on a path to reform, and she wanted swift and decisive action:

> I have attempted to cover the necessary elements for state legislation which I feel the National Association should promote among its state chapters. In addition, there are suggestions for local chapters. In order to implement some of the suggestions, new laws will have to be passed, and new directions taken by local chapters.

Before delivering the report, Betty Jo asked Stella Mullins to review it. As the Dallas chapter's professional program director, Mullins was second in command to executive director Katherine Reed—the fireball attorney who'd been enmeshed in the controversial child abuse matter at Parkland Hospital in 1973. As for Mullins, she had arrived at MHA in 1976 with solid credentials that included a master's degree in social work, experience in the juvenile justice system, a stint as a direct service practitioner in a community mental health clinic, and membership on the city's interdisciplinary child abuse committee. Betty Jo came away satisfied with Mullins' critique of the committee report, having discovered in

272

Stella "... a very smart lady who had a lot of the same concerns I did." This brief encounter led to an instant friendship between Betty Jo and Stella—two women bound by a single cause—which would land them side by side on countless mental health projects and events from that point forward.

In 1979, with the retirement of Katherine Reed, Stella was promoted to executive director of MHA Dallas, but would remain in the position for just two years, moving instead to Austin where her husband, Charles, was set to become the executive vice chancellor for health affairs of The University of Texas System. Once in Austin, Stella applied for and landed the top professional staff position at MHA Texas, becoming the state's executive director in 1982, an achievement made possible in no small part by her excellent track record in Dallas and with the enthusiastic recommendation of board member Betty Jo Hay—who would become state president one year later.

In the meantime, along with the strides Betty Jo was making on the board during the late 1970s, she continued leaving her mark as an effective volunteer leader. In 1977, for example, she raised enough money to bring nationally-recognized social scientists to the chapter's annual child abuse conference in Dallas, where they shared valuable expertise on the issue. Again, to the benefit of many, Betty Jo had gotten results, and a quick glimpse into her fund-raising workshop notes not only reveals her formula, but reflects its single most important ingredient, a skill at which few were better: *"1977—Child Abuse Conference—I raised $6,000 by making ten personal phone calls."* The following year, Betty Jo would take on even more responsibility as chairman of the 1978 child abuse conference.

'78 Conference to focus on growth stages

Child abuse and its effects in the developmental stages of the child through infancy, latency and teenage will be explored at the 9th annual Child Abuse Conference in Dallas on February 16 and 17.

The conference will be held at the Southwestern Medical School Health Science Center, Gooch Auditorium.

Ronald P. Rohner, Ph.D., of the Department of Bicultural Anthropology at the University of Connecticut will be the principal speaker.

Betty Jo (Mrs. Jess) Hay is the chairman of the 1978 conference.

Betty Jo Hay, chairman of the 1978 Child Abuse Conference.

Education and children's issues were matters of the highest order to Betty Jo. In 1978 she chaired the annual Child Abuse Conference sponsored by the Mental Health Association of Dallas. That same year, and in 1979, she served on the National Commission for the Prevention of Child Abuse.

But there would be much more to 1978 than the conference. That year, another challenge caught Betty Jo's eye, this one regarding allegations of inferior services lodged against the Dallas County Mental Health and Mental Retardation agency. The complaints were of such concern that Betty Jo joined an outside task force to investigate, and when its work was done, the group recommended ways to improve the delivery of community care. In a forceful speech before state legislators and county commissioners, Betty Jo presented the group's findings, leaving no one unconvinced as to the seriousness of the allegations or the reality of the substandard conditions that had prompted the outcry. And when she was done, there likely were some Texas politicians in the room—particularly those accustomed to a high degree of citizen deference—who were disconcerted by her straightforward manner, none more so than the Dallas County Commissioners, who were scolded in public by Betty Jo for playing politics with board appointments:

> If you will permit me an aside to the commissioners as related to the MH/MR board, the task force would urge that you come into compliance with House Bill number three and stagger the terms of the board members. . . . You should also realize that when recruiting and appointing board members, you should pick those who will be willing to commit the time necessary to understand the intricacies of MH/MR programs. These appointments are not and should not be treated as political plums.

And if the politicos on the receiving end of that implied criticism thought it was the last they'd heard from Betty Jo Hay and the task force, she put a quick end to that notion:

> You can rest assured that you will be hearing from us, often. We are a dedicated group of volunteers who . . . believe strongly in what we have recommended here today. Please tuck this information away somewhere in your memory so that when these issues come up, you will remember what our proposals have been.

All in all, as she worked to raise public consciousness on behalf of others, Betty Jo's promise was simple and straightforward: If there was one thing upon which elected officials could rely, it was continued scrutiny. And that included state lawmakers, too, who, like their local counterparts, were publicly—and sometimes vehemently—held to account when Betty Jo was on the agenda. Judge Oswin Chrisman saw it with his own eyes on occasion, recalling Betty Jo as a formidable advocate:

274

There was a side to her that was very tough. . . . She didn't mince words at legislative committee hearings. She would tell them, "This is wrong and you're responsible and you're not putting nearly enough money into these programs." She would kind of set her jaw in an interesting way. It wasn't menacing, but you knew you had a worthy advocate. . . . When you had Betty Jo after you, you had problems. If she thought you were standing in the way of something, she would go after you.

She applied those same tough standards to fund-raising. Elaine Shiver—director of the Texas Parents As Teachers program, and Betty Jo's MHA ally and friend—said she admired Betty Jo's direct approach when asking for money, particularly from donors whom she felt had the potential to do more. "There was no better teacher than Betty Jo when it came to raising money," Shiver remembers. "She would remind us that we were not asking for ourselves, but for those who needed our help." American Airlines is a good example. On a quest for a pledge of financial support from the airline giant, Shiver once accompanied Betty Jo to its headquarters at DFW International Airport, a meeting made possible through Betty Jo's acquaintance with CEO Robert Crandall, who, Shiver explained, "arranged for us to meet with the person in charge of their corporate giving program":

> When we arrived Betty Jo and I laid out our request. The gentleman then asked, "Mrs. Hay, how much has American given before?" She looked him in the eye and calmly, but firmly, replied that she had been the president of the local chapter, state organization, and the National Mental Health Association and "to my knowledge American Airlines has never given a dime." I held my breath! Still new to fund-raising, I was in awe of her directness. There was a long pause, and then he laughed and said, "So you're telling me it's time for us to ante up!" Her response? "Yes, I would say so." We got the money.

Tough-minded advocacy not only was Betty Jo's forte, it was her inherent response to the call of those who needed protecting but couldn't protect themselves, specifically children and the mentally ill. "Betty Jo identified with people she perceived as victims," said David Farr. "She had a natural instinct for the common man, for the social victim, and it wasn't in her head—it was from her heart." The same was true when it came to children, said Jess. "She had a mother's instinctive, protective outreach for children, and she became very aggravated by anything approximating abuse of children."

The Mental Health Association's wise reaction to Betty Jo's zeal for mental health advocacy and education was to promote her leadership within the organization. "Betty Jo was always open and she was a natural leader, and she brought a new force to MHA activities," said Hay. "Board members saw her as a leader and wanted to appropriate her capacities in pushing the organization along. . . . She always responded positively to higher office if she felt like she could do the job she was being asked to do."

As a result, beginning in 1978, Betty Jo had an impressive run through a series of chapter and state offices of the Mental Health Association, serving in the following positions: chapter vice president, public information (1978), chapter vice president, development (1979), chapter executive committee—serving on the children's, membership, and nominating committees (1979-1984), state vice president and chapter president-elect (1980), Dallas chapter president (1981, 1982), state president (1983, 1984).

Impressive though it was, a listing of formal titles failed to capture the full scope of Betty Jo's contribution as an influential and important reformer of the mental health system. But that was as it should be, said close friend and board member Elaine Shiver, who explained that titles and job descriptions were matters of little consequence to Betty Jo, who was just as happy in the trenches as anywhere else. "She was front and center in every-thing that went on during those years," Shiver said. "She was in most of the committee meetings . . . whether it was a standing committee or organizing a fund-raiser. For a few years when we focused on serving the needs of homeless families, I remember sitting in many of those meetings with her."

By the time Betty Jo took office as chapter president, she not only had a proven track record as an inspiring leader, but also as a feisty member of the rank and file. "Her style of leadership was to be 'out front,'" said Shiver. "Whatever she asked us to do . . . she was already doing herself tenfold. If it was money she requested, she and Jess had already donated. If it was time—she was committed for the whole project. She expected you to respond. How could you not? It was for the children and those who were unable to advocate for themselves. Betty Jo continually challenged us."

And behind it all, behind the enthusiasm she generated, and the personal commitment she made to each project, were those trademark organizational skills, always there, powering the engine that turned words into action, said Shiver:

She knew how to make meetings run like well-oiled machinery. If you went to a committee meeting Betty Jo was running, you knew things were going to get done and the right people were going to be there. She expected you to show up at every

276

meeting and to be involved every minute of the meeting. But she never wasted your time. You always felt like you were there on a mission and you were doing something important.

Betty Jo and Stella Mullins ran it like a business, and I think that's why the Mental Health Association was strong in those years.

Shiver wasn't alone in her thinking. Betty Jo's matter-of-fact approach to the business side of mental health issues during her presidency also caught the eye of other board members, including Marnie Wildenthal, wife of UT Southwestern Medical Center president, Dr. Kern Wildenthal, who remembers his wife praising Betty Jo's leadership during those years. "She would come back from board meetings and say Betty Jo understands what needs to be done. She has a vision of where we need to go, and she knows how to move the organization in that direction."

Research into the causes and treatment of mental illness ranked high among the priorities set by Betty Jo during her years as MHA president, and in pursuit of knowledge on the subject, she and the Dallas chapter began forging close ties with The University of Texas Southwestern Medical Center at Dallas, the leading medical research institution in North Texas. Their relationship began in the early 1980s, at the onset of research by UT Southwestern's Department of Psychiatry into the biology of mental illness. Recognizing the importance of that research to their mental health mission, Betty Jo and Stella Mullins made a conscious effort to cultivate the friendship of Dr. Kenneth Altshuler, chairman of the Department of Psychiatry, a step that eventually led to an alliance which benefited both institutions. MHA henceforth became a valuable conduit for spreading the word about UT Southwestern's efforts, and the Dallas chapter not only enjoyed the prestige of its association with the city's premier medical research facility, but Dr. Altshuler's presence on its board, as well.

In March 1981, two months after Betty Jo became president, the chapter featured articles about UT Southwestern's scientific research on the front page of its monthly newsletter. One carried the headline, "Research to be focus of annual meeting," describing the event's keynote speaker, Dr. Floyd Bloom, as "a researchist seeking to determine how certain parts of the brain function and how the brain controls man's behavior," and another, "Southwestern Medical a leading research center," began with an editor's note announcing it as the first in a series of stories about the medical center's research programs. The first article contained numerous quotations gleaned from an extensive interview with Dr. Altshuler, who disclosed that, among other things, psychiatry department researchers were investigating "the circuitry of the brain to determine the effects of medications on certain mental disorders." This research was vital, Altshuler said, because "we already know that such diseases as schizophrenia and manic depression are of a biological/biochemical nature."

And Betty Jo didn't stop her information blitz at printed material. Instead, she raised the profile of Southwestern's scientific research to an even higher level in 1981 by hosting a weekly cable television show called *Mental Health Matters,* which featured frequent interviews with research doctors and psychiatric school professors.

The research, meanwhile, was beginning to show that depression, schizophrenia, and other mental conditions were indeed physical illnesses resulting from biochemical imbalances. Betty Jo recognized that the scientific link made between biology and mental illness held great promise for those suffering from psychological disorders, and that future

278

scientific research might lead to the most important breakthroughs of all—more effective treatment and, ultimately, prevention.

In 1983, Jess honored Betty Jo for her outstanding mental health advocacy and service by creating a professorship in her name, which was to be presented through the Department of Psychiatry at The University of Texas Southwestern Medical Center at Dallas. "Betty Jo had developed a very close relationship with Southwestern," Hay said, "so the professorship turned out to be very appropriate because she stayed related to the school and its work for the balance of her life." The $100,000 endowed professorship was awarded to Dr. A. John Rush, nationally recognized for his research on depression and manic-depressive illnesses, and announced by UT Southwestern on the front page of its September 1983 newsletter:

> Dr. A. John Rush, professor of psychiatry, was named Betty Jo Hay Professor of Mental Health. . . . The professorship was given by Jess and Betty Jo Hay of Dallas and named for Mrs. Hay for her work in mental health, says Dr. Kenneth Altshuler, chairman of the Department of Psychiatry in which the chair will reside. The Hays are well-known for their interests in philanthropy and education.

Betty Jo and Jess continued their commitment to UT Southwestern by funding two upgrades to the 1983 endowment, the first in 1988, which established the Betty Jo Hay Chair in Mental Health and provided an endowment of $500,000 to support the psychiatry department's research. Once again, word of the gift was acknowledged in the UT Southwestern newsletter: "Dr. A. John Rush, who previously held the Hay Professorship, has been named holder of the Hay chair," the story read. For Dr. Rush, the new chair represented not only a significant increase in funding for his research, but a vote of confidence in his work. The second and final upgrade, at the $1 million level, followed in 1991, and again was made public through an elaborately-printed brochure:

> Mental health and education—Betty Jo Hay's major civic and philanthropic interests—come together with the endowment of the Betty Jo Hay Distinguished Chair in Mental Health at UT Southwestern.

**THE
BETTY JO HAY
CHAIR IN
MENTAL HEALTH**

THE UNIVERSITY OF TEXAS
SOUTHWESTERN
MEDICAL CENTER
AT DALLAS

In February 1983, Jess established the Betty Jo Hay Professorship in Psychiatry to honor his wife for her dedication and service to others. Out of that professorship grew the Betty Jo Hay Chair in Mental Health, with additional support by Jess, then chairman of the Board of Regents of The University of Texas System, and contributions from the matching gift programs of Exxon, MCorp, Lomas & Nettleton Financial Corporation and Southwestern Bell. The chair was established at The University of Texas Southwestern Medical Center at Dallas in February 1988 and announced at a dinner on March 16, at which Betty Jo was surrounded by her parents, family, and friends. Dr. A. John Rush was the first holder of the chair.

In Honor of the Establishment of

The Betty Jo Hay Chair in Mental Health

THE UNIVERSITY OF TEXAS
SOUTHWESTERN MEDICAL CENTER
AT DALLAS

pays tribute to

Betty Jo and Jess Hay

Their significant and enduring contributions to civic and educational causes have distinguished them as leaders in the important areas of mental health and higher education.

The establishment of The Betty Jo Hay Chair in Mental Health is a visible and permanent manifestation of their commitment to research in and the treatment of affective disorders.

The Betty Jo Hay Chair in Mental Health

provides for UT Southwestern a connection with Betty Jo and Jess Hay that is continuous and it will be a reminder of their thoughtful stewardship for decades to come.

Therefore, it is with gratitude and affection that this document is presented on March 16, 1988.

Kern Wildenthal, M.D., Ph.D.

At The Betty Jo Hay Chair in Mental Health dinner-celebration, both Betty Jo and Jess were honored with a tribute document presented by Dr. Kern Wildenthal, which extolled "their significant and enduring contributions to civic and educational causes."

Betty Jo and Jess Hay

Mental health and education—Betty Jo Hay's major civic and philanthropic interests—come together with the endowment of the Betty Jo Hay Distinguished Chair in Mental Health at UT Southwestern.

The medical center's Department of Psychiatry is especially grateful to the Hays for their generous contributions to the field of mood disorders, including depression and manic depression. Those funds played a large part in developing a major research effort that led to the founding of a National Institutes of Health-supported center. When established, the Mental Health Clinical Research Center at UT

The Betty Jo Hay Distinguished Chair in Mental Health at UT Southwestern in Dallas was an up-grade from the previously established Chair in Mental Health in her name. The Medical Center's Department of Psychiatry expressed gratitude to the Hays for their gifts to the research of mood disorders, including depression and manic depression. Income from the endowment was helpful in developing a major research effort that led to the founding of a National Institutes of Health-supported center. When established, the Mental Health Clinical Research Center at UT Southwestern was one of only four in the country founded in the mood disorders. On May 1, 1990, the new Mental Health Clinical Research Center was funded by the National Institutes of Health with almost $2 million. The MHCRC is directed by Dr. John Rush, who until July 2008 was the holder of The Betty Jo Hay Distinguished Chair in Mental Health and a professor of psychiatry at the institution.

The Hay Chair will continue Mr. and Mrs. Hay's support of UT Southwestern's Department of Psychiatry, particularly its research into mood disorders.

...outhwestern was one of only four in the country founded for research in the mood disorders.

"The outstanding researchers in the MHCRC have been working for more than a decade in this area, and their work is recognized nationally and internationally," said UT Southwestern President Kern Wildenthal, M.D., Ph.D.

Mrs. Hay is known as a tireless worker who always gives her best, and the numerous boards on which she serves are proof of her stewardship. These include the Mental Health Association in Texas, the United Way of Metropolitan Dallas, the Advisory Board to the School of Social Work at The University of Texas at Arlington, Baylor College of Dentistry, the Texas Mental Health Foundation, The Council of the Women's Foundation, and the Hogg Foundation Commission on the Mental Health of Children and Their Families.

She has also served on the boards of the Menninger Foundation, the Menninger Fund, the Menninger Clinic and the National Commission on Children, to which the U.S. Senate appointed her in 1989.

In addition to her board member-ships, this outstanding civic leader chaired a Child Abuse Conference for the Dallas County Mental Health Association in 1978 and was a member of the National Com-mittee for the Prevention of Child Abuse in 1978-79. Mrs. Hay played a major role in the work of the National Mental Health Associ-ation from 1978 to 1987, serving as president in 1986. She also served as a member of the Citizens Task Force to study Dallas County MH/MR and

hosted a weekly TV show from 1981 to 1982 on KNBN on mental health issues.

The role the 1952 SMU graduate has taken in education also has been outstanding. From 1980 to 1983 she was a member of the Association of Higher Education of North Texas and served one term as chairman. From 1972 to 1979 she was a member of the Coordinating Board, Texas College and University System, serving as chairman of the Financial Planning Committee and as a member of the Development Committee. From 1976 to 1979 Mrs. Hay was a member of the Council on Post-Secondary Accreditation (COPA). She belonged to the Southern Association Commission on Colleges, in the early 1980s.

Mrs. Hay served on a statewide Task Force on Quality Education at the Baccalaureate Level in 1981, the National Task Force on Proliferation and Specialization of Accrediting Agencies in 1976 and the National Task Force on Accreditation and the Public Interest from 1977 to 1979. She is a frequent speaker at commencement ceremonies at major universities.

Married to Jess Hay, a leading Dallas businessman, civic leader and former chairman of The University of Texas System Board of Regents, this strong woman has taken her place beside him not only in the home but in public life. The Hays are parents of two daughters and have two granddaughters and one grandson.

A. John Rush, Jr., M.D.

A. John Rush, Jr., M.D., has brought international attention to the Department of Psychiatry for his work in the mood disorders, which include depression and manic depression.

On May 1, 1990, the new Mental Health Clinical Research Center (MHCRC), directed by Dr. Rush, was funded by the National Institutes of Health with almost $2 million.

"The establishment of the MHCRC at UT Southwestern is a major step forward in finding answers to the puzzling questions that surround the diagnosis and treatment of the depressive and manic depressive disorders," said UT Southwestern President Kern Wildenthal, M.D., Ph.D. "Now with the establishment of the full-fledged center, the potential for the escalation of knowledge in this field is assured."

Holder of the Betty Jo Hay Distinguished Chair in Mental Health and professor of psychiatry, Dr. Rush has been a leader in depression research for many years. Many of his studies focus on biological and psychological diagnostic tests, trying to find the best treatments for specific kinds of depression and identifying risk factors for developing these disorders.

Dr. Rush graduated from Princeton University and Columbia College of Physicians and Surgeons. He did his medical internship at Northwestern University and his psychiatric residency at the University of Pennsylvania.

Dr. Rush has been a leader in depression research for many years.

282

The medical center's Department of Psychiatry is especially grateful to the Hays for their generous contributions to the field of mood disorders, including depression and manic depression. . . . "The outstanding researchers in the psychiatry department have been working for more than a decade in this area, and their work is recognized nationally and internationally," said UT Southwestern President Kern Wildenthal, M.D., Ph.D.

Dr. Rush's work also was highlighted in the brochure:

Holder of the Betty Jo Hay Distinguished Chair in Mental Health and professor of psychiatry, Dr. Rush has been a leader in depression research for many years and has brought international attention to the Department of Psychiatry for his work in the mood disorders.

While the endowment unquestionably had a long-term impact on the progress of Dr. Rush's professional career, it is not the money he thinks about when looking back on his group's numerous achievements during those productive years. Rather, he remembers Betty Jo—her constant presence, inspiration, and the lasting impression she made on him and many others within the Psychiatry Department:

Betty Jo's support and constant encouragement contributed much to the development of my research. In turn, I developed research opportunities for other people and created the infrastructure that helped build the program. Her interaction with this department, and the endowment, were seminal to our success—absolutely critical.

But not even her fervent commitment to mental health research outranked the cause of children, because where Betty Jo was concerned, nothing was more important than their protection and welfare. "Children's issues are really where I'm coming from," she said in a 1986 magazine interview. "It's my basic feeling that children in this country are our future, and we'd better do a good job with them." And doing a good job meant starting when they're young, said Jess, explaining the high value Betty Jo placed on early childhood development. "She had a deep belief that mental health and productive citizenship . . . begin at a very early age." Aside from it being a deeply-held personal conviction, though, there was solid scientific evidence to back Betty Jo's belief that a child's start in life holds the key to its future. Betty Jo shared some of that evidence with her audience in a 1987 speech:

Why are the early years of life so important? Studies . . . by developmental psychologists and experts in medicine and education showed over and over the importance of the first few years of life in terms of the development of language, intelligence, and emotional well-being. They also found that working with the family is the most effective way of helping children get off to the best possible start in life.

Those were the very principles the Dallas chapter of MHA applied to its programs during Betty Jo's tenure as president, starting with the annual parenting conference which attracted large audiences with an impressive line up of nationally recognized keynote speakers. In 1982, noted anthropologist, social biologist, and author, Dr. Ashley Montagu, addressed the issue of "Parenting in a Violent Society." The year before, in a presentation entitled, "Non-sexist parenting and role free family life," principal speaker Letty Cottin Pogrebin—founding editor of *Ms. Magazine*—provided a feminist social critique. MHA Dallas also supported a Family Advocate Program that offered group parenting seminars and weekly home visits, designed "to establish rapport with troubled families and serve as a 'family advocate' by modeling good parenting skills." Moreover, it sponsored Parents Helping Parents, a weekly self-help group for "abusive, neglectful, or at-risk parents" facilitated by professionally-trained volunteers.

In 1981, MHA Dallas launched an initiative known as WHO—We Help Ourselves—a child victimization prevention program, which was an overnight success. With an educationally-sound curriculum and sensitive, nonthreatening content, the program provided a potential way out for children who needed one. "WHO has three messages for children," one section of the material read ". . . plan for personal safety, have a plan of action, and ask for help." A year later the program was being videotaped and taken to the community by a small corps of volunteers who reached 19,000 children in Dallas County. Ten years after the program's 1981 kickoff, a fact sheet prepared by MHA Dallas attested to its remarkable success:

> At the end of the WHO Program's tenth year, there are now 148 programs located in Texas, Arkansas, Oregon, Oklahoma, Illinois, Missouri, New Jersey, Louisiana, New Mexico, and Georgia. Over one million children have participated in the WHO Program.

284

During the 1980s, as more and more women entered and remained in the paid work force, the issue of non-parental child care became a matter of growing national concern. Debate over the appropriate role of government, employers, and parents intensified as a broad array of special interest groups moved in to address the increasing need for child care support and services. For their part, Betty Jo and Jess realized early on that providing on-site corporate child care would be beneficial, and were anxious to implement such a program at Lomas & Nettleton, but it wasn't practical until 1984 when the company built a service center and consolidated the bulk of its employees at or near the new facility.

Even though 1984 was busy planning for The L & N School, Betty Jo and Jess were also involved in numerous other activities, but found time to participate in one of their passionate interests: politics.

Betty Jo and Jess attended the 1984 Democratic National Convention in San Francisco during the week of July 16-19. With her credentials, Betty Jo not only had access to the convention, but to all related functions, as well. Jess served as a delegate that year. They threw their support behind former Vice President Walter Mondale, though they initially had endorsed U.S. Senator John Glenn as their Democrat of choice for president. In spite of Glenn's withdrawal from the race, he and his wife, Annie, as well as Mondale and his wife, Joan, continued to enjoy a long and sustained friendship with Betty Jo and Jess.

```
1625 MASSACHUSETTS AVE NW
WASHINGTON DC 20036
28PM
```

Western Union **Mailgram**

```
4-185925U241008 08/28/84 ICS WA16614          DALB
00774 MLTN VA 08/28/84
```

```
BETTY JO HAY
7236 LUPTON CIRCLE
DALLAS, TX 75225
```

```
I AM REALLY LOOKING FORWARD TO MY TRIP TO TEXAS NEXT MONTH
-- AND TO MEETING YOU AT A "TEXAS-STYLE" CHAMPAGNE BREAKFAST.

    YOUR ENERGY AND ENTUSIASM ARE CRUCIAL TO OUR EFFORTS THIS FALL,
AND YOUR FINANCIAL SUPPORT OF THIS EVENT WILL ENSURE ITS SUCCESS
AND HELP US ON OUR WAY TO VICTORY IN NOVEMBER.

    THANK YOU FOR YOUR HELP, AND I WILL SEE YOU IN DALLAS ON
SEPTEMBER 20TH.

CORDIALLY,


GERALDINE FERRARO

05133

21:13 EST

MGMCOMP
```

This mailgram from Geraldine Ferraro—Walter Mondale's running mate—was sent to Betty Jo one month after the Democratic Party's nominating convention in San Francisco. In her effort to support the first-ever woman vice presidential candidate, Betty Jo in concert with Judy Tycher set about planning a major "Texas-style" fund-raising breakfast to be held in Ferraro's honor September 20, 1984 at the Fairmont Hotel in Dallas.

Page 10   Sunday, September 2, 1984

PUBLIC EYE

Betty Jo Hay and Judy Tycher announce plans for Geraldine Ferraro's breakfast on Sept. 20 at the Fairmont.

Sporting "Dallas for Ferraro" buttons, Betty Jo and Texas breakfast co-chair Judy Tycher were featured in *The Dallas Morning News* on September 2, 1984 in advance of the campaign event.

286

WALTER F. MONDALE

2550 M STREET, N.W., SUITE 500
WASHINGTON, D.C. 20037

September 17, 1984

Mr. and Mrs. Jess Hay
7236 Lupton Circle
Dallas, Texas 75225

Dear Betty Jo and Jess:

I know that your most fervent wish is that
Gerry and I win this historic election. And, I
am spending every ounce of my energy on the campaign
trail, trying to accomplish that goal.

What I hope I can convey to you in this short
note is that you have my deepest, most intense and
most personal gratitude for all that you have done.
You said, "Yes, I will help," clearly and loudly
when I asked. You stood up to be counted, even
during the roughest of times. And, win or lose,
I will never forget it.

There are only a few individuals who have made
the supreme commitment to me and to this campaign.
You are two of these very special people and I
consider you both to be my closest and most important
friends.

Words can never express the magnitude of my
thanks. So, I hope that in some way in the future
my actions can prove to you the depth of my gratitude.

Joan joins me in sending our warmest regards.

Sincerely,

Fritz Mondale

A heartfelt letter of thanks from Walter Mondale to Betty Jo and Jess for their commitment to his quest for the presidency in 1984.
The letter also reflects the depth of the personal friendship they shared.

By that time, it was too late to help Ramona Taylor, an L & N employee whose life could have been altered significantly by the availability of child care in the workplace. Taylor, who, in addition to being a Lomas & Nettleton senior vice president and corporate secretary, also was a friend, and it was the state of her personal life in the early 1960s which opened Betty Jo's eyes to a vital need that wasn't being met. "I remember when Ramona was caring for her critically ill husband who died of heart failure in 1969, tending to the needs of their two children, Keith and Cheryl, and working at the same time. I thought that was awful; she needed some help," Betty Jo said then. "That got me thinking about corporate child care, and I lobbied Jess about it for years." As usual, Betty Jo's patience and power of persuasion paid off, and when Jess broke the long-awaited news about his plans for a child care program at Lomas & Nettleton, it was a moment Betty Jo would long remember. "He came home one night and said, 'Okay, we're going to do it now.' It was very exciting. I was thrilled to death. I felt like I'd birthed a baby."

Corporate childcare consultant Peggy Wilks soon was called on to develop the program, and once on the job discovered in Jess Hay a business executive for whom child care outside the home truly mattered. "Mr. Hay had very strong ideas about the quality and caliber of the program," remembers Wilks. "He was very direct and straightforward; he wanted it to be the best."

By the time Kate Wheeler was brought in to direct the corporate program in early 1984, she, like Wilks, found Jess's imprint on many of the decisions which had been made regarding the school's day-to-day operation. "Jess already knew what he wanted," Wheeler said. "It would be called The L & N School. He had decided it would be for infants through kindergarten. He wanted it to be a learning center, and not just a care provider. And he wanted the hours of the school comparable to the working hours of most employees." After that, Wheeler—a close friend of Jess and Betty Jo's, and a former teacher and consultant with the Highland Park Independent School District's Talented and Gifted program—fleshed out the details of a program that eventually included an experienced, well-paid staff, low teacher/student ratios, a full-time registered nurse, library, and a parenting program.

The L & N School achieved national recognition in 1986 when it was selected by the National Association for the Education of Young Children as one of nineteen accredited child care programs across the country. The school also was featured in a U.S. Department of Health and Human Services documentary highlighting model early childhood education programs. Jess shared Betty Jo's pride in the school and became a staunch advocate of early childhood education, demonstrating his commitment to addressing the needs of young

288

children and their families by serving as chairman of the Dallas Child Care Partnership, an organization dedicated to improving the quality of child care and making it more accessible.

But Betty Jo's lobbying victories didn't end with the opening of The L & N School. Motivated by an intense interest in the political process, she utilized her uncommon access to lawmakers to achieve similar results with MHA's legislative program, thereby affirming her effectiveness as an advocate. She was called to action in the belief that every citizen should have the right to basic human services, a political philosophy rooted in the New Deal years, and furthered by the empowerment movements of the sixties and early seventies. "We should get involved in the political process," Betty Jo implored, during a 1977 speech to a civic group. "Government affects all our lives from the day we are born until the day we die. To be involved in government is to show concern for our community and for our fellow human beings."

And Betty Jo did her best to make government easily accessible, opening the door to anyone who wanted in. In 1981—not long after she took office as president of MHA Dallas—the chapter devoted a full page of its newsletter to legislative concerns, listing contact information for state and national lawmakers. Those reading the publication couldn't help but feel their participation truly must matter:

> When state legislation is pending in which the Mental Health Association has an interest, your influence is needed. . . . Please clip and save this list so you can become part of the legislative network. . . . *YOU CAN MAKE A DIFFERENCE!*

From her extraordinary ability to mobilize grass roots volunteers, to the friendships she had nurtured with state and national political leaders through years of mutual trust, Betty Jo was always on the move, determined to bring positive change to the policies governing her primary public concerns, and never, ever short of new ideas. One of her most innovative was the so-called Honoring Dinner, an annual affair that eventually replaced the Galaxy Ball as the state MHA's principal fund-raiser. The concept was to hand pick honorees based on their support of mental health issues and, more often than not, on their political connections, which according to Dr. Kern Wildenthal, produced more than just the desired financial result. The dinners were, in his words, "a very effective fund-raising mechanism. . . . Their knack for selecting politically persuasive people . . . was very shrewd. Not only did it bring in money, but it bound political leaders to their cause. The honorees felt good about what they had done in the past and would want to do still more in the future. It was a multiple win."

In 1980, Betty Jo and Jess, together, co-chaired the very first Honoring Dinner, which attracted more than 500 guests and paid tribute to Dr. Wayne Holtzman—president of The University of Texas System's Hogg Foundation for Mental Health.

Three years later, the award went to Diana Hobby, the wife of Lt. Governor Bill Hobby, who downplayed the significance of the achievement during an interview with *Austin American-Statesman* columnist Lee Kelly, and instead gave much of the credit to Betty Jo. "'Frankly, the major contribution I've made is that I have friends who work for good and worthy causes,' Diana Hobby told us in a telephone conversation from her Houston home. 'No, I'm not being modest. How can you say 'no' to Betty Jo Hay?'"

In truth, this was just the latest in a long string of honors conferred on the self-effacing Diana Hobby, who had made consistent and substantial contributions to the cause of mental health over many years, and it was to these achievements that Betty Jo pointed during her own interview with the *Statesman* columnist:

> She has supported day care issues and mental health legislation. Diana chaired the Child Care '76 Advisory Committee that held forums across the state for children, youth, and families. She launched a latch-key children's project in Houston, and helped establish a Title XX Coalition and a working parent seminar program.

Featured as honorary chairmen at the 1983 Diana Hobby Honoring Dinner were three of the heaviest hitters in state politics at the time, and their wives, a who's who of high-ranking brass which rightly caught the eye of *The Austin American-Statesman*: "Gov. Mark and Linda Gale White, Gov. Bill and Rita Clements and Gov. Dolph and Janey Briscoe," the newspaper reported in its coverage of the spectacle. This feat alone was enough to put a stamp of approval on a black-tie event that might otherwise not have received one, thereby transforming the Honoring Dinner into a don't miss, political extravaganza. That, in turn, left Austin legislative lobbyists—aware that the presence of three governors under one roof was akin to winning a trifecta at Churchill Downs on Derby Day—clamoring for tickets, and Betty Jo with a sense of satisfaction that her innovation was working.

"Betty Jo helped generate a broad base of support among the political establishment," said Jess. "She brought together all of our political activity in support of mental health issues. For example, when you had a mental health Honoring Dinner, it would have been very uncommon in those days not to have had the lieutenant governor, governor, all the other elected state officials, and a number of key legislative members present." And it just kept growing. In 1984, when state treasurer and future Texas governor Ann Richards

290

was honored, Lee Kelly noted in her column, "More than 600 people attended the event, which netted more than $270,000 for mental health coffers."

Orchestrating such an event required more than just the time and effort of Betty Jo. It also demanded volunteer talent, and those who answered the call usually found themselves swept up by Betty Jo's enthusiasm and can-do attitude. "Complete belief in what she was doing was contagious," said Elaine Shiver. "Those of us who followed her came to believe we too could accomplish whatever she asked us to do. The message was, whatever the task, we ALL were in it together when we tackled a project. She set the example and we followed."

The Inaugural Committee
requests the honor of your presence
to attend and participate in the Inauguration of
Mark Wells White
as Governor of the State of Texas
and
William P. Hobby
as Lieutenant Governor of the State of Texas
on Tuesday the eighteenth of January
one thousand nine hundred and eighty-three
in the City of Austin

On January 18, 1983, Betty Jo and Jess attended the inauguration of Texas Governor Mark White and Lieutenant Governor Bill Hobby at the state capitol in Austin where they applauded White's defeat of Republican incumbent Bill Clements, Bill Hobby's re-election, and the 1982 Democratic sweep of all state offices.

Galaxy Ball Best Ever

"The Mental Health Association is delighted to report the highest net Galaxy Ball in its twenty year history," said Stella Mullins, Executive Director of the MHA in Texas.

The Dallas Galaxy Ball netted $282,806 of which $144,684 was shared with member chapters of the MHA in Texas.

President Betty Jo Hay expressed her appreciation to all those who contributed to its great success. These included: Governor and Mrs. Mark White, Honorary Chairmen; Former Astronaut Alan B. Shepard and Mrs. Shepard, Special Guests; Kaye Gold, Belinda Weber and Lauryn Gayle White, Ball Co-Chairmen.

Elaine Shiver, Invitations Chairman; Mary Catherine Sweet, Reservations Chairman; Cheryl Hortenstine, Decorations Chairman; Vicki Kessler, John Sexton, H. H. Miller, Jr. and Virginia Morris, Door Prizes; and Nedda and Paul Low, Auction Chairmen.

The 1984 Galaxy Ball will be held March 10 at the Post Oak Warwick in Houston.

In 1983, Betty Jo took the helm of the Mental Health Association in Texas. On March 12 of that year, the organization's principal fund-raising event—the Galaxy Ball—generated an unprecedented amount of money in the name of mental health. The statewide event was held at the Fairmont Hotel in Dallas.

The Governor's Mansion
Austin, Texas
78701

March 22, 1983

Mrs. Jess Hay
7236 Lupton Circle
Dallas, TX   75225

Dear Betty Jo:

Just wanted you to know the Galaxy Ball was not only the most impressively decorated ball I have been to, but we had fun as well.

Everything was perfect! You are certainly to be commended for your accomplishment.

The roses were beautiful too!

Sincerely,

Linda Gale

Linda Gale White

LGW/lmb

Following the success of the 1983 Galaxy Ball, Betty Jo received a letter of appreciation from First Lady of Texas Linda Gale White. She and Governor Mark White acted as Honorary Chairmen of the ball.

And while following Betty Jo's lead may not always have been easy, it surely was rewarding, which reminded Shiver of the time she volunteered to help with a dinner mailing Betty Jo had organized:

> Betty Jo converted one room of her house for the project. As you entered the room you saw work stations for addressing, stuffing, stamping, etc. There were stacks of material on the pool table, bar, and portable tables. She had us organized in shifts and fed us at mealtimes. It was an all day and into the night affair. As with all of Betty Jo's events, it was work mixed with laughter and friendship. You wouldn't want to miss it.

The concept of the Honoring Dinner as a strategy to build legislative support for a single cause paid off in 1983 when Governor Mark White signed into law a revision of the state's Mental Health Code. White's action was the culmination of an effort which had begun a year earlier when representatives of forty organizations banded together to establish the Mental Health Code Task Force. Led by Helen Farabee—a figure of great consequence within the volunteer ranks of the Mental Health Association—the task force had but a single mission: to reform a policy mired in the past, a policy essentially unchanged since 1957.

Many people, including Betty Jo, considered Farabee the grande dame of the Texas mental health movement. Her commitment to the cause started in the mid-sixties when she and future lieutenant governor Bill Hobby joined forces and successfully swayed state legislators to establish the Texas Department of Mental Health and Mental Retardation. Eventually, Farabee's involvement would land her in the top spot at the Texas Mental Health Association, a position she held from 1972 to 1974 and then again in 1985. In addition, she not only was appointed by First Lady Rosalynn Carter to the Public Committee on Mental Health, but she also chaired the Texas Advisory Council on the Construction of Community Mental Health Centers in 1976, and the Texas State Mental Health Advisory Council in 1977. And, as if those commitments were not enough, Farabee served as chairman of the Special Senate Committee on the Delivery of Human Services in Texas, which was instrumental in the creation of the Texas Health and Human Services Coordinating Council, of which she was a member.

Not unlike Betty Jo, Helen Farabee worked in tandem with her husband, Texas Senator Ray Farabee of Wichita Falls, who represented District Thirty from 1974 to 1988, and shared his wife's vision of improved human services for all Texans. In the end, Farabee's tireless efforts on behalf of mental health issues would span nearly three decades and come to a close with some well-deserved recognition, including her induction into the Texas Women's Hall of Fame in 1985. Following her death in 1988, the Texas Mental Health Association established the Helen J. Farabee Public Policy Fellowship.

And so it was that this powerful Texas triumvirate—Helen Farabee, Betty Jo Hay, and Stella Mullins—led the charge for mental health during the 1980s, and through their work dramatically advanced an agenda that had all but come to a halt. "I don't want to sound excessive," said Jess, "but the reality is that Betty Jo, Helen Farabee, and Stella Mullins almost single-handedly awakened the political establishment in Texas to the importance of mental health issues":

> There were major, major positive changes in public policy related to mental health concerns during that period of time. And the woman most responsible for helping define the related public policy advances was Helen Farabee. The most important women, by far, in terms of attracting broadened support for those policies were Betty Jo and Stella.

The three were lauded for their distinguished service by *Austin American-Statesman* columnist Lee Kelly, who covered the October 1982 Honoring Dinner recognizing Helen Farabee, and who lavished praise on each of Texas MHA's top leaders, particularly the guest of honor:

> Meet some superwomen . . . Helen Farabee of Wichita Falls, Betty Jo Hay of Dallas, and Stella Mullins of Austin are our candidates for Superwomen-of-the-Year. . . .

> More than 600 folks jam-packed the Driskill Hotel for a sitdown dinner and toast-after-toast to Helen—she's the indefatigable woman whose work in the areas of child advocacy, mental health, juvenile justice, the aged, and disabled could fill this column.

By the spring of 1983, Farabee and the task force had completed their revisions to the Mental Health Code and the legislature had approved the recommendations, leaving only Governor Mark White's signature to make it official. To ensure his signing of the bill received the fanfare it deserved, Betty Jo lined up former First Ladies Rosalynn Carter and Lady Bird Johnson as special guests of honor at the event in hopes of gaining maximum

294

visibility, which may have done the trick, as news of the landmark legislation was announced on the front page of the May/June 1983 issue of *Advocate,* a statewide newsletter published by The Mental Health Association in Texas:

> A major revision of the Texas Mental Health Code was signed into Law April 27 during Mental Health Association ceremonies at the State Capitol. . . . The code was passed unanimously by both the House and Senate. "It is a credit to the excellent work of the task force, representing over forty organizations, that the bill passed so smoothly and quickly through the legislature," said Betty Jo Hay, President of the Mental Health Association in Texas.

With the legislative side of matters now well in hand, Betty Jo turned to the business aspect of the mental health picture, with an eye toward improving MHA's fund-raising capabilities. Putting her creative flare to work on this most pressing of concerns, Betty Jo, along with Jess, resolved to establish the Texas Mental Health Foundation in 1982. By providing a continuous source of funding "to promote programs of the Texas Mental Health Association and the fourteen chapters in Texas," the foundation served as yet another means of moving the state mental health agenda forward. Its formation aptly coincided with the October 1982 Honoring Dinner for Helen Farabee, which, in effect, became the focal point for raising the foundation's first $100,000—a sum designated as the "Helen Farabee Fund for an Enlightened Public Health Policy." To date, most of the grants allocated by the foundation have benefited at-risk children, no doubt a source of great pleasure to its benefactors.

The legislative and fund-generating expertise of Texas MHA did not go unnoticed by the organization's national leadership, nor did the leadership's outward acknowledgment of that fact get by Elaine Shiver, who distinctly recalls the prestige enjoyed by the Texas affiliate at national conventions in the early 1980s. "Texas was really shining. . . . I remember going to the national conference with Betty Jo, Helen, and Stella, and feeling very proud that I was with a group that people recognized, everybody knew them." As it happened, the high standing Betty Jo had achieved on the state level would have a far-reaching effect on her future within the organization. She progressed through a series of national board committee assignments, from the resource development committee, to the program, finance, and executive committees, and finally in November 1984, the national MHA tapped Betty Jo

Hay for its top volunteer job by naming her president-elect of the organization, a post she would hold for one year beginning that month.

Texas MHA, understandably awash with pride at Betty Jo's election, wasted no time in organizing a reception in her honor. Co-sponsored by the Hogg Foundation for Mental Health, the January 24, 1985 gala featured Hogg Foundation president Wayne Holtzman, who had nothing but praise for Betty Jo's contributions to the mental health cause:

> Betty Jo more than anyone else has been responsible for the revitalization of the Mental Health Association in the past four years. Her work as a fund-raiser has transformed the face of the organization. . . . She has been a real role model for volunteerism in the state, and now the nation.

In response to Betty Jo's new role as national spokesperson for MHA, congratulatory articles and honorary awards began streaming in, and continued to do so for the next two years. She maintained a full schedule of speaking engagements which not only showcased her talent as a gifted communicator, but earned her the admiration of fellow advocates from around the country. Even former MHA Texas president Judge Oswin Chrisman, who had worked closely with Betty Jo for years, continually was struck by her extraordinary ability to deliver an effective message:

> When she gave speeches she always had something humorous to say. . . . She had a good voice, a pleasing demeanor, and a knack for communication—never condescending, always direct and straight.

As Betty Jo's public stature increased in 1985, so did her husband's. In February of that year, the nine-member University of Texas Board of Regents unanimously elected Jess Hay to a two-year term as chairman, after which he immediately issued what amounted to an all-out declaration of war against proposed legislative budget cuts targeting higher education. Shortly thereafter, *On Campus*—a UT faculty and staff publication—carried a story about the controversy in its February/March issue, laying out Hay's position, including his intention to vigorously defend the need for proper financing of the state's colleges and universities:

Resolution

WHEREAS, the Mental Health Association in Texas and the Hogg Foundation for Mental Health wish to commend Betty Jo Hay, a dedicated volunteer committed to children, the promotion of mental health and the prevention of mental illness; and

WHEREAS, Betty Jo Hay, has given untold hours of loyal service to help the mentally ill citizens of Texas and the United States; and

WHEREAS, active in the mental health field since 1972, this distinguished person provided an impetus to improved care and treatment of the mentally ill and for promotion of mental health in children; and

WHEREAS, Betty Jo Hay founded the Mental Health Foundation which provides educational grants for Mental Health Association programs across the state; and

WHEREAS, this outstanding volunteer has worked tirelessly for Mental Health Association goals at the local, state and national levels; be it

RESOLVED by the Mental Health Association in Texas and the Hogg Foundation for Mental Health that Betty Jo Hay, be commended for her outstanding volunteer contributions in mental health for the citizens of Texas and the United States.

Adopted this 24th day of January, 1985

Helen J Farabee
Helen J. Farabee, President
Mental Health Association in Texas

Wayne H. Holtzman
Dr. Wayne H. Holtzman, President
Hogg Foundation for Mental Health

For her outstanding work on behalf of those living with mental illness—in Texas and across the nation—Betty Jo was formally commended by the Mental Health Association in Texas and the Hogg Foundation for Mental Health on January 24, 1985. The resolution was presented in Austin by Stella Mullins, Wayne Holtzman, and Helen Farabee, fellow leaders in the cause of mental health.

CONCURRENT RESOLUTION

WHEREAS, The Mental Health Association in Texas will observe its 50th Anniversary on May 2, 1985, with a celebration in the state capitol; and

WHEREAS, The Mental Health Association in Texas is a nonprofit citizens' advocacy organization dedicated to promoting mental health, preventing mental illness, and advocating improved care of mentally ill persons; and

WHEREAS, Founded in 1934 as the Texas Society for Mental Hygiene, this fine group has actively sought to bring about increased awareness of the concerns of mentally ill persons; by means of an extensive network of publications and educational workshops, great strides have been made toward informing the public of the many services available for the treatment of mental health problems and of the opportunities for careers in the mental health field; and

WHEREAS, The Association has worked through the legislative process to bring improvements in the mental health service delivery system in Texas; it was instrumental in the writing of a new Mental Health Code that was enacted by the 68th Legislature in 1983; and

WHEREAS, The Mental Health Association in Texas has founded many programs to promote mental health and to provide assistance to the families of mentally ill persons; and

WHEREAS, During the 50th Anniversary Celebration, the Mental Health Bell will be rung in the Capitol rotunda; this bell was cast from chains and shackles used to restrain patients in mental hospitals; the inscription on the bell reads: "Cast from the shackles which bound them, this bell shall ring out hope for the mentally ill and victory over mental illness"; and

WHEREAS, The celebration will also include a reception honoring charter members of the Texas Society for Mental Hygiene; and

WHEREAS, The fine work of the Mental Health Association in Texas stands as a tribute to the dedication of those persons, who, over the past 50 years, have devoted time and effort to helping victims of mental illness live their lives with dignity; now, therefore, be it

RESOLVED, That the 69th Legislature of the State of Texas congratulate the Mental Health Association in Texas on the occasion of its 50th Anniversary and commend this outstanding organization for its admirable work; and, be it further

RESOLVED, That an official copy of this resolution be prepared for the Mental Health Association in Texas as an expression of high regard from the 69th Legislature of the State of Texas.

CONCURRENT RESOLUTION

WHEREAS, The Mental Health Association in Texas, on the occasion of its 50th Anniversary to be celebrated this year, is proud to announce the choice of one of its members, Mrs. Betty Jo Hay of Dallas, a president-elect of the National Mental Health Association; and

WHEREAS, Active in the field of mental health since 1972, Mrs. Hay has served continuously on the board of directors of both the Dallas County and Texas associations since 1974, and is past president of both organizations; and

WHEREAS, She has contributed generously of her time to promote awareness of the mental health cause among the public, in the process becoming a capable and compelling spokeswoman on all issues pertaining to mental health; and

WHEREAS, This enthusiastic "role model for volunteerism," as described by the National Association, has focused her efforts particularly on committees relating to children and adolescents; while simultaneously assisting prominently in various association fund-raising efforts; and

WHEREAS, A graduate of Southern Methodist University, she has been honored for her altruism by the academic community through the establishment, within the department of psychiatry of the University of Texas Health Science Center at Dallas, of the Betty Jo Hay Professorship of Mental Health, now occupied by Dr. A. John Rush of that institution; and

WHEREAS, Her exceptional achievements and unmatched energy merit special recognition by this legislature and all Texans; now, therefore, be it

RESOLVED, That the 69th Legislature of the State of Texas hereby commend Mrs. Betty Jo Hay, the 1985 president-elect of the National Mental Health Association; and, be it further

RESOLVED, That an official copy of this resolution be prepared for Mrs. Hay as a token of highest regard from the Texas Legislature.

A 1985 State of Texas resolution marking the fiftieth anniversary of the Mental Health Association in Texas also announced Betty Jo's impending presidency of the National Mental Health Association. "Her exceptional achievements and unmatched energy merit special recognition by this legislature and all Texans," it read in part.

298

THE WOMEN'S CENTER OF DALLAS
CORDIALLY INVITES YOU
TO ATTEND THE

EIGHTH ANNUAL
WOMEN HELPING WOMEN
AWARDS CELEBRATION

THE WESTIN HOTEL, GALLERIA
WEDNESDAY, APRIL 24, 1985
6:30-9:30 PM

HORS D'OEUVRES
WINE AND BEER
(CASH BAR PROVIDED)
FOLLOWED BY HONOREE PRESENTATIONS
AND KEYNOTE SPEAKER,
ANN RICHARDS

1985 HONOREES

ELLA BAILEY
BEVERLY LAUGHLIN BROOKS
BETTY JO HAY
JOY MANKOFF
TEGWIN DYER PULLEY
DAN WEISER, SPECIAL RECOGNITION

Betty Jo was among six women honored in 1985
during the annual Women Helping Women Awards
Celebration sponsored by the Women's Center of
Dallas. Texas State Treasurer Ann Richards delivered
the keynote address at the Westin Galleria Hotel
in Dallas on April 24.

The United Negro College Fund

proudly presents

its Distinguished Leadership Award to

Betty Jo Hay

For extraordinary leadership service rendered,
to the Fund and its member institutions
and for sincere concern for the minority youth
of our nation.

Presented this 10 day of May 19 85

Christopher F. Edley
President

Virgil Ecton
Executive Director

A mind is a terrible thing to waste.

Betty Jo's commitment to the pursuit of quality education for all of our people was one of her passions,
and in 1985 the United Negro College Fund acknowledged that fact by presenting her with its
Distinguished Leadership Award.

In assuming the chairmanship, Mr. Hay noted that "as a first priority, the board must extend its best efforts to continue adequate legislative funding for the components of the UT System and, indeed, all of Texas higher education." He emphasized that "the appropriation proposals currently before the Legislature are well below the levels needed to maintain the momentum of the UT System's academic and research progress, and would severely limit the state's ability to meet the high technology requirements of the future."

During the months that followed, Hay and his allies were able to flex sufficient political muscle to turn back the legislative threat, but not without concessions on both sides. As a result, the way forward became dependent on trade-offs, said Shirley Bird Perry—vice president for development at The University of Texas at Austin—who, at the time, credited Hay for paving the middle ground:

> Jess Hay runs a large financial institution. . . . He deals with complex financial matters all the time. He understood what we needed, and he was able to go to the right political figures and say, "If we do this, we can get through to the next legislative session."

When the legislation finally passed on the closing day of the 1986 special session, Betty Jo and Jess were there to celebrate a compromise bill which contained fewer budget cuts than initially proposed, but most significantly, cuts well within a range Jess and the Board of Regents could live with for the remaining months of the 1985 - 1986 biennium. On that successful note—and believing that what had been trimmed from the budget would be restored during the next regular session of the legislature—they held an impromptu victory party which was covered by news reporter Lawrence Biemiller, who'd been following the ongoing budget battle. The triumphant gathering, wrote Biemiller, was held "in the Lieutenant Governor's apartment behind the Senate chamber. . . . The visitor begins to appreciate the role of socializing in the legislative process. Mr. Hay and his wife, Betty Jo, are holding court in front of a table on which sits an arrangement of fresh flowers."

That Biemiller would paint Betty Jo and Jess in terms befitting royalty was not far off the mark, considering that period of time in their lives. "They were at the top of their game," said a close friend from the mid-1980s. They had, after all, attained positions of the highest profile and, to their credit, were using those positions to effect large-scale, meaningful change within institutions long overdue for both. Yet beyond their exalted status, beyond the tremendous political clout they now wielded and the regard in which they were held by friends and admirers, lay a simple truth about Betty Jo and Jess: they had not arrived at this point alone. Instead, Hay said, theirs were the accomplishments of many. "Our effectiveness invariably is so intertwined with the efforts of others that any honor, praise, or notice always appropriately should be a shared experience rather than an individual endowment," he explained.

Nevertheless, their growing prominence continued to attract attention, and was on full display in a November 1986 issue of *The Houston Post* which featured a story under the headline, "Betty and Jess Hay":

> In the small fraternity of the state's most powerful men, he [Jess Hay] stands near the top. One of twenty people included in a recent Texas Business magazine article entitled "Who Really Rules Texas," Hay is chairman of the powerful University of Texas Board of Regents. . . . *Dallas Morning News* political reporter Sam Attlesey calls Hay "the reigning king of the kingmakers among Democrats seeking office. Hay's prowess in raising money for candidates has made him a political legend."

> Betty Jo, a vivacious, outgoing woman . . . is a power in her own right. As president of the National Mental Health Association, she had been instrumental in raising millions of dollars on the local, state, and national levels for mental health research and related initiatives.

While he and Betty Jo clearly had acquired a heaping helping of it, Jess invariably viewed power as something of an illusion, fairly easy to sustain he said, "so long as the individual does not seek, to any material degree, to exercise it for his or her own personal benefit." Which explains why he bristled at the notion of individual recognition when it came his or Betty Jo's way. It simply wasn't the Hay style. To the contrary, he and Betty Jo believed firmly "that, as individuals, we seldom function effectively in isolation. Rather, we work in community, in relationship with others. Thus, the product of a particular effort normally should be credited to the group rather than to any single participant. The generation of perceived political power, for example, normally is the result of shared endeavor, and, therefore, should be thus attributed."

Today

The Houston Post
Sun., November 9, 1986

SUPER TEXANS

Betty and Jess Hay

He is known as the reigning king of kingmakers among the Democrats. She has raised some $5 million for mental health associations.

EDITOR'S NOTE: *Periodically, Today reporters take a close-up look at some of the state's super achievers to help explain the impact they have and how they earned their success.*

By ELIZABETH BENNETT
Post Reporter

DALLAS — Jess Hay's power of concentration is legendary among his employees at Dallas-based Lomas & Nettleton Financial Corporation, the world's largest mortgage banking firm.

Standing in a buffet line for lunch recently, L&N's chairman and chief executive officer was deeply engrossed in a political discussion with several company officials. Nearing a large caldron of hot vegetable soup, Hay reached down for a saucer and — forgetting the cup — ladled out a full portion of soup. He didn't miss a beat in his conversation until the steaming liquid started filling up the saucer and overflowing onto his shirt sleeve, grabbing his attention.

"Something like that happens to Jess all the time," recalls an amused John Sexton, the company's chief financial officer. "He also has trouble with cars. One time Jess parked his car at Texas Stadium and walked away, when suddenly it caught on fire and people started yelling and screaming at him. He's had three cars burn up on him like that. I know in my heart he caused it somehow because he was thinking of something else."

But if Jess Thomas Hay, 55, can't concentrate on the small stuff, he has no trouble with more demanding matters.

In the small fraternity of the state's most powerful men, he stands near the top. One of 20 people included in a recent Texas Business magazine article entitled "Who Really Rules Texas," Hay is chairman of the powerful University of Texas Board of Regents, even though he had to defeat Gov. Mark White's pick for the job — and even though his own alma mater is Southern Methodist University. But Hay's real political clout lies in his ability to raise money for Democratic politicians, with the able assistance of Betty Joe, his wife of 35 years.

Since the two first started working together on political campaigns at SMU in the early '50s, the Hays have labored quietly behind the scenes to support — and elect — Democrats of their choice: Gov. Mark White, Lt. Gov. Bill Hobby, Railroad Commissioner Jim Nugent, U.S. Sen. Lloyd Bentsen, and former president Jimmy Carter.

Senators, governors and celebrities have been frequent visitors in their Dallas home over the years. Carter, who appointed Hay finance chairman of the Democratic National Committee from 1977-1979, once gave a campaign speech on the Hays' patio. Carter also has been an overnight guest in their home, along with Bentsen, Hobby and a host of other state and national political figures.

Dallas Morning-News political reporter Sam Attlesey calls Hay "the reigning king of the kingmakers among Democrats seeking office. Jess Hay's prowess in raising money for candidates has made him a Texas political legend."

But unlike a number of other powerful, wealthy Texans — particularly in the world of politics — Hay shuns the back-slapping and limelight. A soft-spoken man who is sometimes per-

Photo by Ron Berard
The Hays, shown by the lake behind their Dallas home where Jimmy Carter was a frequent guest, have worked behind the scenes for decades to support and elect Democrats of their choice.

ceived as cool and aloof, he leaves the small talk to his 55-year-old wife, Betty Jo, a vivacious, outgoing woman who is a power in her own right. As president of the National Mental Health Association, she has been instrumental in raising millions of dollars on the local, state and national level for mental health research.

Working together, the Hays have created a lifestyle that includes frequent escapes to their luxurious, six-bedroom house in Acapulco, complete with a houseboy, cook, two maids and a gardener.

The couple's names are on every party planner's guest list, from Nobel Prize awards ceremonies to receptions for the visiting Prince Charles. They recently attended opening ceremonies in Atlanta for the Carter Presidential Library — for which he raised nearly $2 million in pledges — and were frequent guests in the White House during both the Carter and John Kennedy years in Washington.

"But Jess never goes any place just to be seen," says Jack Wheeler, a Dallas consultant, lobbyist and old friend of the Hays. "They could go to a gala every night, but they'd rather stay home and eat turnip greens and play bridge — both of them. They have no social climbing in them. In the world they live in, which is certainly different from mine, they're as comfortable sitting down with the president of the

> **Mother said when I married Jess, I did real good. I got a Democrat and a Methodist.**
> — Betty Jo Hay on her choice of a husband

Betty Jo Hay, president of the National Mental Health Association, urged husband Jess to create The Lomas & Nettleton School, a model child-care facility for employees of his mortgage banking firm.

See Betty and Jess Hay/page 17F

In the Sunday, November 9, 1986 *Today* section of *The Houston Post*, Betty Jo and Jess were profiled as *Super Texans:* Jess as a state political leader and Betty Jo as the newly installed President of the National Mental Health Association. The two made an impressive team, and through their combined talents and efforts The L & N School was established. It was a model child-care facility for employees of the Lomas Financial Group. The school was one of the features in the article.

The National Mental Health Association

Tribute
to
Mrs. W. Averell Harriman

The National Mental Health Association
requests the pleasure of your company
to honor
Mrs. W. Averell Harriman
on Thursday, the twelfth of September
Nineteen hundred and eighty-five
Mrs. Gerald R. Ford
and
Mrs. Lyndon B. Johnson
Honorary Chairpersons
The Honorable and
Mrs. Luther H. Hodges, Jr.
Chairpersons
Mr. Art Buchwald
Master of Ceremonies

Reception at half past six o'clock
Dinner at half past seven o'clock
Gene Donati and His Orchestra
Sheraton Washington Hotel
Washington, D.C.

Reply Card Enclosed   *Black Tie*

In 1985, when she was president-elect of the National Mental Health Association, Betty Jo oversaw planning of a tribute to Democratic political activist Pamela Harriman, wife of diplomat and statesman W. Averell Harriman. The event took place in Washington, D. C. and featured Betty Ford and Lady Bird Johnson as honorary chairpersons. Ten months later in July 1986, Averell Harriman would die.

MRS. W. AVERELL HARRIMAN

DEEPLY APPRECIATES YOUR THOUGHTFULNESS

AND KIND EXPRESSION OF SYMPATHY

Betty Jo -
I am grateful for your sympathy and
that of the Mental Health Association.
Averell did care, and try to help, in the treatment
for America's mentally ill. Sincerely, Pamela

A handwritten postscript from Pamela Harriman to Betty Jo came with this note following the 1986 death of Harriman's husband, noted statesman and diplomat William Averell Harriman. "I am grateful for your sympathy and that of the Mental Health Association," she wrote. "Averell did care and try to help in the treatment for America's mentally ill. Sincerely, Pamela." In addition to serving as governor of New York, the 94-year-old Harriman was a two-time Democratic presidential hopeful who had worked under four U. S. presidents—Franklin D. Roosevelt, Harry S. Truman, John F. Kennedy, and Lyndon B. Johnson.

Still, the accolades kept coming, and on October 18, 1985, Texas MHA paid tribute to Betty Jo and Jess at its annual Honoring Dinner, a spectacular affair which featured a striking assembly of honorary chairmen as a testament to the Hays' longstanding relationship with political power. Included in the star-studded lineup were President and Mrs. Jimmy Carter, Speaker and Mrs. Carl Albert, Senator and Mrs. Lloyd Bentsen, Governor and Mrs. Mark White, Governor and Mrs. Dolph Briscoe, Lt. Governor and Mrs. William P. Hobby. Their headliner status—and that of other leading citizens associated with the black-tie fund-raiser—made the dinner a rousing success, and at the same time helped set a new record in donations to the cause of mental health. As for hard-driving event co-chairs Ann and Bob Utley, netting more than $500,000 after the effort they'd put in was more than sufficient payoff.

JIMMY CARTER

October 18, 1985

To Betty Jo and Jess Hay

It is with great pleasure that Rosalynn and I join your family and friends in congratulating you tonight. We regret that we cannot be with you as you are honored for your untiring public service and devotion to bettering the lives of others.

The Mental Health Association has accomplished a great deal over the years, due in no small part to your contributions and combined efforts. We are pleased that the Mental Health Association of Texas is paying tribute to you who have touched us all by your caring example.

Rosalynn joins me in extending our congratulations and warm best wishes.

Sincerely,

Jimmy Carter

Mr. and Mrs. Jess Hay
La Mansion
Austin, Texas

Though Rosalynn and Jimmy Carter could not attend the Austin event honoring Betty Jo and Jess for their work on behalf of the mentally ill, the former president nevertheless sent well wishes in recognition of what he called their "untiring public service and devotion to bettering the lives of others." The October 1985 function was sponsored by the Mental Health Association in Texas.

STATE OF TEXAS
OFFICE OF THE GOVERNOR
AUSTIN, TEXAS 78701

MARK WHITE
GOVERNOR

October 30, 1985

Dear Mr. Garrison:

Betty Jo Hay, from Dallas, assumes the presidency of your association after many years of leadership at the local, state and national levels. She was a prime mover of the Texas Mental Health Association Foundation which is now at the halfway mark toward a $1 million goal. And, she initiated the first long-range strategic plan for the Association in Texas. We can honestly say that the Mental Health Association is alive and well in Texas because of Betty Jo -- her emphasis on children and adolescents just adds to the litany of accomplishments.

You are fortunate to have her knowledge, expertise and desire to succeed focused on the Mental Health Association. Betty Jo also brings with her the talent, ability and forcefulness of her husband, Jess. Jess Hay makes and takes time from his duties as Chairman of the Board at Lomas and Nettleton to complement Betty Jo's efforts. His visibility with the largest mortgage house in the country and the extensive network developed by his professional and political involvement are an invaluable asset. Together they are an incomparable team.

It is indeed an honor for Texas to have Betty Jo Hay represent a national organization such as the Mental Health Association. We look forward with great anticipation to a banner year for your association at the state level and nationally. Betty Jo's ability to persuade, her understanding in this subject area and her credibility make her an ideal spokesperson for the cause of mental health.

Governor of Texas   Lieutenant Governor   Speaker of the House

This 1985 letter was sent to leaders of the National Mental Health Association in advance of Betty Jo's induction as president, and signed by Texas Governor Mark White, Lieutenant Governor Bill Hobby, and House Speaker Gib Lewis. It contains not only a message of praise for Betty Jo's extraordinary talent, but also a preview of her remarkable partnership with Jess, as well as glowing Texas pride at having one of its own selected to steer the future of a vital national organization.

The festive occasion not only conferred distinction upon the Hays as a couple, it also served as a send-off for Betty Jo who, two weeks later, would travel to Washington, D.C. for her induction as president of the National Mental Health Association during a ceremony at the organization's annual meeting. Once there, however, Betty Jo was more concerned with a congressional reception she was to attend than with the formalities of the ceremony. She viewed the reception as another opportunity to attract political support for MHA, therefore, falling back on her formula of personal letter-writing as a way to ensure

305

the best possible turnout, Betty Jo mailed invitations to key members of the United States Senate and House of Representatives requesting their presence. And as was usually the case, her effort paid off. Massachusetts Senator Edward Kennedy—whose family encounters with mental illness had made mental health one of his signature issues—was among several legislators making an appearance at the reception, after which he followed up with a personal letter of thanks to Betty Jo:

EDWARD M. KENNEDY
MASSACHUSETTS

United States Senate

WASHINGTON, D.C. 20510

November 1, 1985

Mrs. Jess Hay
7236 Lupton Circle
Dallas, Texas 75225

Dear Betty Jo:

I appreciate having the opportunity to spend even a few minutes with you last evening and hope we can have a prolonged conversation in the very near future.

The need for our government to address the tragedy of mental illness in this country is perhaps greater than it has ever been and only through a combination of public and private efforts can we effectively provide help to those people unable to help themselves.

I assure you this issue will always be high on my legislative agenda and I look forward to continuing to work with the National Mental Health Association, and you, to that end.

I am sending under separate cover copies of some recent legislative initiatives in which I am involved. I hope you find the material useful.

Next time you are in Washington I hope we can spend some significant substantive time together on this issue.

With best wishes,

Sincerely,

Edward M. Kennedy

I look forward to working with you

Massachusetts Senator Edward Kennedy attended a reception during the National Mental Health Association's 1985 convention in Washington, D. C. at which Betty Jo formally accepted the presidency. This personal follow-up letter reveals Kennedy's eagerness to work with Betty Jo on concerns related to mental illness, a signature cause for a U. S. senator whose family had encountered its share of the disease.

I appreciate having the opportunity to spend even a few minutes with you last evening and hope we can have a prolonged conversation in the very near future. The need for our government to address the tragedy of mental illness in this country is perhaps greater than it has ever been. . . .

I assure you this issue will always be high on my legislative agenda and I look forward to continuing to work with the National Mental Health Association, and you, to that end.

In addition to the reception they attended, MHA delegates also had the chance to spend time on Capitol Hill visiting with members of Congress in their offices. Texas Senator Lloyd Bentsen received one such visit from a delegation that included Karen Hale, a Texas MHA professional who had worked closely with Betty Jo and Stella Mullins. On this particular day, Betty Jo happened to be with Hale's group, which was ushered into the office by a Bentsen aide who then seated them in the senator's conference room. Moments later, Hale remembers, Bentsen himself entered the room, turned to Betty Jo—the newly-elected president of MHA—bowed at the waist and said, "Your Eminence." "It was a beautiful gesture on his part," she said. "It demonstrated the esteem he held for Betty Jo."

And so, having now gone the distance, Betty Jo Hay became president of the National Mental Health Association in November 1985, and soon would begin taking up the challenges of her office with characteristic determination and optimism. In a moving acceptance speech at the annual meeting, she offered words of hope and encouragement to a roomful of hard-working, dedicated volunteers, words that expressed her profound belief that the whole truly is only as good as the sum of its parts, a message she had delivered countless times before:

In a world of problems, each one of us can be a part of the solution. Each one of us can be a candle in the darkness of current conditions for the mentally ill in America. . . . A simple postage stamp is useful because it sticks to one thing until it gets there. If we stick to it—if we persevere—we too, will get there.

Over the next decade, darkness would threaten the issues Betty Jo cared most deeply about—mental health, education, and children—but she was not to be deterred. Holding fast to her resolve even in the face of great odds, Betty Jo would reach inside herself and beat back the darkness with her single most powerful weapon: the bright flame of increased commitment.

PHOTOGRAPH ALBUM
5

JANUARY 1971
through
NOVEMBER 1985

"Betty Jo Hay is 40 Today." After a ride around town on the bus, the party arrived at Ned and LeAnn Harris' for her birthday dinner. Ned with Wrinkles, the dog, Betty Jo, Patty, Debby, and Jess. June 6, 1971.

Jess sent Betty Jo 40 beautiful red roses on her birthday. June 6, 1971.

Betty Jo in a tropical setting outside their tree house. She and Jess liked #10 at Little Dix Bay on Virgin Gorda, Virgin Islands. November 1971.

The Summer 1972 *Mortgagee* featured "LNF-Recognition by the Big Board." From left to right: NYSE President Robert W. Haack welcomes LNFC chairman and chief executive officer Jess Hay and president Gene Bishop to the trading floor the day LNF was listed.

The Hays spent three weeks in Europe after the Democratic National Convention. Mrs. Dean, a London history teacher and tour guide, informs Patty, Jess, and Betty Jo about Eton College. England, Summer 1972.

Linda Boggs, Cokie Boggs, her daughter (later known as Cokie Roberts the journalist), Betty Jo, and Mary Albert at far right. Jess Hay was a delegate at the 1972 Democratic National Convention in Miami.

Betty Jo and Jess with Debby, waiting for Santa on Christmas eve. 1972.

Margaret Crow and Betty Jo at a party hosted by the Crows for Debby. 1973.

Ted and Bess Enloe, Jess and Betty Jo, New York Stock Exchange official, John and Nancy Sexton. Listing ceremony for Lomas & Nettleton Mortgage Investors at the New York Stock Exchange. Circa 1969.

Dr. Willis Tate, president of Southern Methodist University, Carl Albert, and Betty Jo
at the SMU Umphrey Lee Associates dinner. 1974.

En route from France to Switzerland, Betty Jo is having
her only fling with a cigar. 1974.

Jess and Betty Jo with Jim and Rand Sale, on the Hay's 23rd wedding anniversary trip to Las Vegas. August 3, 1974.

Betty Jo, Al Rohnstedt, and Ramona Taylor enjoy the moment at
Al Rohnstedt's retirement party in New York City. 1974.

After the ball in Debby's honor, Betty Jo and Jess relaxed in the
foyer of the Regency Room of the Fairmont Hotel, Dallas.
December 8, 1973.

Betty Jo at the Royal Hawaiian Hotel in Honolulu.
November 1975.

Betty Jo at Hana Ranch, Maui, a Hay family favorite.
November 1975.

Betty Jo at Kahala Hilton Hotel in Honolulu.
November 1975.

Governor Dolph Briscoe presenting
a proclamation to Betty Jo.
Spring 1976.

Governor Jimmy Carter
and Betty Jo exchanging greetings
during his successful campaign
for the presidency. 1976.

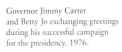

314

John Dalton was one of the Carter delegates who defeated the Bentsen delegates, including Betty Jo, in the 16th Senatorial District of Texas in the March primary of 1976. Thereafter the Hays and the Daltons became good friends.
From left: Travis Johnson, Betty Jo, John and Margaret Dalton, Lloyd Bentsen, and Jess.
May 1976.

After the 1976 election campaign, when Lloyd Bentsen ran for president, the Hays relaxed with Lloyd and B.A. on their boat moored in Annapolis, Maryland. May 1976.

Senator Lloyd Bentsen with many members of his Senate office and Presidential campaign staffs, following a luncheon meeting in Washington, D.C. Circa 1976.

Frank Moore and Betty Jo at Jess's birthday
dinner in Washington, D.C.
January 22, 1977.

The bridge group celebrating Betty
Jo's 46th birthday which will be
on June 6, 1977. Rand Sale, Jeanne
Scott, Jerry Johnson, Charlene
Miller, Jerry Pittman, Betty Jo,
and Peggy Smith.

Patty and Betty Jo at Betty Jo's
birthday dinner in Washington, D.C.
June 6, 1977.

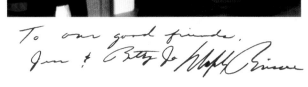

To enable his assuming duties as Regent of The University of Texas System at Austin, Jess's oath of office is administered by then Secretary of State Mark White, with Betty Jo in attendance. Inscription: *Jess–while serving as regent you must learn the "Hook'em Horns" sign. Mark.* January 1977.

Arleigh Templeton, Betty Jo, and Bob Hardesty, in back, at a dinner at Bauer House in Austin. 1977.

Betty Jo, Janey and Governor Dolph Briscoe, and Jess at a reception in the Governor's Mansion, Austin. January 1977. Inscription: *To our good friends, Jess & Betty Jo. Dolph Briscoe.*

Betty Jo and Jess sailed as guests of Margaret and Trammell Crow on the *Brave Goose* departing from Sicily to Dubrovnik, Yugoslavia. Also aboard were Roger and Pauline Sullivan, Sue and Bill Dillard, Marian Nichols and a crew of eight. Summer 1977.

Aboard the *Brave Goose*. Trammell Crow, Betty Jo, Sue and Bill Dillard, Margaret Crow, Roger Sullivan, Marian Nichols, and Jess. Summer 1977.

Jess's cousin Mary Lee and her husband, Dr. Brad Reeves, with their two children, Bradie and Kathryn Reeves. Circa 1977.

Harry and Frances Provence, Betty Jo and Jess at the party for Harry Provence on his
retirement as chairman of the Coordinating Board, Texas College and University System,
held at the lieutenant governor's apartment at the capitol. All the current and
some past members were present. 1978.

Sis Meyers and Betty Jo at Harry Provence's retirement party. 1978.

With their first grandchild, Jessica, Betty Jo and Jess have a
new experience. She was born June 30, 1978. July 1978.

Betty Jo and Jessica with "High High," A.K.A. Mickey Mouse. January 1979.

The U.T. Regents and their spouses. Standing: Howard Richards, Sterling Fly, Jess Hay, Betty Jo Hay, Tom Law, Jimmie Powell, Nancy Powell, Dan Williams, Roland Blumberg, Judy Newton, Jon Newton, and Ross Sterling. Seated: Bobbie Fly, Jo Ann Law, Caroline Williams, Jane Blumberg, and Maude Sterling. March 30, 1979.

Betty Jo and Jo Ann Law at a party for U.T. Regents. March 29, 1979.

Betty Jo receiving formal recognition and thanks for her service as a member and Vice Chair of the Council on Post-Secondary Accreditation. Betty Jo also was presented a key to the city of Arlington from the mayor. 1979.

PRESIDENT JIMMY CARTER'S
VISIT TO THE HAY HOME
JULY 1980

Preparing tables and chairs for President Carter's visit.

The pool and decorative cart were made ready for the special occasion.

Betty Jo had the pool area beautifully planted with flowers to entertain President Carter and his friends on their visit.

Jess, Bernie Rapoport, President Carter, Audre Rapoport, and Betty Jo
at the function for Carter.

The Reverend Robert Price, Arnita Brown, and President Carter with Betty Jo.

*With best wishes & love
to Betty Jo Hay
Jimmy Carter
'80*

President Carter, Betty Jo, Jessica, and Jess at the Hay home.
Inscription: *With best wishes & love to Betty Jo Hay. Jimmy Carter '80.*

It was an evening of affirmation honoring Speaker and Mrs. Bill Clayton at the Fairmont Hotel, Dallas.
Senator Peyton McKnight, Anne McKnight, Jess, Speaker Billy Clayton, and Betty Jo. December 10, 1980.

At the White House Oval Office. Harry McAdams, Jessica, held by Jess, Rosalynn Carter, Betty Jo, President Carter, Debby, Chuck Werner,
David Hopp, and Patty. December 14, 1980.

Betty Ann Thedford, Jane Blumberg, and Betty Jo at U.T. Regents retirement party. Betty Jo with "Hook'em Horns" sign. Chancellor Don Walker is in the background. January 10, 1981.

Betty Jo, Vice President Walter Mondale, and Jess. Inscription: *To Jess and Betty- with admiration. W. Mondale.* January 17, 1981.

"FIFTY YEARS IN POLITICS!"
THE DALLAS COUNTRY CLUB
JANUARY 20, 1981

Betty Jo gave a surprise party for Jess's 50th birthday, which was two days later.

Betty Jo and Jess having fun.

Nonie Bramblett gives her nephew, Jess, a birthday kiss.

Betty Jo and Jess enjoying the program at his party.

Kathryn Peacock dancing with her brother-in-law,
Edgar Peacock, Betty Jo's uncle, at the celebration.

Betty Jo with Keith and Norma Foreman Glasgow at a Mental Health dinner honoring
Wayne Holtzman at the Driskill Hotel, Austin. 1981.

Betty Jo presiding at a Mental Health dinner
honoring Wayne Holtzman at the Driskill Hotel,
Austin. 1981.

Betty Jo. 1981. Photograph by Gittings.

Betty Jo with Thelma Garvin, and other Exxon wives, in Kuala Lumpur on the Hay's
first Exxon trip to Malaysia. 1981.

Betty Jo and Bill Banowsky. Carl Albert Center at
Oklahoma University, Norman. 1981.

Betty Jo and Speaker of the House Tip O'Neill. Carl Albert
Center at Oklahoma University, Norman. 1981.

Jess with his girls. Patty, Betty Jo, Debby, and Jessica. 1981.

Betty Jo, with her parents Kathryn and Duncan Peacock. 1981.

BETTY JO HAY'S SURPRISE
50TH BIRTHDAY PARTY
AT THE DALLAS CHAPPARAL CLUB
JUNE 6, 1981

Betty Jo and Jessica with Jess celebrating her birthday.

Can you believe it? Betty Jo is 50! Jess and Betty Jo danced at the surprise party.

Betty Jo and Jessica celebrate together by blowing out candles on her large birthday cake.

Betty Jo and Jess were still dancing by the end of the party. It was a day filled with happy memories.

Four of Betty Jo's dear friends, helping to celebrate her birthday. Stell Chappell, LeAnn Harris, Maxine Tadlock, and Frances Thomas.

Jim Wooten, Stella Mullins, Betty Jo, and Jerry Pittman.

Betty Jo in Washington, D.C. with the Mental Health bell. June 1981.

The metal that went into the bell came from mental hospitals in all parts of the country at the request of the Mental Health Association. It was melted down at the McShane Bell Foundry in Baltimore, Maryland, on April 13, 1953.

The 300-pound bell bears this inscription:

Cast from the shackles which bound them, this bell shall ring out hope for the mentally ill and victory over mental illness.

Betty Jo and Jess were back in the states following the Exxon board trip to Hong Kong, Malaysia, and Australia. Summer 1981.

A Chinese dinner in Betty Jo's honor was held on the evening prior to her christening of the *Esso Spain,* hosted by chairman of the Chinese shipbuilding company in Taipai, Taiwan. May 1982.

In commemoration of Betty Jo's christening of the *Esso Spain,* she received a necklace from Exxon's Lee Hamilton. May 1982.

Betty Jo and Charlene Miller with a group of Exxon and Chinese shipbuilding company representatives, just prior to the christening of the ship. May 1982.

Buddy Miller and Jess met Charlene and Betty Jo in Honolulu after the ship christening. Summer 1982.

Malcolm Milburn, Betty Jo, and Jane Blumberg at a function of U.T. Regents. 1982.

Six of the Dallas contingent of the Ponder Group: Jack Wheeler, Betty Jo, Jess, Kate Wheeler, Vicki and Ron Kessler en route to Austin to have dinner with other members of the Ponder Group, namely, Diana and Bill Hobby, Kay and Ray Hutchison, and Stella and Charles Mullins. Summer 1982.

THE GALAXY BALL
FAIRMONT HOTEL, DALLAS
MARCH 12, 1983

Betty Jo and Jess at the Ball.

Jess, Linda Gale White, Governor Mark White, and Betty Jo.

Former astronaut Alan Shephard and Betty Jo share the podium.

Linda Gale White and Lucien Flournoy at the Ball.

334

Betty Jo, Rosalynn Carter, Helen Farabee, and Governor Mark White on the occasion of the temporary placement of the National Mental Health Association's Liberty Bell in the chamber of the Texas State Senate. April 27, 1983.

To honor Diana and Bill Hobby, a dinner was held by the Mental Health Association in Texas at the Wyndham Hotel in Austin. Lucien and Maxine Flournoy were in attendance with Betty Jo and Jess, who chaired the event. September 23, 1983.

Kathleen and Bob Krueger at the MHAT Hobby dinner. September 23, 1983.

Ray Farabee, Betty Jo, and Patty enjoy the Hobby dinner. September 23, 1983.

Frances Thomas, Betty Jo's
dear friend. 1983.

With their guide, Betty Jo and Jess at the Sphinx at Giza in Egypt.
They were on an Exxon trip to Saudi Arabia. November 1983.

A visit by Mary Agnes Hilmer, Betty Rawl, Betty Jo, and Geneva
Grandy to the Sphinx was part of an Exxon trip to Saudi Arabia.
November 1983.

Betty Jo, Senator Lloyd Bentsen,
Jess, and B.A. Bentsen. Circa 1983.
Inscription: *To Jess and Betty Jo—
With admiration and appreciation for
a wonderful couple. Lloyd & B.A.*

Debby and Betty Jo at the Gourmet Gala.
1983.

Betty Jo and Webb Spradley, her
future son-in-law, in a festive
mood aboard the Stella Solaris.
New Year's Eve 1983.

A riverboat excursion, for Betty Jo,
Jess, Jessica, and Myrtle Hay, was
part of a family cruise through the
Caribbean and up the Amazon
River to Manaus, Brazil.
December 1983-January 1984.

ANNOUNCING THE BETTY JO HAY PROFESSORSHIP IN MENTAL HEALTH FEBRUARY 4, 1984

Attending the function announcing the Betty Jo Hay Professorship in Mental Health at The UT Southwestern Medical Center at Dallas. Clockwise: Jerry Pittman, Stell Chappell, Chili Clark, Duncan and Kathryn Peacock, Jo and Roy Guffey.

Betty Jo receiving accolades from Dr. Charles Sprague.

Betty Jo when she first heard the news of the establishment of the Professorship. Standing: Dr. John Rush. Sitting: Marnie Wildenthal, Betty Jo and Jess.

George Bramblett, Betty Jo, Buddy Miller, and Pedie Bramblett at the dinner. Since 1972, the Brambletts and Hays have been good friends and allies on many fronts.

338

Jill and Amy Bramblett, daughters of Patty and Richard Bramblett. Circa mid-1980s.
Photograph by John Haynsworth, Inc.

"Champagne and Gershwin" benefiting the Mental Health Association in
Dallas. Erin and Elaine Shiver, Jess and Betty Jo. 1984.

Betty Jo with Senator John Glenn of Ohio during his 1984 campaign for president.

Betty Jo and her two daughters,
Patty and Debby, enjoy a summer's
evening. June 1984.

Betty Jo and her cousin,
Mary Frances Albert.
July 1984.

Re Ruru's farewell party at the Hay home.
Jess, Patty, Re Ruru, Jessica, Betty Jo,
Cindy Simmons, Debby, and Jane Garner,
Jessica's nanny from 1983 to 1990.
August 1984.

The Hay's party during the Democratic Convention in San Francisco, aboard a yacht furnished by their friend, Ron Volkman, a fellow Democrat who then resided in Northern California. Betty Jo, Senator David Boren, Jess, Governor Jerry Brown, B.A. Bentsen, Garry Mauro, and Senator Lloyd Bentsen. 1984.

Jess, Walter Mondale, and Betty Jo at Mondale's fund-raising dinner at the Fairmont Hotel in Dallas. September 1984.

MENTAL HEALTH ASSOCIATION IN TEXAS
HONORING ANN RICHARDS
OCTOBER 26, 1984

Jim Wooten, Betty Jo, and Marjorie Wooten attending the dinner in Austin.

Ann Utley, Stella Mullins, Ann Richards, Diana Hobby, Joanne Smerdon, Betty Jo, and Betty McKool at the dinner.

Lady Bird Johnson, Betty Jo, and Pamela Harriman enjoyed the occasion.

342

John Albert Baumert, son of Polly Albert, at the Presbyterian Church in McAlester, Oklahoma, where he attended the Peanut Butter and Jelly Preschool. November 1984.

Betty Jo and Ann Richards at the Dallas for Ferraro breakfast rally, held for Geraldine Ferraro, the 1984 Democratic vice presidential nominee. Walter Mondale was the Democratic presidential nominee. Fall 1984.

Ann Richards, Geraldine Ferraro, her husband, John Zaccaro, and in back Carl Albert, at the Ferraro breakfast rally. Fall 1984.

Betty Jo with Diana Hobby, Chet Edwards, and Julie Brice at a political gathering in Dallas, one week prior to the national election. Lowry Mays is in the background. November 1984.

Betty Jo and Jess with
The University of Texas
System Chancellor Hans Mark
and his wife, Marion Mark.
December 1, 1984.

Jess and Betty Jo hosted a
dinner honoring Governor Mark
White. Betty Jo with Linda
Gale White, Texas First Lady.
The couple to the right is
Dorothy and Luther Campbell.
December 4, 1984.

Jess and Betty Jo with Janis
and Howard Richards at a
Regent's party at the Bauer
House in Austin.
Circa 1984.

Betty Jo chatting with her friend, Buddy Miller, at a tribute to Bernice and Lee Mulder, Lois and Ernest Turnbull, Anette and Frank Comroe, and other tenured officers and employees of Lomas. January 21,1985.

Betty Jo receiving a special commendation from The Hogg Foundation for Mental Health and the MHAT. Presented by Stella Mullins, Wayne Holtzman, and Helen Farabee. Austin, January 24, 1985.

Stella Mullins congratulates Betty Jo on receiving a special commendation from The Hogg Foundation for Mental Health and the MHAT. January 24, 1985.

Betty Jo with Dr. Ira Iscoe, then the director of Plan II at The University of Texas at Austin, being honored by The Hogg Foundation for Mental Health and the MHAT. January 24, 1985.

Honoring volunteers at the annual
meeting of the Dallas County MHA
are Luther Campbell and Betty Jo.
February 1985.

Paul and Nedda Low at the annual meeting of the Dallas County MHA.
February 1985.

Betty Jo and Tom Rhodes were in attendance at the Dallas County
MHA annual meeting honoring volunteers. February 1985.

Vivian Castleberry, Don Weiser,
and Betty Jo at a reception for the
"Women Helping Women" award.
April 24, 1985.

Celebrating MHAT's 50th anniversary, Betty Jo and Jess admire the Mental Health
bell in the Texas Senate Chamber. Helen Farabee in back. May 1985.

Senator Gary Hart and Betty Jo prior to a MHAT related
luncheon in Austin. May 1985.

Enjoying their score sheet after an afternoon of bridge at the Dallas Country Club.
Katherine Bauer and Betty Jo. 1985.

U.T. Regents dinner honoring Priscilla Flawn and her husband Peter Flawn. Betty Jo, Tyrell Hill, Betty Ann Thedford, Marcee Landram, and Priscilla Flawn. August 8, 1985.

Betty Jo and Jess greeting Priscilla and Peter Flawn at the U.T. Regents dinner honoring the Flawns. August 8, 1985.

KATHRYN AND DUNCAN PEACOCK'S 50ᵀᴴ WEDDING ANNIVERSARY
SEPTEMBER 22, 1985

Betty Jo and Jess hosted a surprise party at the McAlester Country Club in Oklahoma.
There was a gift from Betty Jo and Jess: a 17 day cruise to Brazil with 2 friends.

Kathryn and Duncan Peacock on the occasion of their anniversary.

Betty Jo passed soft drinks to the riders on the chartered bus bound for her parents wedding anniversary.

Betty Jo is a super hostess. Ed and Elaine Haines, front; Jimmy Thomas and Jerry Pittman, middle; and Sally Brice, rear.

KATHRYN AND DUNCAN PEACOCK'S 50ᵀᴴ WEDDING ANNIVERSARY

Patty, Jessica, Debby, and Betty Jo at the celebration.

Betty Jo with her parents, Duncan and Kathryn Peacock.

Betty Jo, Duncan, and Kathryn with the 50th anniversary wedding cake.

Betty Jo and Jess with her mother and father.

KATHRYN AND DUNCAN PEACOCK'S 50ᵀᴴ WEDDING ANNIVERSARY

Betty Jo presiding at the ceremonies.

Kathryn Peacock, Edgar and Ruth Peacock, and Duncan Peacock enjoy the toasts from family and friends.

Earl, Kathryn's brother, and Doris Albert.

Kathy Albert, Polly Albert, Patty Hay, and Pat Haines enjoy the party.

KATHRYN AND DUNCAN PEACOCK'S 50TH WEDDING ANNIVERSARY

Susan and Scott Wilson with Jerry Pittman.

A portion of the Haines family:
Pat, Eddie, Elaine, Terry, and Cumalee.

Betty Jo with her uncle and
aunt, Carl and Mary Albert.

KATHRYN AND DUNCAN PEACOCK'S 50TH WEDDING ANNIVERSARY

352

Betty and Budge Albert having fun and dancing.

Good friends make for good times. Betty Jo and
Jimmy Thomas catch their breath after dancing
the Charleston.

Jack and Kate Wheeler with Jess.

KATHRYN AND DUNCAN PEACOCK'S 50TH WEDDING ANNIVERSARY

Earl, Polly, Nancy, Kathy, Chris McMullin, Linda Callahan and Amanda Albert Winn.

Duncan, Betty Jo, Kathryn, and Jess as the anniversary party was drawing to a close.

The assembled cousins. Kathy Albert and her daughter, Amanda, Nancy Albert, Patty, Jessica, Debby, and Polly Albert.

MHAT DINNER HONORING BETTY JO AND JESS IN AUSTIN
OCTOBER 18, 1985

354

Celebrating the special tribute. Roddy and Rhonda Harlow (the Hays nephew and niece) and Patsy and Don Harlow (Jess's sister and brother-in-law).

Duncan Peacock, Betty Jo, Jessica, Kathryn Peacock, Myrtle Hay, Debby, and Jess.

Betty Jo, Ken Ashworth, and Jess.

Cecile Bonte and Elaine Shiver.

MHAT DINNER HONORING BETTY JO AND JESS IN AUSTIN

Lowry Mays, Ramona Taylor, and Joe Penland.

Betty Jo and Jess enjoying comments made by Bill Hobby, Ann Utley, and Lloyd Bentsen.

A presentation by Bob Utley was made to Jess and Betty Jo at the dinner. Bob and his wife Ann were co-chairs of the dinner.

MHAT DINNER HONORING BETTY JO AND JESS IN AUSTIN

356

Papa and Jessica enjoying a dance.

Betty Jo, Roland and Jane Blumberg, and Jess.

Dr. Bill Ross with Betty Jo.

MHAT DINNER HONORING BETTY JO AND JESS IN AUSTIN

Dallas County Commissioner John Wiley Price and his date with Betty Jo.

Tu and Jessica share an animated conversation at the dinner.

Patty and Betty Jo with the CEO of the NMHA, Preston Garrison.

Betty Jo, David Farr, Debby, and Sondra Farr share a fun moment.

Betty Jo dancing with Lieutenant Governor
Bill Hobby at U.T Regents dinner honoring him
with the Santa Rita award. October 23, 1985.

Senator John Glenn with Betty Jo, Annie Glenn, and Don Tobias, president of the
Ohio MHA. 1985.

Texas delegation to the 1985 NMHA. Seated, left to right: Elaine Shiver, Dallas; Virginia Barlow, San Antonio; Stella C. Mullins,
Austin; Betty Jo Hay, Dallas; Helen Farabee, Wichita Falls; Dora McBride, Houston; Kathryn Hall, Dallas.
Standing, left to right: Patricia Looney, Wichita Falls; Joanne Smerdon, Austin; Karen Hale, Austin; Peggy Greenspan,
Beaumont; Kathy Edwards, Austin; Laura Richmond, San Antonio; Cecile Bonte, Dallas; Betsy Swartz, Houston;
Ann Utley, Dallas; Alisa Larson, Houston; Hal Haralson, Austin.

BETTY JO'S INSTALLATION AS PRESIDENT OF THE NMHA
NOVEMBER 2, 1985

Friends gathered for Betty Jo's installation as president of the NMHA. Virginia Barlow, Stella Mullins, Helen Farabee, and Karen Hale. November 2, 1985.

The National Mental Health Association and the Mental Health Association in Texas cordially invite you to a reception honoring
Betty Jo Hay
1986 National President
Saturday, November 2, 1985
5:30 to 7:00 p.m.
Presidential Foyer and Cabinet Room
The Washington Hilton

Invitation to Betty Jo's installation as president of the NMHA.

Betty Jo delivering her inaugural address as president of the NMHA.

360